A HALF CENTURY
OF THEOLOGY

A HALF CENTURY OF THEOLOGY
Movements and Motives

by
G. C. BERKOUWER

translated and edited by
Lewis B. Smedes

William B. Eerdmans Publishing Company

Copyright © 1977 by Wm. B. Eerdmans Publishing Co.
255 Jefferson Ave. S.E., Grand Rapids, Mich. 49503
Printed in the United States of America

Translated from *Een halve eeuw theologie: motieven
en stromingen van* 1920 *tot heden* © 1974 Uitgeversmaat-
schappij J. H. Kok, Kampen, Holland

Library of Congress Cataloging in Publication Data

Berkouwer, Gerrit Cornelis, 1903-
    A half-century of theology.
    Translation of Een halve eeuw theologie.
    Includes index.
    1. Theology, Doctrinal—History—20th century.
I. Title.
BT28.B44713   230   76-56798

ISBN 0-8028-1688-6

Contents

Foreword

WHEN I ENDED MY REGULAR LECTURES AT THE FREE UNIVERSITY OF Amsterdam with a brief survey of the movement of theology since 1920, I was asked by many friends to expand the lectures more fully. Now that I have fulfilled the request, I am quite conscious that the result is still very incomplete. I am also sensitive to the fact that my review is closely bound up with my own experiences and my own encounters, both with persons and with books. In short, my own personal and, therefore, limited assimilation of this fascinating and dynamic period is what has gone into this study.

Movements and Motives! With this subtitle I am protecting myself a little against the charge of setting my own limits, of being selective, and thus of ignoring factors that have challenged and stimulated others. I have personally experienced this half-century of theology – I became a theological student at the Free University in 1922 – as a continuing event, and I am sure that everyone who really entered into it will have experienced it as something that has carried him along in continued and growing interest. Perhaps my account is the result of sustained curiosity. The word *curiosity* may sound odd here, since that is not always a great virtue. But I believe that without genuine curiosity – a sense for news – theology will not do well. I regret every sign that theologians have lost their curiosity. It happens when we are satisfied with a small territory we have carved out for ourselves and lose our feel for new perspectives and new opportunities for enrichment.

Besides, without the tensions of curiosity there is little hope for any essential corrections in one's own insights. A complacency sets in, a feeling that the gospel has been adequately thought about and understood, and that we can restfully settle down with what has already been said. A curiosity that works itself out in passion-ate study and serious listening to others promises surprises, clearer

7

insight, and deeper understanding — no matter from which direction they come. And so curiosity brings a certain joy as we walk through the challenging terrain.

We can easily make mistakes; errors are possible at every turn. But mistakes need not be our destiny.

As we oversee the period from 1920 to 1970, and try to bring the whole picture before our spirits, we will probably conclude that there is more doubt and uncertainty in theology now than there was at the beginning. What dogmatic themes and what churchly confessions are not being discussed these days in terms of "new questions"? And where will it all end, as we plow our way through what some people call the wilderness of our time? Consider for a moment, without trying to be complete, the theological problems on the agenda: the Holy Scriptures and their authority, infallibility, and trustworthiness; the difficult questions of exegesis and hermeneutics; the confessions regarding God, creation and redemption, christology, divine election as the heart of the church; and, not least, eschatology in a world threatened more acutely than when Oswald Spengler shocked us all with his *Decline of the West*. And these are not all of the questions that hover around the theological discussion table.

Some people have experienced the development of this half-century with deep anxiety, and in their anxiety are not able to keep curiosity alive, except to ask how all this is going to end, where the church and its theology are going, and how soon the progressive loss of certainty will result in the loss of faith itself. I must say that I have not experienced our half-century in this spirit. I do not mean that theology is not vulnerable. Quite the contrary! And I certainly do not mean that all the problems we face are free from danger for those who deal with them. I see little ground for theological optimism. But the hesitations and doubts that are indeed present at many points do not in themselves indicate a deep and final uncertainty, least of all an alienation from the gospel, on which everything stands or falls for everyone. If it is true, as it must be, that theological reflection cannot survive as a repetition of the past, a preservation of once-for-all achieved and now unchangeable dogmatic systems, then continued testing and probing are an unavoidable mandate. And surely Reformation thinking is by definition willing to accept the challenge.

Sustained by this conviction, I will try to give an overview of the fascinating events, with all their struggles and discussions, of the theology of this half-century. I will try to indicate aspects — always incompletely — that, as I see them, are still profound and important, and, far from disappearing, still meet us as we scout today's theological arena. I do not mean that nothing much has really happened since 1920. But I do mean that even at the beginning questions were being raised and answered that are still nagging us today and will be around for some time to come, even if in other forms and against other backgrounds.

That we are wrestling today with questions put on the agenda a half-century ago commends modesty in our address to today's challenge. But it may also encourage us to accept that challenge with a curiosity aroused by that which is truly new, the gospel of Jesus Christ who makes all things new, the gospel which theology is dedicated to understand and translate for our generation. Awareness that theology is not the new thing and need not be, but is only a servant of the new, makes theology, with all its questions and uncertainties, a work of joy.

1

Background and Beginning

As I think back on my theological beginnings, and focus on the situation in my own church, the Reformed Churches of the Netherlands, I do not recall that the church and its theological life at that time were marked by quietness and certainty. Herman Bavinck died in 1920, but theological issues he raised kept stirring the minds of others. New perspectives and attitudes were forming, especially among the younger men. Questions about the confessions of the church arose, and it was asked whether a new confession was not demanded. There were questions about the role of the church in the world and about cooperation by the Reformed community with others who thought differently about things than we did. These and other questions seemed to raise a more basic question still: What does it mean to be Reformed? (This was the title of a pamphlet written by J. B. Netelenbos in 1920.)

What was then called "ethical theology" was a prominent issue for conservative theology in 1920. "Ethical theology" was not easy to define precisely. There were leftist ethical theologians and rightist ethical theologians, which complicated things. But generally, "ethical theology" was characterized by the slogan: "not dead doctrine, but the living Lord." It was an anti-dogma slogan, and the false antithesis it implied was roundly criticized.

The biblical question was in the air at the time also. In fact it became the focus of an ecclesiastical debate in which Netelenbos was accused by the general synod in 1920 of holding faulty views of biblical authority, namely those of "ethical theology." At that time the issue seemed crystal clear to many people. But others were wrestling with problems of the Bible and its inspiration, and a single synodical judgment did not put these questions to rest. It was Herman Bavinck who had placed them on the agenda. Such questions never cast a shadow over his own faith, but the way he raised them showed that the question of Scripture was never wholly answered in his own mind.

Bavinck did not confine himself to discrete dogmatic questions, however, but concerned himself with the broader issues of the role that the church should play in the world, and with the nature of the church's catholicity. He never stopped wrestling with them. The beauty of catholicity, a beauty he saw continually threatened and disfigured in history, captured his mind and affected his approach to theological problems. His objections to the synod's decision in 1920 were related to his view of the church and his view of theology's relation to culture. A galaxy of questions hovered in the atmosphere and were raised in endless discussions and student conferences. They all impinged on the church's tradition, though none of the people involved had the slightest notion of deserting that tradition. But their allegiance to the tradition was not slavish, and they felt personally responsible in facing the "renewal" that Bavinck desired, a renewal that would affect the relation of the tradition to other traditions, to other people, and to other churches.

The way into the future was not clearly marked out. Questions about theological isolationism and contact with other churches pushed their way into the minds of young theologians. Sometimes they evoked fear for the loss of theological identity. But they also raised the fear that identity in isolation would be bought at the cost of shrinkage of their catholic faith.

The influence of Abraham Kuyper was no longer as powerful as it once had been. There was doubt about his doctrine of common grace, doubts about his view of the antithesis between Christianity and other life-views, and doubts about the polemics that these views had aroused. Without denying the necessity of polemics, people wondered whether they ought not be carried on more carefully and more modestly. And on this point, a subtle difference between Bavinck and Kuyper began to show itself. Kuyper had said: "When principles that run against your deepest convictions begin to win the day, then battle is your calling, and peace has become sin; you must, at the price of dearest peace, lay your convictions bare before friend and enemy, with all the fire of your faith." But who was the enemy? And who was the friend? That was the question, as I recall it, that occupied the minds of many Reformed people in 1920.

At the time it was no easy task to get at the truth of things. For instance, on one hand people heard Kuyper's battle cry for principles, and, on the other, they heard criticism that his doctrine of common grace led to a secularized Christianity. Attacks against Kuyper were confusing for many people; for instance, it was said that he had himself adopted a modern world-view, but this sounded strange when set against the vivid accounts of his conversion and his own attack against modernism. It was he whose brand name for modernism had become a kind of battle slogan. *Fata morgana,* he called it – a mirage! How could this man have a modern world-view? But a W. J. Aalders was more subtle: Kuyper, he said, was both modern and anti-modern. It was true that he repudiated traditionalism, which for Kuyper meant a stubborn loyalty to a creed that had no bearing on one's own time and place. He was convinced that the Christian community had a calling "to infuse the Christian consciousness expressed by the creeds into the consciousness of our generation until its own consciousness becomes specifically Christian." But this vision hardly struck people as suspect. His goal was grandiose, perhaps, and even arrogant, but hardly deserving of indictment as modernistic. It was not a concession to modern consciousness, but a summons to overcome it. But it did imply the challenge of connecting Christian faith with modern thinking. Bavinck, too, had spoken of the need to make contact with the "consciousness and life of the times within which (theology) . . . labors." This motif was going to assume larger proportions in the midst of still more problems in relating theology to culture. At any rate, awareness was growing that isolation was no longer possible, that the times and the calling were bound together. But some saw Kuyper's philosophy of culture – his vision of a revival of Calvinism in the Western world – as an effort to culturize Christianity. And they thought Bavinck, too, had capitulated to modern thought after he had taken the chair of dogmatic theology at the Free University.

The relationship between Kuyper and Bavinck is interesting in itself. We cannot go into their individual influences on the half-century that lay ahead, but they were considerable. Kuyper's influence worked through the development of the Philosophy of the Law-Idea. But Bavinck raised theological questions that continued to play a crucial role in mainstream theology after he had gone. Some of these were the same questions that "ethical theology" specialized in, the relationship of Christian faith to culture and science, and the analysis of the *experience* of salvation within the human heart.

In spite of his objections to experiential theology, Bavinck did not think that the purpose of this theology was to make subjective, pious experience the criterion of religious truth. Kuyper was more critical of experiential theology, and thought Bavinck's critique was too mild. He suspected that a pantheistic streak ran through experiential theology. Bavinck, on the other hand, was more sensitive to the dangers of dead orthodoxy, of a confession that one believed in place of a living faith that one confessed. Great theologian that he was, Bavinck certainly was aware that the Christian had to reflect about the manner in which divine revelation entered convincingly into human consciousness. And in this regard he acknowledged an important truth in experiential theology. Relativism had no part in his theology, yet he always carefully analyzed theological opinions he did not share in the tension of a tightly drawn line between appreciation and criticism. His successor, Valentin Hepp, remarked that Bavinck probed the outer limits of appreciation in the work of those with whom he disagreed. Contact *and* encounter: this was the vocation he felt was a challenge to conservative theology for the new era. And all the while the challenge of catholicity fascinated him.

Besides "ethical theology," the beginning of the twenties was also marked by the presence of modernist theology. The conflict between orthodoxy and liberalism has always figured large in the history of the Reformed Churches. Kuyper, in 1871, branded liberalism as a mirage, a *fata morgana*, within Christendom. It was, he said, beautiful and seductive, but empty of reality. In view of his radical opposition to liberalism, his noting its beauty is remarkable. His admiration did not, however, weaken his antipathy to liberalism. Much rather, he experienced its blandishments as a summons to fight: "There is courage in our blood again, and luster in our mild eyes. We have learned to venture again, and to admit that our enemy is riding high in the saddle." And still, he talked of the beauty of liberalism.

The beauty he saw lay in the early deterministic phase of liberal thought, a determinism that "chases free will out of the church and glorifies God's determination of life." There was beauty, too, in the optimistic confidence that the "holy things" would prevail in the human heart. It was, he said, a most unusual phenomenon that "the strictest Reformed people, of the old stamp, at first

accepted the preacher of liberalism as one of their very own."
They actually dreamed "that the truth of God was breaking
through in the church of the fathers." Divine sovereignty, irresistible grace, predestination — all of it was articulated so well
that it seemed as if the most rugged sort of orthodoxy (supralapsarianism) was about to have its day. This early liberalism, full
of color and smacking of energy, grasped again for principles, for
roots and relationships within what had become a tragic, melan-
choly religious environment; it impressed people as a powerful
faith, a faith that really expected divine rescue in times of ship-
wreck, a faith that was jubilant about the love of God. It was
able, with its grasp for depth, to form a partnership with the
thought of the age, and offered the promise of filling the depths of
the human heart.

We cannot say that this side of the liberal mirage was long
appreciated by Reformed people as time went on. Kuyper's appreciation for it had little echo later on, especially as objections grew
to the very determinism that he admired within all those principles.
And what we remembered of Kuyper's response to liberalism was
not his early fascination, but his insight into its illusory character,
its seductiveness as a mirage. Other facets of liberalism came to the
fore, quite unrelated to its determinism, and these were seen to
be antithetical to historic Christianity.

Bavinck's lecture on *Modernism and Orthodoxy*, given in
1911, set the tone for Reformed criticisms of modernism.
Here there was nothing of Kuyper's appreciation of modernism's deterministic penchant. Bavinck set the two in sharp
opposition, based on the uniqueness of God's revelation — a
matter of life and death for Christian faith. He typified
liberalism as "anti-supernaturalist" in that it recognized no
reality beyond and above nature. But even Bavinck refused
to be totally negative about liberalism. He spoke of the "tremendous problems in the facing of which Christianity had more than
ever before to demonstrate its catholicity; it had to demonstrate
that the gospel is a word for all people, all times, and all circumstances." He was especially intrigued by the expanding knowledge
of a world rapidly opening its secrets. We had no right, he said,
to "despise the knowledge that God in his providence is dis-
closing to us from all sides in this century. We must use every
means that science and culture make available for a better understanding of God's truth in general revelation." Moreover, we

should study "the psychological and historical conditions under which revelation, inspiration, incarnation, and regeneration took place." And he saw modernism as at least attempting some of these things.

Bavinck did not speak as romantically about modernism as Kuyper did, and was little interested in the aspects that fascinated Kuyper. He did refer to the "apparent overlapping of determinism and the doctrine of predestination" but thought there was a fundamental difference between them (*Gereformeerde Dogmatiek*, 1906, II, p. 330). He was concerned with other things, with the encounter between the church and modern culture, with the call to catholicity; and he saw these in terms of a profound calling. He was fascinated with the themes that arose in the thought of his time, and, though critical, was open to the questions posed by the confrontation of science with faith. His judgments of how others dealt with the problems were influenced by his own sense of the importance of the problems themselves. In the case of "ethical theology," his opposition was tempered by awareness that it was trying to understand something of how men actually experience God in this world. It was the same in his opposition to modernism; his critique was never merely negative, and he knew that the issues were not simple and transparent.

Bavinck's students (I never knew or heard Bavinck personally) recall a kind of tension in the man. "Outwardly he gave the impression of spiritual peace and balance. But one could not help feeling that behind that image lay a deep, nervous tension that sometimes erupted in angry words at people who shared his convictions but understood nothing of his problems" (G. Brillenburg Wurth). We ought not explain Bavinck's tensions in terms of his personality. They were part of the theological problem that he lived and thought.

The tensions came out in an incident when, after his studies at the University of Leiden, he prepared to take his ordination exams. He was assigned to preach on the blind guides of Matthew 15:14: "Let them alone; they are blind guides." He suspected that the text was assigned him with his professors at Leiden in mind. Impulsively, he began his sermon, in pique, with the remark: "Why this text was given to me is not hard to guess. The phrase about leaders *of the blind* was purposely left out of the assignment. It would have been natural to include it. But that no one dared to do." This was the Bavinck of tension, not the Bavinck of spiritual patience. He had written to his friend, C. Snouck Hurgronje, that he had learned at Leiden to try to understand his opponent. And his friends did not always understand him in doing so.

The influence of his early years at Leiden did not diminish, and it made a difference in his approach to the problems that engrossed him increasingly in the later years. Toward the end of his life, he wrote a report on the question of expanding the church's creeds. Among other things, he said "that in the almost three centuries since the writing of the confessions, errors have increased, on one hand, and on the other our insight into some areas of the confession has grown more clear." So integrity and truth compel the church, he said, to give an account to those outside the church as candidly as possible. Continuity of faith within all the changes of time — this is what Bavinck was concerned to express. But he touched here a problem that had played a role in the rise of modernism and in the development of biblical criticism. He was aware of this and it had the makings of a challenging confrontation.

These were questions that also fermented within the Roman Catholic Church of the time, since the turn of the century, in fact, when modernism began to invade the churches. A sharply condemnatory encyclical was issued from the teaching office in 1907 and an anti-modernist oath was published in 1910. But later, after 1920, Catholics began to step back a pace from earlier condemnations of modernism. They asked themselves whether Catholic reaction to modernism had not been too negative, whether it had not failed to take account of real problems, and whether those same problems would not come back to rap at the portals of the church with more force later on. The anti-modernist oath was followed by intense fear lest the enemy show up inside the church itself. It was a period of suspicion and insinuation, the day of what came to be called "integralism." Integralism stood for a demand of absolute purity in the church over against all modern errors, and for absolute clarity on the traditional inheritance of faith that was entrusted to the church to be kept unchanged for all time.

As far as I know, Bavinck never spoke publicly about Catholic integralism, though he must have known about it. Clearly, it came from a spirit foreign to Bavinck. Integralism closed the ranks against everything that looked new or strange; it helped

create an epidemic of suspicion. Bavinck declined to take this
route. And he did so for the sake of the truth.

Catholic voices were raised against the negativism and reactionary spirit of integralism. The question was raised as to
whether Pius X was not too one-sided in his denunciation of
modernism. Cardinal de Jong spoke out against the "wheels that
grind too finely," and his biographer recalls how he filled an
integralist journal with ironic jottings indicating he saw it as little
more than rumor-mongering. To be sure, Pope Benedict XV, as
early as 1914, had rejected integralism in a summons to greater
love among Catholics.

As students in the twenties we were little aware of all that
was going on in the Catholic world. Later we would learn something of the harshness and grimness of it all, and would discover
that there was a common problem that Catholics and Protestants
shared as they sought the right way for the church to travel
"between the times." In all this, it is no wonder that Bavinck
became a model of how theology could be done with commitment
to the truth combined with openness to problems, and carefulness
in judgments against others. And we understood that this posture
had nothing to do with relativism.

As we hesitatingly sought a way for Dutch theology after
1920, understanding little of the complexities of the whole theological question, we encountered a duality within the circle of
modernism itself. I will characterize it by referring to a professor
at the University of Leiden, K.H. Roessingh. I recall the impression that Roessingh made on me as a theological student. His
untimely death at the age of 39, in the midst of a stormy theological development, shocked many of us, not only because an
impressive writing career had come so early to its end, but mostly
because of the new sounds he made that caused us all to wonder
whether Kuyper's label — mirage — for modernism was wholly
accurate. When Roessingh died, I wrote in our student paper:

> The effect of his work was not to make everything clear and cer-
> tain; much more he made it plain to us that it was the paradox of
> wrath and grace that was the most important thing in life. He
> witnessed to the paradox during his final days. He said: "From
> God comes judgment *and* forgiveness, the never ended struggle
> and the ever renewed victory, the despairing cry from the depth of
> misery to him on high and the Hallelujah for the help he
> gives below."

For us, this was a new form of modernism. It was what Roessingh called a "modernism of the right." The term "right" gave us problems. We had gotten used to distinguishing between the right and left in "ethical theology," even though the distinction was often hazy. Besides, it was pretty hard to see the difference between leftist "ethical theology" and plain modernism. But how could modernism contain a right and left wing? This was the question for us in the Reformed tradition: What must we think of modernism of the right?

Was the self-styled rightist of modernism still the same old modernist, only with a different style? Were all the familiar convictions and motives of modernism still there? Or was a new stream loose in theology? What was clear was that right-wing modernism had no intention of being annexed by orthodoxy. While it may have been *rightist* modernism, it was still rightist *modernism*, and intended to be. But what characterized it was its unabashed willingness to go anew in search of a theology.

One thing was clear to Roessingh. Liberalism had been a spiritual necessity. Liberalism was not a catalogue of liberal ideas; it was an attitude, a disposition of critical openness and of integrity toward the result of modern science. He admired modernism's effort to bridge the gap between faith and culture, and to accept the problems that bridge-building entailed. He refused to accept what Moltmann would later call "the cold schism" between faith and culture.

Anyone who knew Bavinck would recognize a kinship between his attitudes and Roessingh's. Bavinck, too, knew that the facts of science "compelled respect," as he put it. So Bavinck was fascinated by Roessingh; he admired Roessingh's interest in various areas of cultural activity, his respect for science, his unwillingness to eschew its results in order to protect the flanks of faith.

But Roessingh, while affirming the stance of classic modernism with respect to culture, questioned whether modernism had a foundation from which to face the crucial questions of the time. It was at this point that he went his own way, seeking and testing the spirits. In 1924 he wrote: "I am seeking a synthesis between the principles of idealistic philosophy and the principles of Reformation Christianity." But he conceded: "the synthesis I seek may never be found."

His search drove him to concentrate on christology. We know about Barth's radical shift (from his *Prolegomena* of 1927 to the

Church Dogmatics of 1932). But even in some of the words used,
Roessingh's shift was parallel. In words similar to the title of H.
Berkhof's book: *Christ, the Meaning of History*, Roessingh wrote:
"Temporality means decay: the eternally shifting play of history.
But Christ is Lord over all and in all. He is the meaning of history
for me. And so the restless, apparently meaningless passage of
all reality has no dread for me anymore." The heart of modernism,
he thought, was its vision of God at the center of realities, holding
all things together. For Roessingh, this bond was Christ: "For
me everything comes together in Christ." He sought a christology
that would be the foundation for critical theology, a christology
that would show the centrality of Christ's significance. "God
works in history. God shall lead Christ to victory in history. But
this is Christ as he really is, as he truly is in timeless perfection,
not merely as I or someone else sees him." Roessingh wanted a
pastoral christology, and he warned against nonexistential preoccupation with theology. He liked to recall General Booth's
good-by to a journalist: "Don't forget your soul," said the founder
of the Salvation Army. "Let that be said to us, too," Roessingh
added. And he cautioned against branding such talk as pietistic,
or "sickly" as they put it then; "Work out your own salvation,"
Roessingh reminded us, "with fear and trembling." For what is at
stake "is the most precious thing God can give: trust in him." He
enjoyed quoting hymns in his addresses, like "Rest My Soul, Your
God Is King." He sprinkled his scholarly lectures with urgent talk
about prayer for God's grace, prayer that Christ might become
king over this bewildered and rudderless earth.

Is it surprising that, as students of theology, we wondered
how Kuyper's characterization of modernism as a mirage could
apply here? Was this nothing but mirage, a specter with no reality
to it? Was this not a very different modernism from the image we
had grown up with? Christ as the turning point in my own life,
and the turning point in world history — was this only a mirage?
Roessingh cited and then anathematized, in the style of papal
anathemas, a sentence from a contemporary modernist. "Christology, however it is clothed, has no place for a faith that is based on
modern insight." The notion had taken root in modernist
circles, but Roessingh was no longer able to breathe in that
atmosphere. He did consider it imperative that we be honest;
and he emphatically took his position against orthodox christology.
While he saw no reason to deny the historicality of Jesus, he

wanted his christology to be independent of this question. Christology, he thought, should not be tied to past history; theology should focus on the cosmic Christ. Still, he found his resources exclusively in the New Testament. He was intrigued by the historical-critical question of how much Jesus' real self was actually reflected in the New Testament profile. But he preferred the language of trust and commitment. "Christ — I can venture with him." There was always a tension at the point where theological problematics met personal piety, maybe even a pietistic strain. But his piety did not turn him away from the problems. He felt kinship with Ernst Troeltsch in this. He experienced his own development as a kind of conversion: and the turn was to a modernism of the right.

Roessingh saw the old modernism primarily as anti-supernaturalist. Its anti-supernaturalism was expressed in making rejection of miracle a kind of shibboleth for modern theology. Old modernism, he thought, was a monistic religion. It had no place for duality, no place for discontinuity and newness. The old modernism assumed a cause-effect nexus in the world that allowed for no genuine breakthrough into the interlocking connections of history. Roessingh wondered whether we do not live in constant experience of breakthrough from another world.

Old modernism tended to equate sin with nature. But Roessingh insisted that sin had no natural residence in the world. In the modernism of the right, sin again became an active negation; it was a destruction, an enigma, and more, hostility toward God — and this was something other than a "not yet" factor in human development. With this renewed awareness of the destructive power and guilt of sin, the theologian's concern had to be with saving grace. This brought the old modernists down on him, roughly at times. He responded to one modernist critic in these words: "And so, in the high moments of our preaching, we are brought back, almost against our will and intention, to the orthodox home." He admitted that he was in rapport with ethical orthodoxy, and challenged old modernism with two points: our own human sinfulness and God's great love, revealed above all in Christ. In short, his difference with old modernism was summarized by sin and grace.

His objection to old modernism was not that it tried to be scientific. He too was fascinated by theoretical questions of reason. He gave an address, once, on the problem of truth in the new theology. But he accused old modernism of a naive trust in human reason. This is the source of his doubts about the quest for a synthesis. He had great respect for Allard Pierson, the man who resigned from the ministry and left the church once he was convinced of liberalism. But he did not follow Pierson's example, and went his own way within the church to wrestle there with the problems of faith, science, and honesty.

The questions of sin and guilt, novelty and continuity, were also part of his vision of the world and history. He was branded a pessimist by old modernists. But he rejected this label, even though he had deep reservations about human progress. Spengler had written his *Decline of the West* in which he talked about the destiny that carried every culture toward its decline and destruction. But Spengler did not consider himself a pessimist, even though his analysis of history seemed singularly pessimistic. Roessingh wrote a critical review of Spengler's work right after hearing Rudolf Otto plead for an "organization of all the good will that exists in the world." He asked whether Spengler was not a hundred times more correct than all the talk about our good will and our good intentions. But still he saw Spengler standing at a relativistic point "where I do not choose to be." He refused to adopt a full-scale historicizing of life, such as that of Theodor Lessing (*Geschichte als Sinngebung des Sinnlosen*, 1919). Certainly a lot of old certitudes have been taken away. But in place of Spengler's apocalypse he posited "our apocalypse" — the biblical hope: "See, I make all things new." Here "decline" cannot be the last word; a new creation is the final reality.

Not surprisingly, the advent of dialectical theology did not come unnoticed by Roessingh. Most old modernists saw nothing in it but a repristinated orthodoxy, an anti-modernity, anti-culture movement. But Roessingh saw things differently. He could grasp Karl Barth's radical criticism of culture and his eschatological accents; he saw these as the most serious attack on humanistic religion that was ever launched. He was fascinated with Barth's assault on liberal theology for having turned faith in the living God into an idealistic cultural optimism, with the attendant loss of the paradox of sin and grace. His response to Barth betrayed some of the tensions that had always kept his theology vibrating. Remarkably, he explained his response to Barth partly in terms of the Dutch character. Holland did not have the great tradition of Kant and Hegel behind it, and was never affected as much as

Germany by dialectical tension. "Erasmus is our forefather, and like it or not, we cannot drive him out of our character."

The First World War was over. Theology was seeking new directions. Roessingh had experienced the dark and irrational sides of reality and felt himself confronted by the very deepest questions in human life. But he was sustained by hope. "The time is close at hand," he would say, and he spoke about being homesick in the fashion of the biblical prayer: "Maranatha, even so, Come Lord." "The perfect is coming," he would say, "and the tensions will be lifted: I do not know how or when. . . ." At the height of his christological and eschatological questioning, Roessingh died, at the age of 39, in 1925. (Roessingh's works were collected in five volumes under the title *Verzamelde Werken*, and published between 1926 and 1929.)

We who were students at the time followed Roessingh's venture with no little amazement. We could hardly guess that what we saw in Roessingh, both his hesitations and his assertions, would hold our attention and demand our response for years to come. I am thinking of the question of supernaturalism, of the relationship between history and proclamation, of the quest for the historical Jesus and historical criticism, and of the eschatological dimension of faith with its implication for the meaning of human life in the midst of dark and evil powers. And in all of this, there looms the question of the truth and credibility of the Christian faith in our modern world. These are the questions with which both Bavinck and Roessingh wrestled. Is there a way for Christian faith to give an answer by way of an honest and authentic analysis of man and his world? Or ought faith and religion to retreat into their own isolated enclave, busy with things that have little to do with what modern man confronts in his world? The question is hardly new, nor was it new in their time. Schleiermacher had been beset all his life with the question of faith and religion in relation to culture. At the end, Schleiermacher was ready to put the question aside: "I do not care to experience this time anymore; I can set myself peacefully to sleep." But, he wrote to Lücke, "You, my friend, what will you do with the tradition?" Is it a fable from which nothing more can be minted, no matter how much history lies at its base? Or is it really filled with perspective and responsibility? He summarized it all in his famous question: "Shall the knot of history come apart in this way, that Christendom is for the barbarians and science for the unbeliever?"

The relevance of his question prevailed as theology sought its way after the First World War. And it remained relevant through the Second World War and into our own time. Those who answered Schleiermacher's question with a courageous No back in 1920 might have predicted that the way ahead would be difficult. And they would have been right. For the way since then has been charged with conflicts and tensions, sometimes without perspective and sometimes with hope, sometimes exciting and sometimes shocking, but always challenging.

2

The Era of Apologetics

WHEN I FIRST BEGAN TO STUDY THEOLOGY AT THE FREE UNIVERSITY in 1922, we were immediately forced to ask what sort of discipline dogmatics really was. We knew that Bavinck had written his highly esteemed dogmatics and that Kuyper had published a huge number of dogmatic studies and that, indeed, his published lectures had become a sort of dogmatics even though he did not consider them a finished piece of work. Dogmatics came to us as a rounded-off and finished system that we had to master for church examinations; we had to demonstrate that we would be capable of passing the material on to others. But later we came in touch with all sorts of doubts and uncertainty about facets of the system; problems and questions unsettled us. We did not know then what Bremmer said about Bavinck much later, that "he had lived the last years of his life in a theological vacuum." Nor did we then know what the call for theological renewal and for further reflection on the church's confessions would mean concretely for us in the days ahead.

What did happen immediately was that Hepp, Bavinck's successor at the Free University, gave an inaugural paper on Reformed Apologetics (1922). Apologetics had historically been a subsection of dogmatic theology, and Hepp had no doubts about the place of apologetics within dogmatics. But he figured that the time had come to concentrate more attention on apologetics. He rejected the notion that apologetics was a defensive undertaking, as most of us had assumed; he considered defensiveness a sign of hesitancy and weakness, a willingness to sacrifice successive points in the line of defense as they came under attack from critics. Kuyper had earlier expressed his own negative feelings about apologetics; he saw it as being "bereft of a boldness that dared everything, lacking a high sense of confidence, and without a flaming readiness for battle; it was more like a timid

25

readiness to sacrifice the outposts and the valleys and then retreat into the fortress of the inner heart to protect oneself from a
frontal assault." Kuyper did not see apologetics as a means for
winning back a lost spiritual militancy. But Hepp saw the situation differently. He thought the church needed apologetics des-
perately if it was not going to lose its power among the intellectuals. Moreover, he assessed the status of Reformed theology in
particular as being very favorable for apologetics. Its system had
won the jealousy of others; had not Ernst Troeltsch been impressed with the excellence of Calvinism over against Catholicism
and Lutheranism? Apologetics, then, not as a defensive movement,
but as a courageously ventured witness to the truth in the
strength of the Christian faith — this is how Hepp saw it. He had
in mind not a general apologetics for faith, but a specific Reformed apologetics.

Bavinck too was better disposed toward apologetics than
Kuyper was. It deserved more serious development, he thought,
and had the potential of enormous blessing for the church. Apologetics, in his judgment, forced theology to account for its own
foundation; it compelled Christian theology to move out of the
mystique of the heart into the full light of reason. It could teach
us that Christians need not retreat humbly into silence, need not
feel foreign and isolated in the world. Bavinck had a vision of an
intellectually aggressive Christianity.

Hepp likewise thought that apologetics lent courage to theology. It was very evident in Roman Catholic apologetics, which
had aggressively gone into battle against the anti-faith forces of
the nineteenth century. Thus, he rejected any devaluation of
rational thought; it could be used to give form to what Paul
said about the gospel being "worthy of all acceptance" (1 Timothy
1:16). This apologetics wanted to build a platform for discussion
and encounter with critics of faith — dialogue and encounter, on
the level of reason, over against the isolation of a strictly personal
and individual piety for which faith was a miraculous gift of God
and not a belief that blossomed with rational thought. Apologetics
was set against the notion, then, that one could talk to other people about faith only in the style of a personal witness.

The First Vatican Council (1870) said that God could be
known from the world of created reality through the natural light
of reason. The anti-modernist declaration of 1910 spoke assuredly of
the possibility of proving God's existence. Thus, opposed to timidity

and silence, the church called for courage in confrontation. This motif played a big role in Hepp's summons to the apologetic task. He even wrote, in his Stone Lectures (*Calvinism and the Philosophy of Nature*, 1930), about Calvinism's affinity for a philosophy of nature. In all this, he stressed above everything else the need for a specifically Reformed apologetics.

This vision of a specific, unique Reformed apologetics made itself felt in many ways during the decade of the twenties. This was true not only with reference to dogmatics and churchly confession, but in the total life-and-world view of Calvinism. In 1925 Herman Dooyeweerd began to write about the need for a Christian statecraft, in which Troeltsch's analysis of Calvinism and capitalism, and of historicism and supernaturalism, came to view. Anyone stimulated by Dooyeweerd's analysis of history, who then turned to Troeltsch, had to come to grips with the special character of Calvinism. Dooyeweerd had concluded, from a study by Matthias Schneckenburger of the comparison between Reformed and Lutheran thought, that the Reformed idea of the law — which Schneckenburger had thought to be central to Reformed thought — had a universal significance. The notion of law espoused by Calvinism had potential to become far more than a facet of dogmatics and ethics. Schneckenburger (and Troeltsch) had seen the law in Reformed life as a legalistic tendency; but Dooyeweerd saw it differently. He saw the law as a boundary between God and creature, and came to a philosophy of the law-idea as central to an "eternal, unchangeable world-order."

Later, Dooyeweerd's views were the center of much discussion, especially with regard to the centrality of the law-idea and the relationship between philosophy and theology. But at the beginning, what was impressive was the research into the unique dimensions of Calvinism as well as of Reformed theology. This also helps explain the movement toward apologetics. When Hepp called for a Reformed apologetics, one which would speak in absolute tones, the question naturally arose as to how this absolute and positive attitude could be united with what Bavinck said about dogmatics — that it was not the Word of God, but only a "vague image and a weak correspondence, a fallible human undertaking in which one tried to think through and translate what God had said beforehand and in various ways. . . ." What meaning might this modest limit to dogmatics have for the positive, confident, and courageous language of apologetics?

Looking back, it was not easy for that generation of theologians to understand this absolutist tone. Still, a summons to appropriate the right to a positive apologetics, especially one oriented to Reformed dogma, gave them something to think about. Understandably, this call to a self-confident offensive could easily raise the image of a defense of dogma as an isolated fortress besieged by alien forces of one's time. Hepp did see apologetics as a "science of the present" courageously encountering whatever criticism the spirits raised in *our* time. But it appeared later, and in fact was true before 1920, that the analogy of the unchangeable fortress being defended from attack was not all that apt; and furthermore, a lot of uncertainty arose as to how best to carry on the defense.

In the area of apologetics — and especially of specifically Reformed apologetics, which Hepp thought others envied — it soon became obvious that there were others outside the circle of Reformed theology who had an equally positive approach. As I recall some of these, the name of A.H. de Hartog, the philosopher-theologian, comes to mind. De Hartog was a crusading apologist of the day. His thoughts and style of witness exuded a magnificently positive manner. He was profoundly convinced of the truth of the Christian faith, and believed that faith did not have to hide itself in some intellectual catacomb, but had every reason to move in the center of the spiritual and cultural conflict.

I have a vivid memory of the circle of students who came under De Hartog's influence. In 1923, when we heard him, he was 54 and in his prime. Seldom have I met anyone who spoke about Christian truth with such fervor and utter certainty. He spoke not simply of a truth that is discovered and experienced only in the atmosphere of a subjective experience, but of a truth that is objective and able to persuade and convince others. He talked in student circles about his epistemology, about Schopenhauer and Hegel, about the reasonableness of Christian faith in an all-good and all-wise God. He talked about all the important theological themes — the Holy Scriptures, the facts of redemption, predestination, and so forth. He also published notes on Calvin's *Institutes* (which we had then not yet read).

De Hartog was present when Barth visited Amsterdam for the first time, back in 1926, and thought at first that Barth was saying the same things he was saying. He thought that Barth's thinking offered the promise of apologetic renewal in Reformed theology. But he was terribly disillusioned, for Barth was saying things quite different from De Hartog's apologetics.

De Hartog was the tireless apologete, fearless in any dialogue, out to demonstrate the harmony between faith and science. When World War One was over, he saw new theological battle lines drawn everywhere. The freethinkers' association called themselves The Dawn; the allusion was to the light of science arising to dissipate the fog of faith. De Hartog began a counter-group called High Noon. In 1929 he wrote a book about certainty in which he tried to show "how the certainty of a higher reality and truth flowed necessarily from progress in the reflections of the human spirit." This was why he was never intimidated by science. What Van de Leeuw said later, that God was not afraid of psychology, would have fit De Hartog's attitude. Facts never threatened him because he was sure that, on deeper reflection, discoveries of new facts could only support faith. He wanted to convince his contemporaries that the All-Energizer ("all" was one of his favorite words) had organized the "all-becoming" universe from before time began. He was fascinated with progress, the ongoing development within the perspective of eternity. With his tendency to take an eternal point of view, he was suspicious of any tendency to look one-sidedly at Christianity as a historical religion. He affirmed the historical facts of redemption; but he did not think it possible to stick with them. They were contingent facts, events of history. One had to go on to see the divine necessity of the appearance of the Christ. From the eternal perspective, he thought, Christianity could bypass Nietzsche. His indomitably positive vision of the "All-Energizer" — on the way to the omega point, as Chardin would put it later — spilled over us all.

"The naked shocks roll over us, the flames burst around us, misery calls out its agony, sin erupts, and hell breaks loose, but the ship of the Eternal Counsel is brought safely to harbor through the ravages of the storms. The sun rises and sets, rivers flow through the valleys, flowers burst forth from the earth, and the power of love radiates into the open heart." This is the way he talked. Seldom have I heard anyone make such a fervent pitch for a theodicy in the midst of a plethora of facts that contradicted it. The sun of love was always breaking through the bitter tears. He was always on the hunt for synthesis, for perspective in the depths and heights. He was often called an eclectic, and he did indeed pluck feathers from many kinds of birds: Von Hartmann,

Schopenhauer, Hegel, Calvin, and Kuyper. And it was for him much more than a matter of theory; his was a deep personal conviction.

In a debate at the Amsterdam Concertgebouw, De Hartog once leaped to his feet like a prophet calling the business to a halt: "Anyone offending my Friend, the eternal, holy God, has to deal with his prophet. Let them put me to the stake — ah, I am already at the stake! It may sound pretentious, but I feel that any man who is jeered (someone had laughed at his words) feels the flames of blasphemy in his face. Shall I let my Friend be derided?" Amsterdam had, for the moment, become a kind of Areopagus, and here was an apologetic with the hot flame of passion and conviction that befit it. No one could deny him this. This was no enclave defense; it was an offensive. The voice was that of a prophet in the world of Spengler's *Decline of the West;* here was the voice of hope and confidence in a time of "fateful necessity" and defeatism.

People have often asked why De Hartog gained no disciples. His synthesis and his forceful thrust toward the deeper rationality of things were not able to entice those for whom the problems of theodicy were not so easily solved as they were for him. We could not follow him as he swept his way through the speculative heights. The rationality of world and life were not all that transparent to some of us.

Toward the end of his life (he died in 1935), De Hartog wrote about "modern paganism." He pointed to a decline into heathenism, and in fact it was not long afterward that synagogues in Germany went up in flames. But De Hartog never basically doubted the truth and reality of his breath-taking vision. In spite of all the obvious differences between De Hartog and Barth, there was something of the triumphant, of the "nevertheless" of the triumph of grace in both. Barth was also able to write that unbelief was "hellish nonsense" in the light of the unconquerable reality. When I talked with Barth in Basel (1954) I admitted that I had more difficulty than he with the joyful "nonetheless." Barth answered: "Yes, yes, I also know about starving Chinese and the wars. But that will pass." Anyone who knew Barth recognized that when he said, "Yes, I know," he was not merely nodding concessions to what he considered trivial information. No less than Paul, when he talked about the "suffering of this present time," Barth took the negatives and pain of life seriously. It was within the awareness of evil that the "nonetheless" broke through. It was the same with De Hartog. We could hear him speak as though he had no doubts at all, hear him give witness to all those who found life tough, but he would witness to the divine perspective, the light in the darkness, the christological *omega* that waits on the horizon of time. Everything in that perspective became deep and irrefutable, universal and meaningful. Everything lay within divine rationality. This was the sphere of apologetics. . . .

Still another advocate of apologetics during the decade of the twenties was that of the fiery apologete, Karl Heim. Heim devoted his whole life to the question of faith's certainty and to the confrontation between faith and modern science and philosophy. As secretary of the Christian Student Association in Germany, he came into contact with all the lively questions, and, for that matter, he himself posed the question of whether unsolved problems form a handicap to faith. The questions that were posed to the church and theology by natural science kept him preoccupied constantly. Dogmatics as such, the exposition of faith's affirmations, steadily lost interest for him. He was fascinated by the answer that his own faith gave to the questions of science, but he was equally interested in the questions themselves.

He never intended to prove the affirmations of Christian faith. He wanted to do a deep analysis of philosophical and scientific thought out of a conviction that Christian faith was the key to an answer for all the questions it raised. The fascinating question-answer correlation, which later would play an ever greater part in theology, set Heim in the midst of the major problematics of his time. He published books about the modern world-view (beginning back in 1904), about empiricism and positivism, about the theory of relativity and, in that connection, about the grounds of faith's certainty. By way of his analysis of reality he tried to lead modern man into a forecourt, where the crucial decisions were made, decisions that could not be made by way of analytical logic, but which were not isolated in the ghetto of pure inwardness either. He moved, he himself said, within the arena of "extra-Christian general philosophy." He wanted to think through the consequences of relativism — that of Einstein as well as Spengler — in order to find the absolute in the encounter with Christ within the situation of threatening doubt. "The fact that we are rooted in God or that we must assume his reality is made clear in no other way than by pointing to the situation we were in when we had to conceive of God in this way." Analysis of human thought was taken up into theology and apologetics as part of the "questionableness" of all human life, as an open question that deserves answering.

Much later, S.M. Daecke talked of the commonality between Heim and de Chardin; indeed the similarity was noted earlier. He called Heim the only Protestant theologian who devoted himself to the question of faith's relationship to natural science and did it, not in general terms, but out of a sense of the primacy of Christ. Heim seemed to Daecke to live more in tension and conflict than Teilhard did, with his optimistic evolutionary vision of the omega point. But the points of contact between them were nonetheless real: no dualism, no unavoidable schism, but a confident search for communication and response in what one might call an indirect, preparatory apologetic. This is why he kept speaking of the leap of faith in which the decision — for or against Christ — was made, a leap that was not made in darkness, even though made in the midst of all problems, threats, and struggles with relativism, nihilism, and secularism.

Yet, one cannot avoid the impression that Heim's influence — like that of De Hartog — was very limited. When I was studying for my doctorate with Hepp, I had to write an exam paper on Heim's book, The Certainty of Faith. For a time I considered writing a dissertation on Heim and I entered into correspondence with him. From his letters, it appeared that the glory-period of full lecture halls was at that time (1927) in decline. He wrote to me that he was thankful that there was still interest in his theology in Holland, and added a wistful note to the effect that "my involvement in the certainty question was being vehemently opposed in Germany by dialectical theology." There were other interests being awakened than those of how a meaningful relationship between faith and science could be nourished and how the Christian faith could be defended. That theological attention was shifting from Heim to dialectical theology is understandable when we consider what this theology had accomplished during the twenties. It is clear that Heim blamed Karl Barth for the exodus of students from apologetics.

But dialectical theology itself brought forth a summons to do apologetic theology. It came, not from Barth, but from Emil Brunner. In 1929 he wrote a much discussed article about "The Other Task of Theology" (in Zwischen den Zeiten), in which he contended that a place had to be created alongside of dogmatics for apologetics. Apologetics should be a theology that entered into the problematics of the day, especially those of natural science. We were reminded of Heim's concerns; but with Brunner it involved first of all not a quest for a synthesis, but an offensive, an attack that theology would launch against the presuppositions of faithless reason. He called this apologetics an "eristic theology" (*eris* means "dispute"). He also called it a "missionary theology," in view of its venture into the total problematics of the thought of the time. Theology, with its concern for the internal structuring of the truth of faith, could not, in Brunner's view, afford to isolate itself from the problematics of science and philosophy. While he certainly recognized the intrinsic value of dogmatics, he thought that his situation made encounter with disbelief the more urgent demand. To reject the summons, he thought (and here he surely had Barth in mind), was to imitate Chinese wall-building. Theology may not — indeed, cannot — speak in the air; it has to speak in a space filled with the theories and assumptions of modern men if it is to be listened to and taken seriously. Brunner — no more than Heim — had notions of proving the truths of faith to natural thought, but he wanted to oppose the axioms of modernity that were basically untenable. In this sense there was similarity between him and Heim, since Brunner also wanted to show that the gospel does give an answer, that it is the solution to the contradictions and antinomies in which the thought of natural man always and necessarily becomes stuck.

Though there is no direct coupling between theology and modern thought, there is a possibility for indirect communication between them, a communication in the form of struggle. Illumination will come, perhaps, out of the struggle; and in this way theology can prevent itself from being locked in the ghetto of inwardness or . . . the ghetto of dogmatics. Early on, before 1929, Brunner's theology showed eristic traits (in *Die Offenbarung als Grund und Gegenstand der Theologie*, 1925, and *Die Grenzen der Humanität*, 1922). They showed through as he came to grips with the harmonistic vision of human life in German humanism, which was less profound than Greek tragedy because it had no eye for the "existential contradiction, the dreadful riddle of Man." This, said Brunner, was why German humanism could speak so simplistically about the progress and continuity of human life and history. Brunner was not trying to prove anything with this; he always believed that faith was paradoxical, miraculous, "the anti-rationalistic, which nonetheless is the fulfilment of all rationality." Faith stood critically against all incursions by reason. In 1925 he wrote that apologetic methods "must not allow revelation to be digested into the system of reason, but contrariwise, reason must be taken into revelation." From this point, apologetics can take the offensive, without fear and without defensiveness that is really a lack of self-assurance. But it must be an offensive that, as with Pascal, is always ready for critical communication. Brunner devoted a large portion of his life to eristic theology (cf. *Der Mensch im Widerspruch*, 1937, E.T. *Man in Revolt*, 1939, and *Offenbarung und Vernunft*, 1941, E.T. *Revelation and Reason*, 1946). He did it always with an acute sense of responsibility. The desire to transcend the closed circle of dogmatics was motivated by a need to liberate dogmatics from its fruitless isolation and to set it in the center of the world's thinking. Here, at the center of the modern thought-world, theology was called to enter into confrontation with self-destructive reason.

During the time that Brunner called theology to this form of apologetics (1929), the conflict between him and Barth was intensifying, and it came to a head in the breakup of the circle of dialectical theology in 1933, when the journal *Zwischen den Zeiten* folded. We will not go into the dispute between Brunner and Barth at this point, though it has much to do with apologetics and the problem of the point of contact. We will only raise the general question that arises out of this early period in the sphere of apologetics: How is it possible that so much discussion could have been provoked by an appeal to "defend" the gospel?

The question is the more interesting because all defenders of the rightful place of apologetics appeal to the fact that the New Testament associates faith with a call to resistance, and to confrontation — a defense that is at the same time an offense. Faith is never isolated; it develops into a movement that is outer-directed. Paul, at the Areopagus and before Festus, proclaimed that he was speaking sober truth (Acts 26:25). Were not the faithful explicitly summoned to give a reason *(logos, ratio)* for their hope (1 Peter 3:15)? And ought not every Christian know how to give a good answer to everyman (Colossians 4:6)?

Why, then, we may ask again, did so manifestly biblical a motif arouse so much debate? It seems so clear: faith is called to defend itself against any critical attack that seeks to negate the meaning, the right, and the truth of faith. Is not eristic theology simply a response to a mandate? Is it not faith's way of showing that it is not ashamed, and that it dares enter confrontation with unbelief?

Right into our own day, the relation between faith and reason becomes a concern whenever we face striking divergence between people who in many ways think alike, but part company when it comes to faith. With this, the problem of communication is put on the agenda: Is faith an irrational and esoteric mystery that has no point of contact with the other person? Can we only *witness* to our faith? Or is there within human thought a possibility for real and mutually understood dialogue?

This is the question that comes to us out of the twenties. We shall have to come back to it, since the relation between faith and reason looms large again in theology. Within the horizon that we have been viewing, it should be noted that the concrete form apologetics takes is always influenced by the presence or absence of certainty and affirmativeness of faith. It can occur that, under the impact of sharp criticism, doubts arise within the circle of faith, doubts that bear on whether apologetics can speak in absolute tones. But whenever certainty is present in times of sharp and widespread criticism of the content of Christian faith, we may no longer be content only to witness — as in "Here I stand, I can do no other." We may feel compelled to ask whether there are not indications in the world of thought available to all that, while not having the cogency of proof, do form "indicators" of the possibility at least, and perhaps the reasonableness as well, of faith.

Bavinck himself was concerned about this question. He spoke of arguments as "indicators" which at least "make an impression." He seemed to respect the value of these "indicators" when it came to certain dogmatic positions. We must keep his situation in mind. Bavinck discerned all sorts of people who in the midst of skepticism hoped "that science would open the inner sanctum of human consciousness and there cultivate the flower of religion." In his book about the certainty of faith, he spoke about the fact that many were ready to sacrifice position after position in the hopes of securing one last-ditch place of safety for religion. He recognized the danger of this fearful attitude, and he preached — in his only published sermon — about the faith that has power to conquer the world (1 John 5:4).

Bavinck was set against all dualism between faith and science. He refused to adopt an isolationism that turned faith into an irrational mystery which could be accepted only in mystic silence or witnessed to only with a "tongue-speaking" that the world could not make sense of. He responded with enthusiasm whenever a critique of the gospel, on second look, was shown to have arisen from prejudice rather than from a responsible argument. He used to sound very much like an apologete, even for the virgin birth, which was being roundly ridiculed in the nineteenth century. A certain theory about the transmission of life led him to write that while there was doubt whether this theory could be directly applied to the virgin birth, it could be said that "should the old struggle between spermatists and ovarists be settled in favor of the later, the working of the Holy Spirit might be physiologically clarified" (*Gereformeerde Dogmatiek,* III, p. 275). This is one of the most remarkable passages in his dogmatics. No one would want to operate with such considerations today; but it is a hint of how Bavinck looked for lines of contact between science and faith with a clear apologetic purpose.

Another instance touches on the doctrine of original sin, one of the most difficult parts of dogmatics according to Bavinck. He felt the hot breath of critics here too; but he thought he saw some relief. The truth of original sin, he thought, was supported by such people as Darwin, with his theory of descent in which inheritance plays such a large part. He offered the thesis that "science in our time offers support for the churchly doctrine of original sin." The philosophy of Kant, Schelling, and Schopenhauer, too, offered the doctrine unexpected support, as did the doctrine of the descent of man. "When theology rejected the doctrine, philosophy took it up." Bavinck indeed reckoned with the possibilities of change and self-correction in science.

What we see in these efforts is that theologians are trying to create room within the total world of human thought for Christian faith. When this is seen it becomes clear that in the background of eristic theology is the conviction that faith has no reason to shut itself off from the world of human thought and, in particular, from science and philosophy.

Among the reasons why apologetics has been in disfavor and why it meets theological resistance is that it sometimes leads to an unattractive militancy which is hard to harmonize with the Christian style. Eristic theology (which Brunner also calls polemic theology) has not always been free from a spirit of conflict that irritates its hearers, with the result that instead of opening doors it turns away potential participants in dialogue or provokes them to counterattack. When the New Testament summons us to struggle and resistance, it leaves no doubt as to the choice of weapons: the breastplate of righteousness, the helmet of salvation, and the sword of the Spirit (Ephesians 6:14ff.). This gives the struggle and defense a special kind of style. But if apologetics becomes a fight over a system, or a gnosis, it becomes something very different from the "giving an answer" for faith that the New Testament asks for. The struggle may not be waged for the sake of a fight, but only for the sake of the truth. There must, therefore, never be lust for victory in confrontation. Confrontations can easily be waged in a manner that alienates faith from science without the believing disputants ever understanding the problems of science; quick counterarguments are then not even taken seriously by the other side. Apologetics may then celebrate some sort of victory, while in reality it has only exposed its poverty.

Once again Bavinck offers a model that is instructive. It was never self-evident to Bavinck that anyone who enters a crisis with modern science will come back unscarred. In 1883, he delivered his inaugural address at Kampen on "The Science of Theology." His friend Snouck Hurgronje had evidently responded to it critically. Bavinck wrote to him admitting that he had begun with a prejudgment. He spoke, indeed, of a *leap;* but he added that only he who dares can win anything. If Hurgronje thought that theology had to enter discussion with science in suspended judgment, waiting to see what the conclusion would be, said Bavinck, this would be the end of theology. But this did not mean at all that a closed system of theology entered discussion with a simple and clear apologetic. Bavinck recognized his own commitment, as he said, "even though I understand deep down the objections that can be laid against Christian faith." He talked of "difficulties and wounds" that one experiences along the way of dialogue. When the theologian says this seriously and self-critically, all cheap apologetics is ruled out for him, and apologetics is marked by a profound analysis of the critical question that is placed before Christian faith by the world of thought in which we are all sojourners together. Lacking this, apologetics will fall into mere repetition and fail to give a real answer to real questions. The questions themselves must be proved and understood before a genuine answer can be given. Herein lies the kernel of all responsiveness: it rejects apparent, make-believe answers as empty gestures. For this reason, all answer-giving throws us back to a testing of our own faith and thought. This kind of response gradually prevailed in the discussion about apologetics. The conviction grew that only in a self-critical attitude could communication take place with critics.

As we look back on these years that we have characterized as "the era of apologetics," we note that the historical development was overshadowed by Karl Barth's sharp and energetic contradiction of everything apologetics seemed to be doing. He pointed to the many dangers that were hidden in apologetics, dangers of distorting the gospel, dangers of letting the answer be determined by the question. In short, Barth feared the danger that revelation would be structured by man, by his experience, his thought patterns, his feel for life and its variously complicated problems. Against this, he proposed that it was not the task of theology "to lighten heaven with earth's searchlights, but rather theology is expected to let the light of heaven be seen and understood on earth." This warning went out against all forms of apologetics that ran the danger of conforming the gospel to the natural man.

We debated for a long time whether Barth's critique was just or not, or whether it was exaggerated — especially with respect to Heim and Brunner. We asked whether Barth's attack left any room for the importance of real questions and whether it did not create a vacuum in communication and dialogue. Could he not have been a bit more Socratic, more dialogical? Was he not too aprioristic and objective? And did not his own style of theologizing risk being "saltless" (Colossians 4:6)?

These kinds of questions played a large role later, when more people began to examine the usefulness of Barth's tremendously influential theology of the Word.

3

The Voice of Karl Barth

IF WE DO NOT DISCUSS ALL THE THEOLOGIANS RECKONED AMONG THE circle of dialectical theology after 1920, it is only because the voice of Karl Barth has dominated the scene, exerting enormous influence into our own time. Brunner, Gogarten, Bultmann, and others who belonged with Barth to the group associated with *Zwischen den Zeiten* will come into view along the way. Though the group later broke up, with each going his own way, all of them kept in contact with Barth, whether in conflict or friendship. Barth was the central figure. I do not intend to repeat all that I have written about Karl Barth in the past; but I will point to certain features that I think, seen now from a later perspective, still have significance for us today. We shall meet Barth again in later chapters, and so this chapter will not tell the whole story. Here we will look at some central motifs of Barth's thought that were received on one hand with great admiration and on the other with intense criticism, both receptions complicated by problems in interpreting his thought.

His commentary on Romans was the work that shocked the theological world. Its reception was an enormous surprise for Barth himself. "As I look back at my pathway," he wrote in 1927, "I look like a man who, groping his way in a darksome church tower, unwittingly took hold of a rope that was, in fact, a rope for a church-bell, and then to his own shock heard the bells resounding over him — and far beyond him." This applied particularly to the second printing. The first edition (which was quickly sold out, and later reprinted in 1963) appeared in 1919; but the second edition (1922), according to Barth, "left no stone of the former edition in it." To analyze the amazing circumstances in which this rapid change occurred would be an exciting adventure — a splendid subject for a doctoral dissertation. What influences worked on Barth in that short time between the editions? Over-

beck's name has often been mentioned in this connection. Barth
himself talked about a visit from Gogarten. In any case, it was the
second edition that made its radical impact on the theological
history of this half-century. This was the book that brought the
phrase "crisis-theology" into common currency as a label for
Barth's thought. Barth, of course, never used that phrase; it was
Paul Tillich who first coined it. However it originated, it was
often taken to mean a negative theology, a theology of the loud
NO, a theology of judgment on culture, morality, and religion —
in short, a judgment on everything human.

When we came into contact with his *Romans* here in the
Netherlands, and tried to understand it (it is, in my judgment,
the most difficult of all Barth's works), we gave it various and
contradictory evaluations. The judgment from Reformed circles
was confused by a comparison between Barth and Kuyper. We
wondered what else, outside of an earthquake (thus one biographer), could be felt in such a dynamic and alarming way. It came
to us with a demand for a whole reorientation in theology. The
first sound from the circle of dialectical theologians was charged
with strong emphasis on the majesty, the holiness, and the
sovereignty of God over against all human pretensions to great-
ness, over against all deification of man or of anything in the
created world. In short, it spoke of the infinite difference and
distance between God and man. Were there not clear overtones
here of what Calvinism had always confessed, particularly as it
was refinished in Kuyper's manner, about the absolute sovereignty
of God?

The discussion was influenced from the beginning by Th. L.
Haitjema's conviction that Barth offered a healthy corrective to
Kuyper's Neo-Calvinism. Haitjema, though an admirer of Kuyper's
vision of a re-Christianized European culture, was convinced that
Kuyper's was not a genuine revival of Reformed theology. He saw
in Neo-Calvinism a deceptive synthesis, an oversimplified connection between Christian faith and culture. Calvin, he thought,
was hard to recognize in Kuyper's summons to overcome the
world for the King. Further, he considered Kuyper's notion of
common grace — set alongside special grace — too simplistic a
justification for gathering all that germinates in worldly soil and
receiving it to the honor and praise of God. Kuyper had digested
much from the culture of the enlightenment that was not usable
within the Calvinistic world-and-life view. Moreover, Kuyper

failed to appreciate the infinite difference between God and man. So, against Kuyper's secularization of Christianity, Haitjema greeted Barth's sharp criticism of culture as a healing corrective. Thus, at the very start we faced questions that would continue to play a large part in the Barth discussions. Many turned away from Barth because they found in him too little concern for the world, or for man in the world. This image was hard for Barth to dispel. Who does not remember Brunner's joy at having discovered what he finally recognized as a *new* Barth in a much later volume of the *Church Dogmatics?* Here he found a more positive Barth, a positiveness that Brunner himself had stressed early on. That was not until 1951, and even then not everyone was as enthusiastic as Brunner was.

In the earliest period, Barth was seen as the theologian of distance, of the *No* and of judgment — of the "infinite qualitative difference" between God and man. But not everyone saw this as a needed correction of Neo-Calvinism's "simplistic" synthesis; some criticized it for being one-sided. Wilhelm Kolfhaus saw an affinity between Barth and Kuyper, especially in their similar stress on the sovereignty and holiness of God. And the appreciation of H. F. Kohlbrügge which they shared only buttressed their similarity. But Kolfhaus' interpretation had little influence with us. The accusation of one-sidedness (transcendence without immanence) was what prevailed. Barth's thought seemed to lack any confidence in the hope of blessing coming from the work of God *within* the world. In short, Barth smacked of dualism. Hepp thought that Barth looked only at the top of the mountain and had no eye for the valley. "He could see nothing of the path leading upward." (This was in 1925.)

In the same spirit, we hastily contrived all sorts of handy characterizations of Barth and dialectical theology. It was a postwar phenomenon. It was a form of desperation-theology, with parallels to Spengler's *Decline of the West.* We had the notion of a theology of catastrophe, of total judgment on all that is human in religion, morality, and culture, and of a radical negation. The same criticism came to the surface in Germany during the twenties. Paul Althaus, for instance, criticized Barth for lacking any positive affirmation of history. Barth could appeal to Ecclesiastes: "God is in heaven and you are on earth" (Ecclesiastes 5:2). But this was not enough for the critics.

The question of ethics came up also. How could there be a useful and concrete ethics, an authentically obedient form of action, if all we have is an absolute judgment on the ethos of men and the world. As a matter of fact, Barth had taught ethics at Münster in 1928 and at Bonn in 1930; but these lectures were not published until much later, so they could not enter into the discussion at the time.

Assessing Barth back then was not easy for those of us just beginning our theological studies. We heard that Barth's theology was one of metaphysical crisis — that is, a theology that judged man as lost because of his finitude. We heard that Barth's dialectics made everything uncertain. We heard about his strange paradoxes that threatened to shake all confidence in faith and believing thought. Later it appeared that Barth himself had little use for the adjective "dialectical." And later we understood that the famous quotation from the commentary on *Romans* ("the infinite qualitative difference," a phrase taken from Kierkegaard) was hardly sufficient to characterize a theology. But who was able to see all this at the time?

Contradictory judgments on Barth kept coming. We were alerted not only to his exclusive stress on crisis and judgment, but also to his "absolute universalism." That is, we were warned of a grace that affirmed everything as well as of a judgment that thundered a *No* on everything. C. Van Til (somewhat later) labelled Barth a "Neo-Modernist" and a "Neo-Manichaeist." A. Jülicher, in a review of the first edition of *Romans,* spoke of Barth's "Neo-Marcionism." All this was even more confused by the voices of liberal theologians who saw in Barth only a resurgence of orthodoxy.

Barth's influence in France seemed at first to be quite limited; French theology was not congenial to Barth's "repristination" of Reformation thought. He was accused of restoring the theology of Luther and Calvin without subjecting them to renewal and without recognizing the significance of the Enlightenment. It was said that Barth was trying to restore a theology of objectivity without allowing it to be refined by the fire of modern thought and criticism. This judgment was given further support as Barth continued to criticize nineteenth-century theology generally, aiming his darts at Descartes and many others who, according to Barth, based everything on the Renaissance discovery that man was the measure of all things.

Barth's attack against Harnack is well known. He began his studies in Bern, where he heard that not a single epistle in the New Testament had been written by Paul. After this he went to Berlin where Harnack taught. He was deeply impressed with the great historian. Yet he slowly came to a totally different vision than was expressed in Harnack's "essence of Christianity" (the Fatherhood of God and the infinite value of the human soul). Years later, the two men met again; the occasion was a student conference in 1920. Harnack had been disturbed by a paper Barth had written, titled "Biblical Questions, Insights and Overview." Harnack called it an offense against religion, a theory that had nothing to do with real life. Barth's ideas, he thought, were like a flashy meteor hastening its way to its own destruction. By abolishing theology as a critical science, Barth sacrificed everything modern thought had achieved. Harnack bristled with anger at this new theological barbarianism that was capturing the minds of more and more students. His criticism was directed especially against Barth's transcendent notion of revelation; it was so transcendent and supernatural that historical and critical thought had to be irrelevant to it. For Harnack the scientific method was the only possible way for theology to make itself "the object of responsible knowledge." Since the eighteenth century, for example, it had become crystal clear that a historical-critical quest for the person of Christ was absolutely imperative. Harnack spoke of theology as the master of its "object," and Barth spoke of the "new world of the Bible" mastering theology. Barth said that the task of theology is one with the task of preaching; Harnack responded by saying that theology's task is one with that of science. No wonder that Harnack confessed that Barth's motives were utterly incomprehensible to him. Harnack once put fifteen questions to Barth; from their nature it was apparent that Harnack considered Barth "the betrayer of scientific theology." He asked what basis Barth had for his affirmations. With respect to Jesus Christ as the center of the gospel, he asked: "How is it possible to lay a foundation for a responsible and universal understanding of this Person other than through a critical-historical study, therewith to prevent the trading-in of an imagined Christ for the real Christ?" And how can we be equipped for such a study except with a scientific theology? When Barth answered that the only way to have a trustworthy knowledge of Christ is through a God-awakened faith, and that anyone demanding any

other way will have to be led by "the science of biblical criticism,"
Harnack was hardly satisfied. Indeed his deep suspicions were
strengthened. He denied Barth's suggestion that modern theology
had wandered from its real theme. He saw in Barth's doctrine
of revelation a kind of occultism (i.e., knowledge through secret
sources), or a form of Marcionism that cut the cord between
faith and the naturally human. And he saw a direct connection
between this and the growing skepticism about the results of
historical research, a skepticism that he suspected Overbeck of
instilling in Barth.

Harnack was wholly alienated by the revelational dimensions
of Barth's theology; to him, it meant the loss of the simple gospel
(cf. Harnack's *What is Christianity?* English title for *Das Wesen
des Christentums*, first published in 1900 but republished in 1964
with a foreword by Bultmann). Harnack, always the historian,
could not grasp the manner in which Barth worked with the history of dogma. Barth wanted to listen to "the voices of the
Fathers" and to every witness that offered a perspective on the
unique content of the Word of God. When Harnack visited Barth
(their relationship remained friendly, just as did that between Barth
and Bultmann) he was shocked to come upon Barth working at a
commentary by Cocceius (who had been mentioned only once,
in passing, in Harnack's *History of Dogma*). Their manners of
approaching the gospel were simply irreconcilable. But the questions that Harnack put to Barth were bound, as they did, to
appear again and again, in other ways, and to lead to ever
sharper discussions.

There is another facet of early criticism of Barth that is
worth mentioning. On one hand, Barth was criticized for coming
on too assuredly, too positively. But he was also criticized for
injecting *uncertainty* into theology. Did he not set all certainty into
crisis? Did he not deny our assured possession of Christian faith
and life? Here we had in mind Barth's protest against the notion
of revelation as "the revealed," as a *given* that we can dispose of.
K. Schilder put this criticism on the agenda early on, and it appeared again in my own book on Barth in 1936. We directed it
against Barth's vociferous objection to an attitude that robbed
revelation of its sovereign freedom and majesty and turned it into
a possession of men, especially of religious men, who from then
on controlled it, rather than let it freely invade our experience as
divine reality in new ways again and again.

In short, Barth's protest against the "blessed possessors" *(beati possidentes)* aroused concern that his theology robbed faith of certainty. Looking back, it seems unsurprising that Barth should begin by criticizing those who appeared to have solutions for all problems. We had met the same criticism in my student days, when we first came into contact with Kierkegaard. During my first year at the University I heard a paper on Kierkegaard, and now recall how sympathetically we responded to his critical attitude toward all religious self-confidence. I recall reading a paper of my own, in 1925, on "Philosophy and Revelation" that ended with this assertion: "Brunner teaches, as does Barth, that we are not allowed the luxury of sitting contentedly on the theologically cushioned seat of the blessed possessors!" (!) I made a connection in 1936 between Barth's "nominalism" and his accents on the absolute freedom of God, which seemed to me then to cross over into arbitrariness. I saw his notion of divine freedom as the unfathomable background for what happens in history and therewith threatens the trustworthiness of revelation. This was hardly an original thought; others had written about Barth's nominalism before. A. Janse saw Barth so caught up in a total "de-certainty" movement, what with the "lightning strike" of transcendence, that all certainty was undermined. I talked about the divine care that overshadowed revelation and set this in contrast to Barth — a point that was caught and criticized at the time by Hendrikus Berkhof. As I see it, the real intentions of Barth were missed most clearly in what I wrote about Barth's answer to the question: "Is there, then, no certainty?" Barth answered: "There is no certainty in faith itself. For God alone gives certainty to faith." I called that (with critical intent) a striking illumination of Barth's whole theology. (This was in my dissertation *Geloof en openbaring in de nieuwere Duitsche theologie*, 1932.)

Afterward I noticed that elements of the same criticism appeared in the writings of others. O. Noordmans, for instance, came to Barth's theology with questions that had to do with the continuity of the life of faith. This was interesting in Noordmans because he also had objections to the continuity-theology of Neo-Calvinism (particularly with respect to the doctrine of regeneration). He was fascinated by the theology of the absolute moment, of the contingency of judgment and grace in the response of God — this in sympathy with Kohlbrügge. But he expressed the fear that Barth's theology endangered the possibility of continuity,

and he missed the "comfort of perseverance" in what he called
Barth's "actualism." Barth, he thought, saw the church as a kind
of "haunted house in which God swept in at unexpected moments."
He asked whether Barth took the doctrine of the Holy Spirit seriously enough. He wondered whether Barth appreciated the "continuing character of grace," or the "more mystical side of the life
of grace." Noordmans did not want to set this continuing life of
grace within the heart of pious man, and was not interested in
anchoring continuity within an anthropological reality. He chose
for Barth against Brunner in the Barth-Brunner controversy, just
as he chose against "the ethical theology of the religious personality." But nonetheless he missed the element of continuity
in Barth.

What was little noticed at the time was Barth's own strong
opposition to theological arbitrariness. He objected strenuously to a
theology that posited the absolute freedom of God and total
discontinuity. Strange, indeed, that we paid little attention
to this, since this theme is what we were objecting to in Barth's
own theology. An example of the confusion is the relationship
between Barth and Hans Michael Müller. Müller criticized Barth's
view of revelation on the grounds that it provided a "theology of
unheard of certainty." Barth, he said, only *appeared* to be actualis-
tic and contingent. Actually Barth taught that man can truly
know God by way of revelation, even though he cannot control
God and master knowledge of him. For Müller our knowledge of
God must be consistently contingent, never sure, never firm, never
continuing. Barth, naturally as we see it now, rejected Müller's
consistent occasionalism. The freedom of God did not mean an
"absolute restlessness" for man; there is a seeking and a *finding*,
there is a faith and *confidence;* there is a knowledge of God which
is the most certain of all knowledge (*Church Dogmatics [CD]* I).
The interesting thing is that, at an early stage in my own critique
of Barth, I saw Müller's "nominalism" as a logical consequence of
Barth's doctrine of divine freedom.

Barth rejected any form of actualism that emptied faith of
genuine continuity. Indeed, his objections grew as he developed
his own understanding of divine grace as the form of divine
freedom. There is an unbroken line from the early through the
later volumes, and it is the life of the doctrine of the freedom
of God's grace. His theme could be Paul's question: "What have
you that you have not received?" (1 Corinthians 4:7). Grace

is given and received, not as a static thing that, once received, never needs to be given again. It comes as manna came to Israel in the wilderness, each day afresh. Barth concludes Volume IV/3/1 with the comforting word that God's grace is in fact renewed every morning. And this is the source of continuity.

We cannot get hold of Barth's deepest intentions unless we keep in view the sharp polemics that he was caught up in, especially in the early period. With enormous vitality, he rid himself of the whole thrust of nineteenth and twentieth-century theology. For Barth, the various theologies of the time were all forms of anthropocentric theology — theology in which not God, but man was the focus. He did not mean that theology had consciously replaced Christian faith with belief in man. In his judgment, it was a very refined undertaking. It had to do with an anthropocentric religiosity in which — in spite of its use of the word "God" — the holiness, majesty, and glory of God, as well as his righteousness and sovereignty, were not taken seriously. The result was that God became a mere means for religious edification, for the nourishment of the pious individual.

Even though we cannot bring Rudolf Otto and Karl Barth under the same umbrella theologically, we must admit that on one level they seemed to us to say pretty much the same thing. The "tremendum et fascinosum" that became a byword for Otto was present in Barth too. It did not come in the form of a metaphysics, or as a datum of the pychology of religion, but as an indication of both the hiddenness and transcendence of God. Barth wrote to his friend E. Thurneysen, in 1919, that he had read Otto's book with "considerable joy" because, though Otto was very "psychologically oriented," he did point "beyond the boundaries to the moment of the numinous," to the "divine in God." And he saw in Otto the promise of a new way for resisting anthropocentrism. His holiness and majesty render it impossible for man, even religious man, to get God in his grasp and so control him.

In my student days we encountered not only Otto's book (The Idea of the Holy), but also an earlier criticism of anthropocentric theology. I refer to Erich Schaeder's Theozentrische Theologie (Theocentric Theology) of 1916. It was pointed against Schleiermacher, Ritschl, and W. Herrmann as well as many others for whom subjective religious experience was given such importance that there was no place for a new, all-determining and

direction-giving Word of God. Against a theology that found its
starting point in man, his need, his longings, and his value,
Schaeder proposed the theocentric as a new approach for theology.
Prior to Barth's critique of Schleiermacher as the "spoiler of reformation theology" Schaeder had written that he was the "man
of destiny for the theology of the nineteenth century." I wrote a
piece in our student paper (*Fraternitas*) in 1926 called "Erich
Schaeder and Karl Barth," in which I noted the similar impression
that both had made on me. But it was not long before divergences
surfaced. When Brunner read Schaeder's book, he wrote: "We
are still looking for an offensive of the right nature." Schaeder
certainly admired Karl Barth, and saw in him a fellow defender
of the overpowering majesty of God. But he also saw the danger
in Barth of a one-sided transcendence that failed to do justice to
the presence of the Holy Spirit in human life, the saving power
of the New Testament period.

   I recall now that, at the time, I thought Schaeder's criticism
of Barth was unfounded and I pointed to Barth's preaching,
particularly his book of sermons, *Come, Holy Spirit* (E.T. 1933),
in which the significance of Pentecost was seen precisely as the
miracle of the Holy Spirit who made Jesus Christ present in life.
The problems seemed to lie at another level than in the dilemma
of transcendence or immanence. At the time his commentary on
Romans appeared, Barth seemed totally unaware that Schaeder
had written against theological subjectivism as he did. In 1925,
Schaeder commented (in the third edition of his book) on the
one-sidedness of dialectical theology, and he thereafter went his
own way. Thus it appeared that the term "theocentric" did not
say enough by itself, and that even though theologians speak in
concert about the majesty of God and the "soli Deo gloria" they
are not necessarily walking the same theological path.

   Thus, the basic motif of Barth's theology was still not wholly
clear. It was apparent even in the early days — in spite of the
difficulties with the *Romans* commentary — that his basic protest
was directed against a theology that had lost its perception of
God's sovereign justification of the godless man (Romans 4:5).
He was opposed to theologies that had drawn a curtain over the
God-ness of God, and that muted the humility men should display
before the God who is the source of all true glory. His protest was
against the hubris, the false boasting, that he saw in the German
church especially, a hubris that was expressed in such slogans as

"Century of the Church" (Dibelius) and "We have the Church."
This protest against all forms of boasting forms the background
for Barth's rejection of any thought that tries to control God and
his revelation as a given that we have in our hands and is ours
to dispose of. His protest against the notion of "revealedness" was
not, as it became increasingly clear, a failure to recognize the
reality of revelation. Nor was it born of a desire to relativize its
truth. But it was a reminder of the permanent dependence of
believers on the free and gracious *gift* of God. Only thus can
we explain the fact that Barth never intended to undermine the
certainty of faith. He was not speaking out of both sides of his
mouth, with a dialectic Yes and No. One cannot, he said, be
finished with the righteousness of God by means of a theoretically
reassuring consideration "that at bottom the righteousness of God
is that of the righteousness of the gracious God" (*CD* IV/1,
p. 540). It was not as though we could view his righteousness
and see in it "that the *real* thing which is meant and intended in
God's judgment is his grace." The Yes of God is without dialectic,
without balancing constructions, but also without self-evidence.
There is no way leading from us to grace, not via dialectics, not
via paradoxes, not via a theology of crisis, not via our humility.
That, Barth insisted, would be the worst kind of Pharisaism, indeed the Pharisaism of the publican (*CD* IV/1, p. 617).

This is the context of Barth's protest against self-styled
"blessed possessors," against all false boasting, and against the
attitude of the Laodicean church: "I am rich and I have made
myself rich and I lack nothing" (Revelation 3:17). At several
conferences between 1920 and 1930 this frontal assault against
false certainty came to the fore. The difference between security
and certitude was the question. Frontal attacks against certainties
can be a fad; everything can be brought into crisis in a way that
discerns no nuances, thus forfeiting all legitimate positiveness.
The danger was not imaginary that the protests against false
boasting were distorted by their very faddishness, and that in
reaction to the faddishness of it, the real biblical protest that Paul
delivered in speaking of the core of the gospel of the cross would
be neglected. God had chosen the weak of the world to conquer
the strong and thus to take away the power from the strong so
that there is only a boasting in the Lord (1 Corinthians 1:27).
This is the protest that might be forgotten when "protests" become fads.

Against this background, it is important to notice how Schilder took up his stance in the discussion about the "theology of crisis" and the fear of false boasting. Being "in crisis," he wrote (*Tusschen ja en neen*, 1929), was not a matter of jingling slogans at conferences, but of being set under the cross as creatures who face the contrast between eternity and time and as creatures en route to the eschaton. He saw Barthian criticism of the "theology of glory" as vacuum-creating theology. He acknowledged, of course, that we must "be serious about the testing, the assessment of our spiritual capital," but he thought Barth lacked the necessary seriousness. At the same time we note in Schilder, in other places, a deep awareness of the danger of false boasting. And as he thought about it, he attacked with an aggressiveness no milder than Barth's. A sermon he preached on Amos 9:7 in 1926 brought to life Amos' startling assault on the self-boasting of the "elect people." Amos sets the fact of the election of the Moabites, the Philistines, and the Syrians under the noses of Israel's self-confidence. Schilder describes the controversy that Yahweh had with his people in this humiliating comparison between Israel and the heathen nations. Israel with its religion and cult, its precious altars, the finger of God stretched out over its history, its spiritual songs — this Israel on a level with Philistia? Amos does not disregard Israel's privilege in salvation history, but he scourges the claims and self-evidence of Israel's "deadly pride, the misunderstanding Israel had of its election, a misunderstanding that had made a 'right' out of what had been given it." Now Yahweh wipes all the misunderstanding away as he turns against Israel; he is now not for them, but against them in angry judgment. We recall Schilder's sermon because it is not merely a recollection of a dramatic moment in Israel's history, a dramatic representation of that moment when Israel bled under the whiplash of Amos. The text is directed to the church of today. "If he takes away Israel's hope, he takes away our hope." Everything hinges on Amos' word, for us as well as for Israel.

The sermon is full of judgment — on us — not in the form of an absence of grace, not as an isolated No, but as the opening of a way: "Come back and let God judge with you. Why does he come down on us so hard? Not to take something away from us, but to give back to us what we ourselves wanted to throw away." Barth doubtless never heard of Schilder's sermon, but one wishes he had read it. What Barth did read was Schilder's "Neo-

Calvinistic" critique of Mozart, to which he reacted in such intense anger. Schilder's Amos sermon would have sounded differently in his ears. In any case, Schilder's sermon — preached to
Neo-Calvinists — would have perfectly matched Barth's own as-
sault against religious self-boasting. It is no accident that Barth was also fascinated by Amos. He
devoted some six pages (in small type) to Amos' "judgment ser-
mons." With his "one-sidedness and emphasis, the protest of Amos
is something entirely new" (CD IV/2, p. 447). It was a protest
against inhumanity and injustice, not merely against the abuse,
but against the very use of divine service; it was thrust against
the house of Israel in "a demonstration of churchmanship." God
did not forget his covenant. On the contrary! But the grace that
was pushed aside had to become judgment again ("Seek me and
live," Amos 5:4). Judgment had to come again "in its uttermost
sharpness over them just because they were his people," said Barth.

Barth's motives were the same as Schilder's; they both protested against all false boasting and criticized a simplistic appeal
to the finger of God in history. Later these thoughts became terribly urgent in the actual lives of both men. With Barth they came to
life in his view of history that led to his role in the Barmen declaration against Hitler. With Schilder they came to life in his resistance
to National Socialism. In both cases, the enemy appealed to
"God and history" and branded as blind those who failed to see
the divine summons in all that was happening around them.

In 1954, when I wrote another book about Barth, I did not
use the issue of transcendence as the key to understanding him.
Nor did I see the paradox or the "crisis" element as the key.
Barth's intentions, at least for me, had become clearer precisely
regarding those matters having to do with certainty. It became
clear to me that he was not, any more than Schilder, "de-
certainizing" faith, but was securing certainty within the only
possible way that faith can be certain, the way of "faith alone
and grace alone." It became steadily clearer that my earlier characterization — the sacrifice of the correlation between faith and
revelation — did not match the real state of affairs. Barth was,
with enormous emphasis, calling attention to the relation between
faith and revelation; faith was not a contributory factor, nor one
component in salvation, but our response to the gospel. This response was so real that the old notion of faith as "hollow space"

or Calvin's metaphor of the "empty hand" were no longer necessary to indicate the unique character of faith.

The whole development of Barth was defined by the manner
in which he refused to attack anthropocentric theology in the abstract, but concentrated on its threat to sovereign grace. He recognized the threat in Roman Catholicism as well as in modern
Protestant theology. He saw this danger especially in Rome's
doctrine of the analogy of being; here it was implicitly assumed
that man as man had the ability to know God before God revealed
himself in grace. From this fundamental point his passionate
struggle emerged against all natural theology as the "discovery
of the Antichrist." He understood nineteenth-century theology as
making man the starting point, man the actual *a priori*. And
against this, revelation told us what the situation really was —
man, not as the starting point, but man in desperate need and man
as the question.

This problematic defined Barth's theology until the end. It
also formed the background to his growing opposition to all
forms of apologetics, especially those oriented around man. For
it was *to* man that the gospel of salvation was directed, it was not
man who had the ability to discover God.

As Karl Heim devoted himself to an understanding of modern
man and his thought, he complained that he missed in Barth's
theology the possibility of genuine confrontation. Barth, Heim
thought, restricted himself too one-sidedly to revelation, to "God
has spoken," and did not give credit to the actual encounter between revelation and the concrete man with his questions and
problems. But Barth went on, increasingly setting revealed theology against natural theology, against the knowing and the
information-getting that went on prior to revelation and which
then had to reckon with revelation. In this manner, we would be
forever building bridges between faith and unbelief, ever looking
for a point of contact apart from grace, a point in man that can be
elaborated into a "principle of explanation" as to how unbelief
becomes faith. Though Heim surely did not lead faith out of
human thought, with its own problematics, Barth distrusted Heim's
attempt to bridge the gap between revelation and human questions. It has been put this way: Heim did not want to begin with
the church and the priest, nor with the *a priori* of God's speech
from above; he wanted to begin with man, with modern man,

with his eyes and ears, his questions and problems – to which, thereafter, revelation would provide its liberating answer.

Barth saw this approach as the first step toward the anthropologizing of theology. He was aware that he himself had paid dues to this approach, namely in the first edition of his dogmatics in 1927, where he had said that the human factor in the speaking and hearing of the Word of God should not be minimized. The man to whom the Word of God comes finds himself in a mysterious space between angel and animal and is confused within the contradictions of his in-between existence, estranged from God, and unable to put the two dimensions of his life together. Thus, human existence is posed as a question. And here Barth thought the Heidelberg Catechism was very pertinent by beginning with a question. The word of God is the answer to a question, and this makes legitimate the task of analyzing the nature of the question. This was all put very summarily in that first volume. F. Gogarten reviewed the volume and complained about its lack of an anthropology. Barth's response to Gogarten is interesting: he was very pleased with the review because he thought it indicated that the scandal created by the volume was not all that serious.

Barth did, however, on second thought conclude that he had given too much attention to the existence question, and therewith seemed to make the Word of God somewhat dependent on our analysis of the problematics of human existence. Barth discerned this danger at the eleventh hour, and turned back – via Anselm and the sovereign "God has spoken" – to the *a priori* in which God's Word becomes a predicate of human existence. He saw Gogarten's way as a dead end. Barth had at first high expectations of Gogarten (Gogarten had played a role in the changes in the second edition of *Romans*), but then saw him taking a wrong route. Gogarten's participation in the German Christian movement was seen by Barth as evidence of his theological mistake.

A total estrangement took place between them later. When Barth was in Amsterdam in 1939, he answered our questions about his rejection of infant baptism by warning us against the danger of tying grace to natural occurrences. If we went this way, he said, we would end up with Gogarten, giving anthropology the first word after which revelation would come as a poor second. Barth continued to discern signs in theology that the *a priori* of grace might be undone by an independent concern for the natural, that is, for a pre-theological understanding of man that would then determine the structure of theology.

In an extensive study on Barth and Gogarten, Peter Lange pointed out that Gogarten did not give the same priority to the notion of a "pre-understanding" of the gospel that Bultmann did. Gogarten, he said, did not use a secular anthropology as the basis for theology. This is seen also in Thurneysen's more discriminating judgment on Gogarten. But Barth saw everything in the same line, namely the essential correlation between existence and revelation — which, methodologically, was of utmost importance to theology. Barth, therefore, felt cut off from Gogarten after 1933, after Gogarten began operating with the notion of "creation ordinances." Between 1930 and 1940, he was dead set against what he discerned as the background to a religious kind of national socialism. National Socialism also saw connections between creation ordinances (folk, blood, and soil) and political life, and set all this within an idealistic sense of calling, with men hearing the voice of God in history, a history that then became akin to salvation history. Barth, over against this, insisted on the radical newness of revelation; revelation, he repeated, can never be the conclusion of human thought. It always blazes a new path. Barth refused to think from possibility to reality. The only passable way is that which moves from the reality of revelation to human possibility. We must begin with revelation, and only then talk about possibilities in human thought.

His resistance appeared in his objection to Brunner's apologetics. It came out especially in his attack against the notion of a "point of contact" which Brunner taught so emphatically. Brunner, to be sure, did not mean that one could produce faith out of this point of contact; such a notion was, in his view, the error of Pelagianism. But this did not assuage Barth. He saw Brunner as attempting to create a "possibility" for hearing the Word of God. Brunner's apologetics looked to Barth like a refined way of putting something in natural man's grasp that prepared him for revelation, if not positively then at least negatively. And this, after all, was the basic fault of Roman Catholic thought — though he discerned traces of it even in Kierkegaard and Heidegger. What he saw in the Kierkegaard-Heidegger axis was a connection between the negativity of doubt and the Word of God, a connection that Erich Przywara astutely wove into the Roman Catholic notion of *analogia entis*.

When Barth wrote his famous *Nein* against Brunner in 1934, he said that he would, if Brunner were right, go directly to the Pope and admit that the Reformation had been founded on a huge mistake. Faith presupposed nothing, no answer and no question, no certainty and no doubt. None of these things makes natural man ready — by means of his ability to ask questions — for hearing the Word of God. Faith cannot be made transparent by means of human predisposition (his "revelation-readiness"). Faith can only be experienced as a miracle. In all this Barth did not intend to isolate faith completely; he did not mean to erect a ghetto for irrational faith, to build an erratic bundle of dogmatic thought which would be wholly foreign to ordinary men. Still, he wanted nothing of a contribution that man could make to faith by way of some "remnant" of his humanity.

It is interesting to note Schilder's admiration for Brunner. He wrote that Brunner, in some senses, approached classic Reformational theology in his accent on the "pre-understanding" — as a "hypothesis for the understanding of the apostolic message of faith." But in this area Barth and Noordmans stood much closer together. Noordmans saw the notion of a "remnant" as a leftover of Scholasticism within Reformed thought. And he thought that at that time — in 1936 — it was being used to torpedo the integrity of the church and its theology from the arsenal of culture and politics. The notion of general revelation, he thought, was no longer "a bridge for pagan entrance into the church, but a door for Christians to exit the church." Barth would certainly have understood Noordmans' remark. For Barth there could be no separate task for a theological apologetics alongside the task of dogmatics, not to "accommodate dogmatics to the Chinese," or even to establish contact with one's "contemporary unbelievers." It would not work even if one's aim were to "undermine the axioms of natural reason," as Brunner put it. Theological thought is a way of "being there" as a witness of faith — and even it was "unrighteous in its achievements." This does not mean that Barth wanted no confrontation in theology. His *Church Dogmatics* is full of confrontation with people like Heidegger, Sartre, Nietzsche, and hosts of others. Barth thought it self-evident that dogmatics would "be an apologetic, polemic discourse from beginning to end" (*CD* I/1, p. 31). It was an apologetic that worked independently of dogmatics that he eschewed. For a separate apologetic always seeks synthesis with natural reason, and this is impossible. Dogmatics cannot tolerate an eristic theology alongside of it; it must — precisely in order to be properly apologetic — "stick to its own last." Authentic apologetics can occur only from within the context of the gospel; when pursued in this setting it will not fabricate a point of contact as a *conditio sine qua non.* Nor will it create a prolegomena out of the possibilities of faith within human thought and existence.

To illustrate what was so essential for Barth in his many polemical encounters, we can point to the divergence between him and another theologian who began his pilgrimage on the same route with Barth: Rudolf Bultmann. They remained good friends to the end, and the bond between them was never broken in their intense efforts to understand each other. In their discussion — much of which was published in the form of letters — Barth never tired of laying the accent on the Word of God as that which is "over against" us, as the Word that comes to us from above. He saw Bultmann as a man possessed with another vision of the New Testament, principally because of his notion of the "pre-understanding" that men generally have of the gospel. Barth discerned a substantial loss for theology and for the preaching of the gospel in this "pre-understanding." And for Barth, theology was all about preaching. Anyone reading the correspondence cannot help noticing that this objection dominates all that Barth says. Indeed it was the same objection that he had to Heim, Brunner, Gogarten, and all subtle forms of natural theology.

Barth was concerned to underscore the Word of God in its peculiar sovereignty, the Word that never returns God's promises empty. In the light of this sovereign power of the Word, he insisted, it is not possible to grant an independent significance to the power of reason or to a "pre-understanding" possessed by natural man. Bultmann considered the questions of human understanding — its nature and their possibilities — to be crucially important. He put them on the agenda as a hermeneutical problem of the first order, one which we should take pains not to minimize. He wrote to Barth: "You appear not to have seen these problems as I have, and for this reason you obviously cannot understand me" (*Briefwechsel,* p. 172). Bultmann thought that he and Barth had different views of how to translate the gospel for contemporary persons. To make the gospel understandable, he thought, we must break through the barrier of an antiquated world-view, and do that radically. To bind ourselves to the old world-view is to erect a false offense, an unreal scandal, on the pathway to faith. Bultmann surely was sensitive to a real scandal, an offense that cannot and must not be removed. He wrote about the "strangeness of Christian Faith" (*Glauben und Verstehen*, IV). But everything depends on how we understand that "strangeness" and that "offense." We can try to preserve absolute notions that in fact cast a shadow over the real offense. But modern people must be liberated from having to face false offenses, liberated by means of a "candid and radical critique." The situation in which modern man finds himself simply demands this. It is urgently necessary because we must understand the kerygma as it speaks to us in our existence; therefore, we must never lose sight of the person who is addressed by the gospel.

Barth's criticism of Bultmann focusses on what he saw as a "prejudgment" that Bultmann made in connection with the limits and potential of what is understandable. Bultmann responded by saying that this objection had an "apparent plausibility," but that at bottom it arose from a misunderstanding of the problem of understanding. Bultmann too was concerned with an openness and a readiness to hear the Word of God. He could say, in fact, that this was precisely his concern. But the problem did not lie in the good will of man, his natural readiness to listen to the gospel. It lay rather in his ability to *hear* it. The "pre-understanding," in Bultmann's view, does not suggest that the Word of God would no longer be "a strange truth and reality that runs counter to man's competence to understanding." Indeed, it is just in the right understanding of the Word that it becomes clear how strange it is, and how the kerygma does contradict our own way of thinking. Thus, the problem of the "pre-understanding" is not a matter of making "prejudgments" that we use as a critical standard for all interpretations of the New Testament.

In spite of the vigor with which Bultmann set forth his real intentions, he did not convince Barth, who continued to oppose him. Barth suspected Bultmann's attention to human "self-understanding" in connection with man's understanding of the New Testament message. Barth said he could not comprehend why anyone had first to creep into Heidegger's mind before he was able to grasp the New Testament. He saw in Bultmann a

canonizing of Heidegger's "existentialist analysis," in spite of
Bultmann's assertion to the contrary. And he rejected this existentialist concept as "the obligatory pre-understanding to the understanding of the New Testament" (*R. Bultmann. Ein Versuch ihn
zu verstehen,* 1952, p. 39).

Was Barth fair in this accusation that "self-understanding"
had been canonized by Bultmann into a criterion for understanding
the New Testament? Barth himself often asked this question. But
he always returned to the conclusion that Bultmann really taught
a "normative pre-understanding, indeed one that competed with
the Holy Spirit and, in fact, set up a barrier to him" (*ibid.,* p. 52).
He could hardly have put his objection in sharper form, especially
after all that Bultmann tried to do to explain that he did not at
all mean to set up human "self-understanding" as a critical
standard over against the kerygma. Barth rightly saw that Bultmann, in their entire discussion, never made a genuine concession
and thus could not make good on his denials of Barth's criticism.

Barth felt alien to Bultmann's approach to the New Testament, and wondered whether a person could ever get any farther
with it than his own self-understanding. Barth's concern — and
he stuck with his position in spite of Bultmann's complaints that
he had been misunderstood — is closely allied to criticisms of
other forms of exegesis in which human listening to the gospel
must be fitted into a philosophical frame. Barth referred to such
exegesis as a schema or a suit of armor.

This did not mean that Barth saw no significance in man's
understanding of himself. He was aware that Calvin began his
Institutes by saying that the highest wisdom was the knowledge
of God and *oneself.* Calvin's striking beginning of his masterpiece
has always captured readers' imagination, especially in view of this
sentence: "But, while joined by many bonds, which one precedes
and brings forth the other is not easy to discern." It is understandable why a man like G. Ebeling would occupy himself so
extensively with these comments ("This monumental sentence,"
Ebeling called it). It is also easy to see why Calvin's words are
brought into contemporary discussions about the interconnections
between the knowledge of God and the knowledge of oneself.

Barth, too, explored this sentence in depth (*CD* III/2) and
indicated the problematics hidden in it. But he added that it cannot in any case be read in terms of a canon of a prior "self-
understanding" as the norm for the knowledge of God. Certainly

there is a relationship and, in terms of the New Testament, we can and must look back to anthropology, ethics, and questions of method. But this must be done without the postulates laid down by Bultmann, and without deploying the existence of man as a hermeneutical key or as a canon for understanding. This was, to the end, the crucial point for Barth in his relations with Bultmann. Both of these men spoke of a difference between them that would not be solved in this life. Bultmann looked forward with Barth to asking Paul in the eschaton what "he finally, once and for all, meant." Barth once compared his and Bultmann's relationship with the encounter between a whale and an elephant who met each other with stupefied amazement; but Barth guessed that when they met in heaven they would discover a common ground.

The problem of the hermeneutical key has played a continued role in the discussion of the last decades. It is not limited to the Barth-Bultmann dialogue; it comes to the surface wherever the *proprium* of the Word of God is sought. The same problematic emerged when Jürgen Moltmann accused Ebeling of constructing a "natural theology of modern existence." It is a complaint that points to what Moltmann called "the anthropological verification-schema." "The problem of one's own questionableness becomes the controlling factor in the knowledge of God through revelation." This is a charge like that which Kuitert levelled to the account of Bultmann (cf. H. Kuitert, *The Reality of Faith*, E.T. 1968).

We would free ourselves from the problem too easily if we saw in it only a misunderstanding of what is really a self-evident "pre-understanding." Even though the intention behind the notion of the "pre-understanding" is directed, for hermeneutical purposes, to the possibility of understanding the New Testament, this in no way guarantees that it would not be usable, outside the question of understanding, as a "prejudgment" and as a canon for judging the truth of the New Testament. The history of the close connection between "pre-understanding" and "prejudgment" is too long for us to let ourselves be seduced into thinking that we would be done with it if we let "pre-understanding" alone be a sort of mold into which we poured the meaning of the text. We cannot shove everything into the lap of the question of understanding. When Moltmann turned on Ebeling so sharply, he did not mean that he was altogether on Barth's side. He thought Barth worked with an *a priori* of revelation in which the ontic element prevailed so completely over the noetic that there could be no other kind of verification than that which occurs through the sovereign and free revelation of God himself. This was the *a priori* that Barth was fascinated by in Anselm, and which led him to begin his dogmatics all over again after the publication of the first volume in 1932. Moltmann's path moves in another direction, namely the direction of the future. The future offers the possibility of eschatological verification (an historical future as opposed to the closed circle of revelation). But he saw the problem of an anthropological verification very sharply, and scored it as a new form of natural theology — not, of course, in the old sense of the "proofs for God's existence," but in the sense of a conformity with what is given beforehand in anthropology, in the sense, then, in which Bultmann meant self-evident pre-understanding.

In Barth's mind, the problem of human understanding is a definitive question in all of contemporary theology. It appears, not only in the explicit discussion with Bultmann about "pre-understanding," nor only in the question of natural theology, but wherever the relationship of man to the divine act of salvation comes to view. It comes to sharp expression in Barth's opposition to all forms of individualism and egoism in salvation. Here we touch on the oft-discussed questions centering around the "for me" or "for us" structure of salvation. Barth sees in individualism and egoism an anthropocentrizing of theology, a tendency he discerned even in the bosom of Lutheranism. He saw it in connection with Luther's treatment of the application of salvation, in which christology tends to be digested within soteriology. He thought he understood why Bultmann appealed to Melanchthon's remark that to know Christ is to know his acts (as versus knowing him in the incarnation and his two natures). He also spied it in W. Herrmann's penchant for refusing to talk about "God himself," preferring rather to talk about "God for us." He saw connections here with Kierkegaard as the father of philosophical existentialism.

We might ask whether Barth was doing justice to Luther and Melanchthon, particularly if we take into account their opposition to Scholasticism and especially to the notion of historical faith and implicit faith. But the problem is a real one, one that comes into today's theology in connection with Luther's urgent question: "How can I find a gracious God?"

In our time the question is raised from several corners as to whether our historical experiences of threat and disaster do not push Luther's question about personal salvation into the background. Is Luther's concentration on individual salvation a concern that has "almost completely disappeared" (Bonhoeffer)? Current theology offers a virtual consensus on this point, especially over against the existentialist interpretation of the gospel. This does not mean that the personal dimension of salvation is being wholly excluded or that the central significance of justification is being totally ignored. Luther's question, as Käsemann remarked, maintains its "continuing relevance" (E. Käsemann, *Perspectives on Paul*, E.T. 1971, p. 174). And Käsemann goes on to say that we would make a mistake if we were to "shove the proclamation of Victory Day to the side." This is still true, even if we do not concentrate on the individual as existentialist theology did.

Obviously Barth's concern about salvation-egoism is connected with his sense for the danger in anthropological theology. Barth's attitude is clear, as for instance when he deals with Luther's question about the gracious God with "highest respect," but then goes on to admit that, in European theology in general, but German theology in particular, it has for too long been a nudge toward, a temptation to, a certain sort of narcissism (*CD* IV/1, p. 527). This was in 1953.

Barth was concerned about the danger of salvation-egoism in his earliest period. In Safenwil, under the impression that Blumhardt, Ragaz, and Kutter made on him, he had a keen distaste for individualism, for the isolation of faith within the inner life — an individualism that lost a vision of the wide horizons of the kingdom of God. Barth saw in all individualism traces of a "pre-understanding" that tended to become a standard for measuring salvation. He saw little difference between pietistic egoism and Bultmann's focus on individual salvation. This is a reason why Dorothee Sölle reacted so forcefully against Bultmann, and why Sperna Weiland reckoned his theology as a "dead end."

Barth's opposition is so interesting because, in his reaction, he does not close his eyes to the importance of man's concrete involvement in salvation. He makes a plea for the validity of the deeper motives of Luther's question about how man can find a gracious God. And he is bothered by the thought that, while sixteenth-century theologians busied themselves deeply with this question, modern thinkers mean to transcend such matters and concentrate on radical questions like the "question of God in general and God-as-such." "As though sixteenth-century man with his concern for the grace of God and the right of this grace were not asking about God Himself and His existence with a radicalness compared with which the questioning of modern man is empty frivolity" (*CD* IV/1, p. 530).

While Barth was critical of what he saw as individualism and egoism, even narcissism, in theology's concentration on what happens to man in salvation, he did think the question of man's involvement was important. Grace, after all, did *appear*, bringing salvation to all men (Titus 2:11). It was, as Barth saw it, in grace that the dilemma between the personal and social, the inner and outer aspects of salvation had to be resolved. This salvation, however, does not permit us to be introvertishly preoccupied with ourselves; it is oriented to a goal. He could say that the Middle Ages, with their "spires, their altars, and their painted glass," would not mean much without a St. Francis and his disciples. But salvation does not arrive at anything, neither in the inner self nor in the total reality of personal life, if it no longer has the shape and form of a salvation whose structure is created in mercy and in righteousness. Therefore, the individual is not the key, nor the canon for understanding salvation; the pious man is not the measure of the gracious acts of God. Barth was never fiercer in his criticism of individualistic notions of salvation than when he suggested that egoistic interpretations of the gospel could only provide grist for Feuerbach's mill. The shadow of Feuerbach, of course, meant a religion that was nothing more than a projection of man, and a theology that was nothing more than anthropology.

Before Barth, Kurt Leese, in 1911, had read theology in the light of Feuerbach, and said that indeed many theologies did bear this anthropocentric structure. This, he said, only helped confirm Feuerbach's suspicions and at the same time left theology without a basis for countering Feuerbach. This was Barth's view of anthropocentric theology: and this was one reason why he tried to expose its anemic interpretation of the "for me" and "for us" aspect of salvation as the key to understanding revelation.

The importance of this discussion lies clear before our eyes. This appears in the attention that Ebeling has given to the correlation between man — in his faith — and salvation, especially as it appears in Luther. ("If your faith and trust are sound, then your God is true. If your faith is false and untrue then you have a false God. For the two belong together, Faith and God. Where you set your heart and give it over . . . that is really your God" —

Luther.) When Ebeling cites such passages out of the Larger Catechism, he speaks of "dangerous texts" — "One can almost hear Ludwig Feuerbach," Ebeling says: "God as the projection and product, yes the essence of man." The answer is not to deny the "for-us" aspect of salvation in order to honor the objectivity of salvation, but to make clear that the orientation of faith to salvation illuminates that salvation (cf. G. Ebeling, *Luther: An Invitation to His Thought*, E.T. 1970).

This, of course, is related to Barth's rejection of natural theology. The objection was to the notion that the Word of God has no analogy in any natural knowledge of God with which the revelation can make contact. The result of its isolation from man, according to Ebeling, was that revelation remained foreign to human experience (Ebeling, *Wort und Glaube*, II, 1969, p. 429). The objection did not arise only from those doing "hermeneutical theology." Barth's theology was typified as one of estrangement and lack of contact, by such observers as H. Zahrnt (*The Question of God*, E.T. 1969).

Zahrnt accuses Barth of espousing a revelation that remains "a monologue in heaven" with which there is no contact in human existence. It suggests a "trinitarian carillon" that chimes high above a godless world. Zahrnt echoes many other objections when he speaks of an "affair in eternity," of a drama that is played out among themselves by the triune persons, and thus of a theology that provides "no way for the Bible to come into our lives." He speaks of a "history-less" theology and a theology that knows no dialoque, no correlation between man's question and God's answer.

This was the same issue that separated Paul Tillich from Barth. More than forty-five years after their early dispute these two were again in confrontation with respect to the problem of question and answer. Barth refused to take this problem seriously, whereas Tillich made it the very key to doing theology.

Schaeder made a plea for the "validity of the subjective," and wondered whether Barth, in his legitimate dispute with Cartesianism, did not nonetheless have to give account to "the believing subject." He did not focus the problem sharply with this, but his unwillingness to be content with the purely objective shows that the discussions about Feuerbach bring us face to face with a very modern problem. The problem of the nature of the correlation between faith and revelation will not go away; its persistence suggests that the subjective is not to be seen as a competitive

factor that subverts objective revelation, but rather it demonstrates man's involvement in it. It is this involvement that —
Feuerbach notwithstanding — will not let itself be scuttled. Only
in recognizing the involvement of the subject in revelation is the
superficiality of Feuerbach's criticism of religion exposed.

In this connection, Moltmann has discerned two lines extend-
ing from the group that began dialectical theology around 1920.
One of them is a theology of proclamation. The other is the
theology of hermeneutics. Though Ebeling has insisted that these
two cannot constitute a dilemma (*Wort und Glaube*, II, p. 108),
many have seen them as a dilemma in respect to Barth. Barth
was criticized for having continually reverted to proclamation, to
the *a priori* "objective" revelation, as a reality that made superfluous any serious concern for the human being to whom the
Word of God was given. We recall the argument of 1923 when —
in a remarkable twist of theological criticism — Tillich said that,
in Barth's theology, the positive note of the gospel was muffled in
the No of judgment. How strange it was, responded Barth, that
Tillich would suppose that he, Barth, had not heard the positive
words of the gospel (as the disciples of John had never heard
of the Holy Spirit, Acts 19). Barth pointed out that the real
question was what sort of positiveness was intended. He mis-
trusted a christology that became a universal, everywhere occur-
ring salvation-event, an event that occurred in the power of symbol.
He was skeptical of a christology that resisted "slicing off" a
particular place in history in order to preserve the universality of
symbolic revelation that could occur anywhere and everywhere.
Barth saw in this an anti-orthodox hysteria, a hint of modern
man's overreaction to Dostoievski's Grand Inquisitor. He distrusted, and could make nothing of, Tillich's notion of the "unconditional" in which he saw little more than a metaphysical
abstraction. ("Why this hide-and-seek game with the icy monster
called 'the unconditional'?") Barth had a good feel for the warning against authoritarianism that Dostoievski was giving. But he
also wanted to preserve "the indissoluble correlation between
theological concepts and the concepts of church, canon, and the
Holy Spirit."

The discussion was futile. But it did open up the large lines
of the problem that Barth was wrestling with in all its variations.
Since then the contours of the objections to Barth's *a priori* and
positivist notion of revelation have changed. We know what

Tillich's theology developed into as he worked out the notion of "the unconditional" into the theology of supra-theism and the "God beyond God." And in the last volume of his dogmatics, Barth summed up what he was after when he spoke of God as "more than the epitome of the 'really real,' but the absolute beginning, the transcendent, the one who embraces all, the 'wholly other' . . . known in his work and his word" (*CD* IV/4, p. 161). He was working with this kind of positivity, which was most concrete. How vague and abstract is Tillich's "ground of being" in comparison with Barth's theology of the "perfections of God."

In 1928, Paul Schempp wrote a "Critical Review of Barthianism" in which he called for an existential discussion that would take place in full seriousness and without "accolades and cryings of woe." Barth certainly was not beyond criticism in this regard. When he addressed, not the "by-standers," but those who in his view were teaching unacceptable theological distortions of the gospel, he could be terribly severe. At unexpected moments he would use such labels as "antichrist," as for instance when he talked about the doctrine of the analogy of being. And he was not beyond warning of the sin against the Holy Spirit (as he did in connection with anti-Semitism).

Barth seldom reacted more sharply than he did against what he called Bishop J.A.T. Robinson's "flatfooted" theology; here he saw a plain jettisoning of faith and doctrine. Robinson's appeal in *Honest to God* (1963) left him stone cold. The German title (*Gott ist anders*, "God is Different") smacked of Barth's own "wholly other God" — from his early days — but Barth saw it only as a dead end. He expressed amazement that Bultmann had spoken of Robinson's book with "mild approval." Barth expressed his feelings in irony. Robinson's book, he said, reminded him of a man sipping the foam from three full glasses of beer, with the etched-on initials R.B., P.T., and D.B. respectively, and then claiming to have discovered the theological miracle drink, which "would be consumed by hundreds, yea ten hundred thousands of jubilant consumers."

Barth's disgust was provoked, in part, by the way Robinson weaved Dietrich Bonhoeffer into the mixture. Robinson had taken Tillich's view of the abyss and ground of our being and joined it to Bonhoeffer's concrete positivity, in a total distortion of the Christian passion that motivated Bonhoeffer to the end. Indeed, Robinson thought it possible, once he had done away with supernaturalism, to synthesize any or all views. It was this project that pricked Barth, and he reacted with a gesture of contempt, wiping this form of pseudo-theology from the theological discussion table. He was unusually forceful and abrupt. But this did not keep him from thinking hard about the transcendence of God (the "God out there" in Robinson's book). He reflected on the caricatures often made of transcendence — including a transcendence that ignores immanence. Anyone who has read his volume on divine providence will recall how he speaks of "God as Lord" in a manner totally alien to the concepts of supernaturalism that Robinson declared obsolete. But he was equally removed from Tillich's "ground of being."

Barth's fierce response came from a conviction that Robinson was doing theology in a way that would destroy theology, and he wanted to remove all possibilities of misunderstanding by being pointedly clear. Barth's response — coming from one who was often very gentle — was not well taken. Polemics have their own psychological flavor, but Barth was saying that compromise has its limits, and was laying an ethical claim to our duty to be aboveboard with the reality we are dealing with. Our business here is not to discuss *Honest to God,* but only to comment on Barth's occasional and sudden displays of aggressive and indignant rejection of someone's ideas. We must see them in a prophetic dimension. His indignation arose from intense conviction and certitude.

Barth's occasional indignation was rooted in his intense theological convictions and certainty. (The complaint that Barth expected certainty from theology was related to his polemics in the beginning stages of his development.) When Barth reflected on his own development (in the Foreword of *CD* III/4) he recalled that his "NO's" were never meant as the "supreme art" of theology nor as "the overthrow of all false idols." And he added, "I have gradually acquired more and more feeling for the affirmations by which we can live and die." That he could "still enjoy debate," however, was amply demonstrated as time went on. He still looked sympathetically into the deepest intentions of theology and church, as he did after his visit with the Pope in 1967. But he could also radically and unhesitatingly reject ideas that seemed to him to impinge on the heart of the matter. He did not share Bultmann's enthusiasm for Gabriel Vahanian's book on the death of God (*The Death of God: The Culture of Our Post-Christian Era,* 1961).

Bultmann thought it "the most exciting theological book that I have read in recent years," but Barth reacted very negatively. We find in Barth, then, an undiminishing enthusiasm for theology, not as the "queen of sciences," but still as a beautiful science that responds to the beauty of God. "In such a sphere," he said, "extreme barbarism" is indeed "sad." But he was willing to risk a certain inelegance out of a concern that we might lose perspective on the gospel, a tragedy, when it happens, for both preaching and theology. With Barth, outbursts of indignation arose from a care for the gospel of God's gracious mercy, of the triumph of grace, not as an *a priori* principle from which theologians can deduce their own conclusions, but as the reality of Immanuel: God with us.

When I had occasion, in 1954, to speak with Barth extensively about my book, *The Triumph of Grace in the Theology of Karl Barth* (E.T. 1956), he expressed a concern that the title might create misunderstanding, as though grace had to do with a new methodological principle. He had spoken of this in Volume IV/3 of the *Church Dogmatics*. I was at first somewhat surprised at his reaction to the title, for I had never thought for a moment that Barth's doctrine of grace was an abstraction from which theologians were free to make their own deductions. Barth guessed that I had perhaps taken the title from Hans Urs von Balthasar's remark that, for Barth, Christendom was a "triumphal affair." But von Balthasar's words had struck me as being too "triumphalistic" for Barth, especially in reference to Christendom. I had in mind what Barth himself had written: "This history is a triumph only for God's grace and therefore for God's sovereignty" (*CD* II/2, p. 194). But here, the triumph is not of Christendom, but of the acts of God in Jesus Christ within history. Clearly the "triumph of grace" (including the title of my book) can mean only the grace of Jesus Christ the Lord. Barth recognized that "one could speak of it this way." And one must recall the "triumph" in which Christ leads us (2 Corinthians 2:14), after the disarming of and triumph over the principalities and powers (Colossians 2:15).

Anyone tempted into fascination with such victorious thoughts can count on being criticized for "exaggeration," for "overstressing" the triumph. Gustav Aulén learned this when he set the "victory motif" at the center of the doctrine of atonement. But one must tune himself to the forceful language of the New Testament, which, after all, proclaims more than a mere dialectic between the "already happened" and the "not yet happened." Barth was fascinated by these New Testament voices, so much so that everyone who got to know him was amazed — even sometimes embarrassed at his certainty and affirmativeness about "Jesus the Conqueror." He was always grateful to J.C. Blumhardt, who refused to capitulate to the grim "reality" that lay before us in its crusty unchangeableness; and he felt nothing for Bultmann's reaction to Blumhardt: "Blumhardt's kind of history is an abomination to me." Barth affirmed, rather, the cosmic, world-historical decision made in the "name of Jesus," a decision in which Barth — in spite of his opposition to the notion of power as an abstract "ability to do anything" — saw an authentic triumph of power.

In this context, we cannot create a dialectical balance between an optimistic and a pessimistic accent unless we are willing to do the same with Paul's doxologies, uttered as they were too in a time at least as unhappy as our own. Barth expressed surprise that older Protestantism (even Luther and Calvin) could have overlooked this message of the liberation from corruption, death, and evil. He wondered how it could speak so often of the kingdom of God in lusterless fashion, and "overlook this dimension of the gospel which is so clearly attested in the New Testament — its power as a message of mercifully omnipotent and unconditionally complete liberation from death and wrong as the power of evil" (CD IV/2, p. 233). Western Catholicism, too, in spite of its saints and its miracles, manifested the same lack of enthusiasm for victory in Christ, in contrast to the Eastern church, which never stopped listening and talking about the triumph of Colossians 2:14. From this thought came a powerful philippic against modern interpretations of this event as myth. The church knew a decisive turn in history had taken place in Christ's death and resurrection, in "the revealing and saving power of God" that was revealed in Christ for all time. Here was positiveness, in the face of everything that seemed to contradict the reality of this power and against all the struggles within, and moreover as authentic "illumination" for faith. It came from Barth as a doxology reminiscent of the bewildering word in Psalm 8 that speaks of the glory of God's name over all the earth, a word that can be read in the light of Hebrews 2, which talks about what we have not yet seen.

This positiveness is rooted in the gospel. It confronts all that gives reason for uncertainty and ambiguity. The kingdom has come, and everything has been done that needed to be done;

herein lies the ground for rejecting "all pessimism, all tragic views, all skepticism," said Barth. Looked at this way, the accusation made by Barth's colleague at Basel, Karl Jaspers, that the Christian message is bound by "exclusivism," is seen as absurd. When Barth lamented that the church did not always absorb this joyful message, he made an exception of the Heidelberg Catechism and the classic hymns of the Evangelical church, in both of which he heard a direct echo of the New Testament witnesses. We need not recall all the New Testament expressions that proclaim the triumph of Christ. Question marks are placed after them often, in view of the bitter reality of evil in the world. They are not just theological question marks. They come from life's experiences, from shocking encounters with the powers of evil and corruption. How can we harmonize the reality of life's experience with Barth's notice that "no praise can be too high for the mighty and triumphant grace of God in the atonement as the fulfilment of the covenant" (*CD* IV/1, p. 69)?

Is there, then, perhaps reason for speaking about exaggeration in these unambiguous doxologies, not only in theology but in the letters of Paul? It would be untrue to say that Barth's convictions of the triumph of grace led him to underestimate the seriousness and radicality of sin and the measureless effects of evil. Van Til's judgment that what Barth says about them "is calculated to lead men to think they are not sinners" is simply incomprehensible. Barth's teaching about the offense of sin ("the loathsome") as sloth, pride, and as lie is just too clear for this. The real questions that have been raised, from various corners, come from Barth's stress on the triumph of Christ amid the evil of the world's sin. I raised such questions myself in my own book on Barth. And Otto Weber, whose theology is most congenial to Barth, suggested that Barth developed the doctrine of providence with hardly a consideration of sin and only later added a doctrine of sin (Weber, *Grundlagen der Dogmatik*, I, 1955, pp. 557ff.). Barth had, in fact, spoken of this division in the preface to III/3 of the *Church Dogmatics:* "I wanted as little as possible to mention God and the Devil in the same breath." And he goes on consistently in his perspective of Christ's triumph to which sin (and all that goes with it) can no longer be a genuinely competitive force. In answer to my own questions he wrote that his concern was to say we should think about evil now only from the viewpoint of "the vigor of the *rejection* of evil as it is seen in

Jesus Christ" (CD IV/3, p. 178). Barth wrote to me, in his first
response to my book, that he had once said to a Scandinavian
colleague who somewhat disagreed with him: "The entire North
criticizes me — and the criticism gets heavier the closer we get
to the North Pole." "I think that we are still one in Christ, but
not one in the Devil."

I suspect that deep questions will always arise as we experience the tension between everything that surrounds and oc-
cupies us and the confident glory of Psalm 8 and Hebrews 2.
When Barth retired in 1962, he still had occasion to lecture.
Choosing as his subject "Introduction to Theology," he spoke of
the "risk of theology." He wondered aloud whether theology still
made sense in our world. Does not a theological existence look
like monasticism? And is it not squarely opposed to everything
that is real in the world? There is a "sea of suffering and misery"
that engulfs the world and mankind — the insanity of dictators,
the intrigues of nations, the murders and the murdered of the
concentration camps, the hunger, the wars; Hiroshima, Korea,
Algeria, the Congo. And while all this storms around us, there is
some demythologizing going on in Marburg and "a little Church
Dogmatics in Basel," the rediscovery of the historical Jesus, and
"that glorious new discovery of the 'God beyond God'" (Tillich).
Is not all this theology an expendable luxury amid all these
terrible shadows of our time; is theology in these times perhaps
only a device to "flee from the living God. . ."? "I am only raising
the question," said Barth. Well, I suspect many have instinctive
sympathy with such questions, certainly when we speak positively
about "Jesus the Conqueror" and talk about his triumph in very
grim voices. Questions arise because we know that — as Barth
certainly knew — there is a large place in life for the reality of the
"not yet" of Christian hope.

In this situation, Barth called us back to the study of the
Scriptures in the knowledge — which we possess in "patience and
forbearance" — that the No is only the vessel of today and that
God's Yes will finally and forever burst every vessel. We know
this only through constantly keeping attention on the witness of
salvation. That Barth throughout his career was oriented to this
witness is of itself no guarantee of the validity of his dogmatics.
But it does mean that all criticism of his work must be governed
by the same orientation if it is to be fruitful criticism. Whenever
this is not the case, when the concrete witness of Scripture is

THE VOICE OF KARL BARTH

forsaken, and the biblical answer is not decisive in the question-
answer correlation, a loss of communication is inevitable.

There is, as I see it, something puzzling in Wolfhart Pannenberg's criticism of Barth's view of the correlation between question and answer. Barth had, as early as his commentary on
Romans, spoken about the correlation: "God has answered before
you asked and only for this reason do you ask at all." This is
hardly a device peculiar to Barth; we find it in Paul (Romans
10:20) and in Isaiah (65:2). Pannenberg thinks that not only
Barth, but Tillich, Bultmann, and Ebeling alike allow the question
to be defined by the answer. These four, without qualification,
under the general category of correlation make a surprising package. Anyway, Pannenberg criticized all four for not paying adequate attention to the "structure of questioning in human
existence." It is, according to Pannenberg, impossible for theology
to "begin talking about God, unperturbed, as if nothing had
really happened" (Pannenberg, *Basic Questions in Theology,* II,
E.T. 1971, p. 189). We cannot "pursue theology from the heights,"
he warns, "if we do not want to land in an isolation ward where
we speak in tongues from above and lead the whole church into
this blind alley." I do not know if Barth read Pannenberg and,
if so, ever made a judgment on his work. But I think that he
would have been as critical of Pannenberg as he was of his own
Prolegomena of 1927 and of Gogarten, and I suspect he would
have asked Pannenberg — as he so often asked others — for more
exegesis, more understanding of the *Word.*

If Barth was influenced less than some others by hermeneutical
questions, it was not primarily because he was turned away by
what Ebeling called "the appearance of hermeneutical chaos"
(*Wort und Glaube,* II, p. 101). It was a notable trait of his theology from the beginning. Ebeling was sure that methodological
and hermeneutical questions were not a cover-up for the real
issues. But Barth's greatest fear was that they might just be. He
was convinced that just this sort of cover-up was a supreme threat
to any and all theology. He was occupied along a way that was
constantly open to new and uncontrolled encounters from the
Word itself. We were not accustomed to this readiness for rediscovered novelty, this tension-filled waiting, this willingness to
break through all traditionalism; it was such a radical contrast to
tendencies to control the Word of God.

We find these elements of extreme tensions and surprises in the Japanese theologian Kazoh Kitamori's book, *Theology of the Pain of God*, set into English in 1966. That God could be inwardly moved, said Kitamori, was his life's greatest discovery. He spoke of Jeremiah 13:20: "Is Ephraim my dear son? Is he my darling child? For as often as I speak against him, I do remember him still. Therefore my heart yearns for him; I will surely have mercy on him, says the Lord." It was this divine yearning, which comes out again in Isaiah 63:15, that amazed him. "My amazement at the mystery of this word became more and more profound as I discovered the relationship between this word and Isaiah 63:15." To be sure, the sense of having made a discovery makes one vulnerable; but one's own discoveries are correctable only by walking over the same paths again — that is, only by restudy of the same Word.

We find the same sense of amazement in Barth, from the beginning. He was amazed by Paul, by what "knows no comparison, by what totally surpassed . . . my standards for thought." And the biblical writers? "Eyes and ears were not really adequate to their descriptive expressions of alarm, affection, overwhelmedness, enthusiasm." And alongside of Paul, there was John with "the true vision" of what it means to see and hear. And Luke, "far more than a religious and socially minded physician," also witnesses to the same "hearing of the unheard of." Here, in what he called the "new world of the Bible," lies the origin of Barth's skepticism about all the questions of human reason. It was not a romantic spiritualism nor exegetical occultism, but a product of his constant return to the Word of the Scriptures. It was in this mood of biblical surprise that he felt his disappointment with modern theology. To Thurneysen he commented on his study of Romans: "I began to read (Paul) as though I had never read him before." And so it went, step by step. "What lies behind all this?" he wondered in reference to Romans 3:20, and, in amazement, at Paul himself: "What manner of man was this?" but especially in response to Paul's message: "What realities were these that set this man in motion?" This was back in 1916 and 1917. But the openness to surprise never left him.

Barth spoke of feeling depressed over our limited ability to let the Bible speak. On reading Romans, he remarked: "This afternoon I have merely translated, in a wonderful movement from word to word, letting the man carry on his unique conversation with himself." The first half of Romans 6 he found "terribly difficult." "I am getting hardly anywhere, and had to go back yesterday to verse eight and begin all over again." Then he was busy trying to comprehend 1 Corinthians and worked through the whole book, in a kind of "running exercise," in order to get at the depths of 1 Corinthians 15. He felt enormous respect for the mysterious "over against" that is so much more than our heart with its dwindling perspectives can contain. Sometimes we notice a marked reserve as he felt as though he were standing before an avalanche about to roll over him. There is nothing here of a schema determining his exegesis beforehand, or of a dogmatic tradition in which he had already digested the witness of Scripture. Here was confrontation with a witness whose amazing word overwhelmed him.

Once he asked Thurneysen (in 1919) to substitute for him at a lecture. He felt, he said, like an invalid in dealing with 1 Corinthians 15; he was like a man struck by lightning, paralyzed by what "burns so fantastically here." Had he lectured himself, "I would have struck them dead, as Moses struck the Egyptian, with great damage to my soul and great silence in heaven." Those who feel that Barth's dialogue with Bultmann about "pre-understanding" leaves many questions unanswered must first understand this background to Barth's disquiet, this profound experience with the Word that led him to a deep fear of temptations to control and master the Word. He did not want the gospel to become an echo of what was present in our heart before we came to it, a rewording of what we had already thought. We must keep thinking about this, as we come into contact with hermeneutical questions, even as we respect their importance. In this context, Barth spoke about Bultmann's demythologizing program; it left him cold. It was a humorless undertaking "all too easily recognized" for what it was, poorly suited for a real dialogue with modern man, and all too quickly degenerating into a deeply suspicious apologetic undertaking.

And then finally he wrote, looking back, about existentializing theology. He said that he was aware long before, even before he read Kierkegaard, what "existential" signified. Wilhelm Herrmann had hammered it into him: "You must act." But existentialist theology aroused his increasing resistance. He recalled a visit by Bultmann (in 1922), and how Bultmann spent hours talking about Heidegger's lectures. Then he felt that he faced a decision. He did not want to raise himself above all hermeneutical questions; certainly he did not want to spiritualize or theologize as a docetic, and did not want to carry on a "monologue in heaven" or talk in "strange tongues." But he did feel a summons to come to terms with the meaning and consequences of the Reformation rule: "Holy Scripture is its own interpreter." This is what he was busy with when he discovered the powerful witness of the "tremendous" Word that always speaks against us so that we can learn to stop speaking against it.

4

The Heart of the Church

ANYONE WHO TRIES TO CLEAR A PATH THROUGH THE UNDERBRUSH of the past half-century's theology, and tries to find the central motifs, discovers very soon that theology has not been a clear, single-lined process. As a matter of fact, it has never been that way, neither in theology nor in the church. The notion of a movement from implicit ideas to explicit doctrines, of an unbroken evolution of dogma, is a myth. All sorts of nonchurchly and non-theological factors have intruded into the theological scene. Even one who is convinced that theology cannot or ought not be a reflection of the prevailing thought of a given time cannot deny that theology is in fact influenced by events of its time. (Cf. my *Wereldoorlog en theologie*, 1945, E.T. *World War and Theology*). This can lead to a multifaceted development, since the historical events are actually experienced by persons and then filtered through their theological thinking in varied ways. We can say at least this, that particular theological themes impress themselves on us in view of our history, while other themes that once occupied theologians with great relevance fall into the background.

There is a kind of hierarchy, a sort of order, in theological priorities. And it is possible that long-neglected problems can suddenly become unexpectedly clear and pressing. It is not hard to locate examples of problems that have suddenly demanded intense attention in our time. We will list a few of them.

We can note first the profound interest in the authority of Holy Scripture, its trustworthiness and its infallibility, in short, its character as divine revelation. The background of our modern concern is the historical-critical research that gained a crucial place in biblical studies during the eighteenth and nineteenth centuries. A barrage of new problems bombarded the church — problems of method, of how to approach the Scriptures, of hermeneutics, and the like. They created grievous tensions in the church, Protestant and Catholic both. For they called believers to give an account of the truth, the power, and the validity of the ancient confessions which, with no hesitation or struggle, testified that the Scriptures were the very Word of God.

Second, there is a striking and increasing concentration on the place and the nature of faith in the midst of a world where communication is of utmost importance. In our world "believer" and "nonbeliever" walk together into the future, but as they walk and talk together they find that they are divided at a given point by the fact that one of them has made what appears to the other a strange decision of faith. More and more, the question must come up as to whether there can really be communication between them at this point. Does faith inject itself as an irrational phenomenon in our world, a feature of life that withdraws from all rationally responsible accounting for itself, and is left only with a witness that has no rational self-defense? Thus the question of communication and dialogue looms large. What is the possibility of a genuine relationship between faith and reason?

A third theme is eschatology. The way for it was blazed by the "quest for the historical Jesus" in the early part of the century. When the "quest" failed, the consistent eschatological orientation of New Testament proclamation was "discovered." About 1920 the conviction grew that eschatology meant much more than an innocent "little closing chapter" of a dogmatics (Barth), and since then eschatology has emerged as a central theme of theology. It has raised questions about life today and in the future, and has come to full expression as the basis for a theology of hope.

We cannot pass through a half-century of theology without bringing all these important questions within the horizon of our discussion.

But there is another theme that demands our attention. It is not strictly a theological theme. It has to do with the concern, even unrest, that is experienced in the churches about the very faith, the dogma if you will, of the church. Here we must speak of doubt and uncertainty that theology has created. Our purpose will be to examine the theological sources of the unrest. They cluster, for the most part, around the reinterpretation of dogma, particularly that of christology and the trinity.

All these themes lie before us in later chapters. Here, we will concern ourselves with one theme that really lies at the bottom of everything else — the question of the living God, the reality of his revelation within our world. I do not mean to speak of the background of the so-called "death of God" theology nor of the questions that surround modern atheism. But I do want to point to various questions and struggles that have loomed within the church itself, and within theology itself. They are questions that hover over our universal experiences of life in our time; but they have their own special character as we ask how the church and its theology have tried to speak of the Lord God with a voice that could truly be heard and understood by "the world." "Who is God?" "What do we mean by his presence in the world?" "Where does he reveal himself here and now?" These are questions that plague many people, and often receive something less than a concrete answer. This question, "Who is God?" is asked in the midst of doubts about all sorts of "God concepts" that men have created. We find ourselves here in quite a different atmosphere than that in which Micah asked: "Who is a God like thee, pardoning iniquity and passing over transgression. . . ?" (Micah 7:18). In Micah's question there is a latent doxology, a "rapturous hymn" (A. Weiser), that leaves all doubt behind as it revels in admiration of the reality of Israel's God. Many of the questions of our time arise not in doxology but in doubt.

Today's questions are more like Job's than like Micah's. For with Job the question is that of God's absence, not of the wonder of his presence. Theology's question of God is a most existential and relevant question, one that casts doubt on all that we had learned and accepted from our childhood days. It is not a theoretical question about God's existence as a "thing," an "X" out there somewhere. Such questions were on the agenda when dialectical theology came to us with its finger pointed to the transcendence of God. Dialectical theology shook people's confidence that God was to be found within the world. Many asked whether it thus left ample room for the reality of his immanence within the world, and whether it was not one-sidedly entranced by the hiddenness of God, hidden as it were in his unapproachable light (1 Timothy 6:16). Naturally, we all knew that the Scriptures testified to a God who was separate from the world, separated from it in his acts and his judgments. But we did not want to be caught by a fixation with the "unknown God" as we thought about the reality of God in his grace and judgment. We wanted to keep open the passage from the "unknown God" to the "revealing God." We wanted to preserve the connections Isaiah suggests as he speaks out of a knowledge of God and yet says: "Truly, thou art a God who hidest thyself, O God of Israel, the Savior" (Isaiah 45:15).

To be sure, we can say in the midst of these questions that the church has given a definite confessional answer to the existence of God. We might think of the Belgic Confession's affirmation of the "one only simple and spiritual Being, which we call God; . . . eternal, incomprehensible, invisible, immutable, infinite, almighty, perfectly wise, just, good, and the overflowing fountain of all good" (Article I). But this stream of words does not automatically answer every modern problem. It is not clear to everyone, in the midst of his actual life, what these impressive words really mean. What is this "simple and spiritual Being, which we call God"? What significance does this wisdom, justness, goodness, this fountain of all good really have for us? Questions arise, not out of a spirit of criticism, nor out of a mood of rebellion, but as earnest calls for an answer, desires to understand, longings for such words to speak to us concretely and comfortingly. Such questions have been given new shape and form within theology, as the problems of theism, of transcendence and immanence, of divine presence and hiddenness have been thrown on the theological screen again.

The hiddenness of God has played an important role in the history of theology (and the church) in connection with a specific "teaching" of the church, a "teaching" in which all the questions of God converge at a single cutting edge. We refer to the teaching of divine election, often referred to as predestination. In the Netherlands, about 1920, the church's confession of election was frequently and extensively elaborated. I do not refer simply to the discussion about supra- and infralapsarianism, which was dealt with by the Synod of Utrecht in 1905. This argument never became a live issue within the life of congregations — and anyone who gets very far into this interconfessional controversy is not surprised that it did not awaken response within ordinary believers. But the confession of divine election did come to the fore in a very direct pastoral way; people in the congregations have been plagued by questions concerning election and human responsibility, questions about the certainty of one's own salvation, about the "book of life" in which names of only certain persons had been written, and questions about the secrecy and mystery of election. We constantly encounter attempts to remove the "contradictions" and to show how we could think about election without being threatened with loss of certainty about our salvation.

For this reason, we wanted to remove the caricatures that have often plagued the doctrine of election. It may be asked whether questions about election are still relevant, whether even the question of faith's certainty is important, and whether the church's confession of election cannot be placed on a back burner. But the questions in fact have not evaporated. They keep coming back in new forms within our talk about God. And they often are directed most critically at what the Reformed churches of earlier days confessed about election. Thus, if we take seriously the conviction that election lies at the *cor ecclesiae*, at the heart of the church, we find ourselves at the center of the church's faith when we focus on the question of election.

Bavinck spoke of the trinity as the heart of the church; it is the confession, he says, with which the whole of Christendom stands or falls, "root of all dogmas, substance of the new covenant," the heart and essence of the Christian religion. Yet, he talked about election too in firm doxological terms, about its "glory" (*Gereformeerde Dogmatiek,* II, p. 368) and about the inexpressibly rich comfort of the counsel of God (*Magnalia Dei,* p. 251, E.T. *Our Reasonable Faith,* 1956, pp. 268-269). Clearly, the analogy of the heart points to the central and huge significance of this confession. In the light of history, it is intriguing and provocative that election should be seen as the *essence* of Christian faith, and that it comes to us as comfort. For this doctrine has sometimes been all but comforting; it has aroused endless controversies that have, for many, been much more confusing than comforting. It may seem strange, then, that election should be taken seriously as the heart of the church. Undeniably, this "cardinal confession of the Reformed Church" (A. Kuyper) has been an offense, with no real liberating and tension-relieving power. For many it was only a sign pointing to a dark, hidden, mysterious, and arbitrary decision "behind the scenes" of the history of every child of man, a decision that was extremely difficult to rhyme with a gospel of love comforting to the heart. Is not this dogma more complex than we, in our praises of God's antecedent love, could have imagined? Does it, then, not make more sense to keep the Reformation's doctrine of justification by faith in the center of the church? And why is it that the doctrine of election provokes questions and objections that continually overshadow the comfort of faith? And why does the doctrine of election so seldom get preached? Why is it that, in preaching the gospel, we generally shove divine election into the background? Is there a connection between the questions about election and the timidity in preaching it?

A question that strikes deep within our reflections on the subject is whether election can be proclaimed without arousing all sorts of new problems in the mind of the listening congregation. What must we think of what Bavinck said, that preaching the gospel should have nothing to do with election and reprobation (*Gereformeerde Dogmatiek*, IV, p. 5)? Do we not have here the intriguing problem of decisions made "behind the scenes"? And does Bavinck's opinion not lead to a suppression of very real questions that will only resurface at a later time with new urgency? For we stand here before a totally different "behind the scenes" than Philip did when he asked to see the Father (John 14). Philip, too, wanted to know about the reality beyond the scenes which, when it was revealed, he finally would know for sure. But Jesus plucked Philip's question away from its "behind the scenes" context and unmasked its illegitimacy: "Have *I* been with you so long and you still do not know *me*?"

Whenever election is spoken of as something happening "behind the scenes" — as the eternal decree — the impression is awakened that though this teaching has been revealed to us, we are not permitted to speak about it too openly. Within this atmosphere, the doctrine of election gets the stamp of a mysterious hiddenness, of an enigmatic and alienating factor involving those "unknown" names written from beforehand in the "book of life." One can understand, then, that preaching would have to do with other things, things that did not have to be kept in the shadows. In this situation, people were urged by preaching not to let murky thoughts about what happened "behind the scenes" lead them away from the certainty of God's promises and the comfort of pastoral counsel. They were, that is, encouraged to concentrate on what happens out in the open, the means of grace.

Similar problems had emerged in reference to the supra- and infralapsarian debate, when, for example, Spanheim admitted that he was a *supra* in his study and an *infra* in the pulpit. This is a revealing admission, one that begs the whole question of truth. This is consistent with the common pastoral advice for people to be content to stick with the means of grace. But in trying to follow this advice, people found that some aspects from "behind the scenes" kept protruding into life. For it was a "revealed" truth that something "hidden" went on behind the scenes, and this suggested that what happened in the dark background was really more decisive than anything that happened in the openness of history. Many preachers will recognize my own experience in my first congregation, when a baptized member of the church who had broken with the church without having made his confession came to me and, with a certain air of triumph, recalled his early catechism about election. The way he had it figured, nothing could help him "if he were not elect" and his own break from the church could not hurt him "if he were elect." We can easily recognize the caricature in this sort of reasoning. While I remember his question better than I do my answer, I suspect that I told him he was caricaturing, and I probably pointed him to the mysterious relation between election and responsibility; in short, I left election alone and resorted to a pastoral warning. But pastoral warning is really powerless over against this sort of logic. Even if we reject his kind of "heads I win, tails you lose" argument, we still must ask why it always comes back. And all the problems that arise in the pastor's study bring us in theology anew before the question of how people can experience and understand election as an eternal, irrevocable, and, in its factuality, a revealed state of affairs that is settled in the decree of God. When we read in the Westminster Confession about the eternal predetermination of "whatsoever comes to pass" we are forced to think again about the strange tendency to silence the issue, to let it be muted in preaching, and on the other hand to claim that it is the glory of the Reformed confession, the center of the confession which ought to be set in the foreground and preached (A. Kuyper, E Voto, II, 1895, p. 194).

With this, we arrive at the relationship between dogmatics and life within the church. Once we face the fact that election is undeniably exiled from our preaching, we face the question of how it can also be the center of our confession. Does this homiletical scrupulousness suggest that election really does belong to "the theological esoteric," where it is a "plaything of our speculations and debates" (O. Weber, "Die Lehre von der Erwählung und die Verkündigung" in Die Treue Gottes und die Kontinuität der menschlichen Existenz, 1967, p. 27)?

All this is further underscored by the fact that the confession of election is accompanied by a summons to protect it from all sorts of misunderstanding and caricature. The Canons of

Dordt, from the seventeenth century, warn us against horrible misconstruals of the doctrine. One caricature is central here. It is that of election as an arbitrary action of God that would turn him into "the author of sin, unrighteous, tyrannical and hypocritical," that it is "nothing more than an interpolated Stoicism, Manichaeism, Libertinism, Turcism," and, finally, that it "teaches us that God, by a mere arbitrary act of his will, without the least respect or view to any sin, has predestinated the greatest part of the world to eternal damnation, and has created them for this very purpose." Against such caricatures, the church is urged to the greatest care, and to speak "to the glory of the divine name, to holiness of life, and to the consolation of afflicted souls."

The Canons speak of those who consciously oppose the doctrine as "blasphemers." But questions also arose from those who genuinely tried to understand what was really intended with this "heart of the church" and how that heart really beat. In the Epilogue of the Canons, the ministers of the gospel are summoned to avoid "those phrases which exceed the limits necessary to be observed in ascertaining the genuine sense of the Holy Scriptures, and may furnish insolent sophists with a just pretext for assailing, or even vilifying, the doctrine of the Reformed Churches." This reference to "just pretext" is striking because it refers to a manner of speaking by which the right perspective on election could be lost. The warning could be applied to every confession, but here it gets special accent in view of irresponsible "playing," as Kuyper put it, "with dead concepts and a coupling of lifeless syllogisms." It appears to us that in the last half-century a lot of attention has been paid to this very danger, as theologians have tried to plow through to an answer to the question of God. This raises the question of whether the church of earlier centuries was always as careful as it might have been, and whether it gave "just pretext" for caricatures and blasphemy. In our time we face the fact not only that the confession of election comes up in theological discussions, but that critical questions have intruded into the life of the church itself. In fact, questions have arisen about whether the Canons themselves have given "just pretext" for "assailing" the doctrine.

We will deal first with the charge that the confession of divine election is at bottom dominated by arbitrariness. By arbitrariness we have in mind the "once-for-all" decision made in eternity that seals the lot of all people forever. The eternal decree of pre-destination (or predetermination) has its logical corollary in "double predestination" — election and reprobation. The question is: Does not double predestination render pointless everything people decide and do? Intuitively — and biblically — the answer comes easily. Human life is sketched by the gospel in motifs of tension and struggle, in contrast to any self-evident reason for indifference or complacence. Who does not recall, among many examples, the dynamics of Christ's prayer for Peter — "that your faith may not fail" (Luke 22:32). Here that which must yet happen is set in the crucible. But this tension can easily be evapo-rated by the thought of that decree, fixed from eternity, the decree that determines everything and every person, a decree that *must* be realized in history. Is there, within this horizon, still a possi-bility for genuine preaching to summon people to a decision of faith? It would be a mistake to assume that we have to do here only with a question that has become passé, a discussion that was at home in a time gone by when ivory tower scholars debated among themselves about infra- and supralapsarianism. The same problem is on today's agenda and is tackled with every bit as much spirit as it used to be.

This is apparent in A. van Ruler's emphatic defense of the doctrine of double predestination. He talked about "the great Reformed truth of predestination, in the full, Canons of Dordt sense of double predestination." He saw in it "the deepest per-ception of human understanding ever known." He honored Calvin and the fathers at Dordt because "they had the spiritual courage to probe the truth to its heart and then to speak it, to stay with it, no matter how great the tension of human existence was." For Van Ruler, the truth of double predestination can be known em-pirically, "touched with one's fingers." From what happens mani-festly in the lives of people — as they are grasped by faith or by unbelief — it is clear that God works in history through his pre-destining and rejecting of men. Even though the doctrine of reprobation does not appear as often, "or perhaps not at all," in the Scriptures, we cannot capture the full content of the Bible "without thinking along the lines of double predestination." Repro-bation is bound up logically with election, for if there is election there must be non-election. And, he adds, it is only through cowardice that people "want to erase the word reprobation. . . ."

Double predestination as truth and reality — there it is. But what is striking is that Van Ruler uses his endorsement of double predestination as a criticism of the so-called "ultra-Reformed." These "ultra-Reformed" are guilty of having exchanged the truth of predestination for an *idea* of predestination. Predestination was turned into a principle "from which, through logical deduction, the whole system is created." What was forgotten was that the gospel is proclaimed, and that thereby salvation is made present in its fulness for all mankind. The "ultra-Reformed" trade the gospel for logic, and want to think through everything via the *idea* of double predestination. But they only end up in a wilderness of logic. We need, says Van Ruler, to be converted so that "we will stop going around with the predestination-idea, but turn instead to the unfathomable fulness and certainty of the gospel."

We have recounted Van Ruler's view because it reveals some of the tensions that the doctrine of election creates. We have in mind particularly the tension between the proclamation of the gospel (as opposed to logical construction building) and the admission of a logical connection between election and reprobation. Van Ruler says we must persevere in spite of this tension.

In respect to this tension we are reminded of what Van Ruler has written about God and chaos (*Theologische Werken,* 1961, VI). He thinks that we have limited chaos to what men do, while God is seen as only permitting it. Van Ruler says that God himself brings chaos into things. Further, he does so not only in reaction to man (as in the case of the tower of Babel); there is an "intimate relation between God and chaos" in which we can see that chaos is one of God's creative works. "Chaos belongs to the essence of things" in a way that we are unwilling to recognize. But we can never attribute chaos completely to man and his sin.

All this — which runs contrary to the consensus of tradition — is coupled with Van Ruler's understanding of how sin fits into God's decree. God does not only come out in response to sin, dealing with it appropriately, triumphing over it; he does not only expose sin in a way that reveals it to us as our own fault and rebellion. God, in connection with double predestination, wills the eternal outcome of history. Human will does play a role in the historical process. But it works in such a way "that men must respect, even here, the mastery and freedom of God (with Judas as a prime example)." He rejects the word "absurd," as he does the category of the impossible. But there does appear "something of the abyss, the wilderness, the spinning of wheels, and imprudence in the essence of God as well as in his actions." Van Ruler's language is not always transparent. But with double predestination (bringing people in history through guilt and into eternal lostness) the "good pleasure" of God is given sharper contours. "What is left for us but to plunge into the abyss, to wander in the wilderness?" For Van Ruler, this is to win the game of love. But in the background of the game lies a certain image of God that is formed from the mold of a strange hiddenness, which comes out in the features of double predestination and of the inclusion of sin within the decree of God. We land here in a complex of thoughts from which all sorts of conclusions can be drawn, conclusions that are traditionally branded as caricatures of divine election.

We encounter the tension again in what A. F. N. Lekkerkerker writes about predestination. "Sometimes I am inclined toward an absurd doctrine of predestination, but I do not dare to speak about it except tentatively, and then among trusted friends." It is hard to get inside Lekkerkerker's notion of the absurd, but it seems to tie in with the traditional concern to distinguish between the deep motif of God's mysterious election, on one hand, and divine arbitrariness and absurdity on the other, as the Canons of Dordt sought to do. The way Lekkerkerker speaks suggests that he is shocked by his own thought, even though it is only a tentative impulse. In his commentary on Romans (1962-65) he had fastened on Romans 9:16 ("So it depends not upon man's will or exertion, but on God's mercy") and declared that anyone who, on the basis of this text, supposes that our willing and exertion are pointless is caught "in a horrible and obstinate misunderstanding." But when we hear him tell of his inclination toward an "absurd" view of predestination we may suppose that he is shifting toward what he earlier called a "horrible misunderstanding."

The Christian church has set the wisdom of God over against the "absurd." And the slogan *credo quia absurdum* ("I believe because it is absurd") has never been endorsed by more than a few people, probably because one does not like to suppose that he is staking his life on irrationality. We "see through a glass darkly," but what we see only dimly is wisdom, not absurdity.

When the doctrine of predestination is associated with the absurd, it is probably due to God's apparent arbitrariness in double predestination. We need not be surprised that Calvin's views are ushered into this context, nor that his definition of predestination becomes a focal point of discussion. "We call predestination God's eternal decree, by which he determined with himself what he willed to become of each man. For all are not created in equal condition; rather, eternal life is foreordained for some, eternal damnation for others" (*Institutes*, III/21/5). And he adds: "Therefore, as any man has been created to one or the other of these ends, we speak of him as predestined to life or to death." Now, it has been allowed that Calvin's whole view does not come to light in this stark expression. Even the most casual student of Calvin knows that Calvin discusses election in other places where this double-focussed determination does not come in sight. Most discussions of Calvin's doctrine of election fasten on his insight into Christ as the mirror of our election. When he speaks of Christ he warns against intellectualist speculations. In a discussion of faith's certainty he referred to Christ as "the clearest light of predestination" (II/17/1). The metaphor of the mirror seems to release some of the tension created by such images as the hidden book with unknown names written in it from eternity. It gives perspective to faith's confidence. Even in the *Institutes* of 1539, Calvin indicated that faith does not rest in God the Father isolated from the Son. It is this and not the isolated definition of predestination that dominates his pastoral theology. A. M. Hunter has remarked that Calvin was "no more in love with the doctrine of reprobation than his critics." Still, it is undeniable that it was his definition that was worked out into the decretal theology of post-Reformation thought (cf. J. Daane, *The Freedom of God*, 1973) when, for example, it was adopted by the anti-Arminians.

The problem of the relationship between election and reprobation pursues us still. It is the logical connection between them that is the sticky issue. For instance, some fasten on to Calvin's remark that "election itself could not stand except as set over against reprobation" (*Institutes*, III/23/1). For Calvin this was a radical, crucial, profound matter — just as was the vision of Christ as "mirror of our election" — because he knew people who did indeed confess election, but denied that anyone was reprobated. Today, theologians like to appeal to Calvin's pastoral accents in which he urgently warns against getting lost in a labyrinth of speculation. How, it was asked, could Calvin's pastoral counsel make sense, so long as the double decree hovered in the background? How can divine election be pastorally comforting if it is backed by a double-focussed eternal decree in which the destinies of two separate groups are settled forever?

In the notion of double predestination we have something else on our hands than a hymn of praise to God's gracious election. The question is whether the notion of double destiny does not turn divine freedom into divine arbitrariness. The question looms out of the sixteenth century, as Calvin saw himself in confrontation with the "absolute might" of God. Calvin proceeded from the conviction that everything God did was righteous, simply because he willed it, and that no one can probe higher or deeper than this. This is the "bridle" that Calvin sets on human boldness. He adds that he does not "advocate the fiction of 'absolute might'." "We fancy no lawless god who is a law unto himself." But, says Calvin, the will of God is "the law of all laws" (*Institutes*, III/23/2). We may ask whether Calvin also provides us with an answer to the problems that arise in connection with the autonomy of God. And we may doubt whether those who wrestle with the problems are necessarily afflicted with "boldness" or "blasphemy." Calvin, with no hesitation, speaks of people "predestined to eternal death solely by his decision, apart from their own merit." His words jar us as we recall the Canons of Dordt rejecting the "calumny" that people are reprobate "apart from their own merit." From this it appears that we are not moved a step further in our discussions of God by speaking of the "absoluteness" of God's will and then muzzling further discussion in the face of it. Calvin must have felt this himself when he insisted that he did not work with a notion of "absolute might." But the difference between his definition of election and the "absolute might" that he rejects is not at all clear.

Calvin has been rightly defended against the charge that he — with Luther — was possessed by a nominalistic notion of arbitrary will. For Calvin, it is rightly insisted, God's moral will is bound to righteousness and justice. Still, he does not make it clear which caricature is being rejected and which line of thought is being blocked. The unresolved tension — the unanswered question and the unclarified ambiguity — lifts its head again when we think of Calvin's much quoted phrase: *decretum horribile*. He uses the phrase in a striking passage: "The decree is dreadful indeed, I confess. Yet no one can deny that God foreknew what end man was to have before he created him, and consequently foreknew because he so ordained by his decree" (*Institutes*,

III/23/7). In the framework of the "dreadful decree" the question is asked: What is the difference between the "dreadful decree" and the "absolute might" that Calvin rejects? And where is the path from this (dreadful) decree to the *comfort* of election that lies at the heart of the church?

I do not recall my impression on first reading Calvin's words on the "horrible decree." Did it have something in common with the things Rudolf Otto said about *The Idea of the Holy*, a book in which he talked about God not only as the *mysterium fascinans* but also as the *mysterium tremendum* arousing a sense of "horror"? And was this shock the same as Paul's "fear" for the Lord (2 Corinthians 5:11)? Or is there a special kind of horror that is a fitting response only to the eternal decree? May we speak of another shock or fear than that which arises in the face of the righteous wrath of God against all evil (Psalm 7:12)? And is this other shock caused by the *a priori* decree that eternally destines people to one side or the other, a decree that is made known to us so that we may subject ourselves to it rather than blaspheme against it?

Uneasiness about this way of characterizing God's decree is suggested by differences in translation of Calvin's *decretum horribile*. Bavinck said that it was not the decree that was horrible; only the reality of sin and hell was horrible. But Schilder understood the "horrible" as meaning: "dazzling, striking one dumb, and gainsaying all objections." Schilder's perception is true to Calvin; he meant to indicate that the revelation of this decree does indeed demand an obedient silence from us. He warns us to listen to what Paul writes: "But you, O man, who are you to complain against God? Will what is molded say to its molder, 'Why have you made me thus?'" (Romans 9:20, 21). But this is something different from a "horrible decree" that shocks people as they stand before this "revealed" truth of an *a priori* double decree in which creation and eternal destiny are parts of the same package. Is that the absolute privilege of God and the unquestionable mystery? But why then was Calvin so sensitive about the "absolute might" of God? I recall countless arguments about election in which one groped for shafts of light, for connections with Jesus Christ, for a way that did not lead to dead end without perspective. In these discussions there was always a resort to Christ as the "mirror of our election" — a facet of election concerning which Calvin did not feel the urge to be silent.

Almost every discussion of predestination focussed on the problematics of the "background" of election. And the discussions always tended to end in the twilight of mystery. Meanwhile, one returned to the proclamation of the gospel as to an oasis in which one could locate some certainty for his faith, as a light within the twilight zone of predestination. But the oases were only temporary stopping points, because the faithful were nonetheless burdened with all sorts of efforts to explain the relation between election and responsibility. Election was set forth as something that does not undo human responsibility; but the relation between them appeared finally as a paradox, sometimes as a mystery that transcends our thought. And, candidly, the paradoxical relation frequently contradicted the very text that was often quoted, Philippians 2:12, 13, which speaks of God's actions and ours in a way that is definitely not paradoxical. For Paul's "therefore" points, not to a hidden decree, but to the revelation of God in Christ.

Why did we find it necessary to resort to obtuse explanations of the doctrine of election? And why did we feel compelled to strive toward an elusive harmony and synthesis when we worked among the congregations? And, particularly, why did we resort to the christological oasis as though we found there a place that could not be threatened by the doctrine of the decree? We knew we had to go further — in concern for the heart of the church — than the construction of defensive syntheses, and we had a sense that the church in its intuition of faith resisted various "hard sayings." We noticed that people found it a blessing that the Epilogue of the Canons of Dordt qualified the "hard sayings." But which sayings were really "hard"? And were they "hard" in another sense than the sayings of Jesus that the disciples found hard (John 6:60)? How could it be made clear that divine election was not an arbitrary decree that opened the door to a fatalism and determinism in which the events of our time and history were robbed of all genuine meaning? This was Bavinck's concern when he rejected the notion of an "eternal justification"; he rejected it because it suggests that everything, including the incarnation, is really eternalized in a way that made the decisive events of Christ's appearance and the fulfilment of time basically superfluous (Gereformeerde Dogmatiek, IV, p. 200, and III, p. 598).

The problem of the "background" continued to cast a shadow over all the wonderful things that were said in theology about God's gracious election. The struggle was always concentrated on our thoughts of the sovereignty and freedom of God which were affirmed by the doctrine of the divine decree. At this point, we usually spoke about the *absolute* freedom and sovereignty of God, as though to silence the opposition. But adding adjectives was not a sure way of preserving authentic orthodoxy, no matter what impression they make on first hearing. Adding "absolute" did not really make the sun rise over the mystery of divine sovereignty and divine freedom.

It may be useful to reflect on the word "despot" in this connection. The New Testament Greek word *despotes* is translated "Lord" (Luke 2:29; Acts 4:24) and "Sovereign Lord" (RSV, Revelation 6:10). In later associations it became clear that it was dangerous to let this word by itself be a key to understanding God. For "despot" came to mean an absolute and arbitrary ruler; and there was no hint of this in Luke 2:29, the hymn of Simeon, praising God for the promise and the peace of the appearing Messiah. In this context, the word *despotes* was rich and understandable, just as it was in the context of God's holiness and truthfulness which surrounds the word in Revelation 6:10. This reminds us that one has to be on guard against isolating and abstracting words, including the word "sovereignty." If we are not, we may use words that violate the heart of the church. This is not a caveat discovered by later theologians who blazed the trail to a new way of looking at the truth of divine election, one that can fit into the decisions of free men who determine their own destinies. Barth wrote concerning Romans 9:14 that Paul's "by no means" does not refer to what God does by way of his sovereignty "as though it indicates a basis for his good pleasure that is known only to him," but that Paul is pointing to God's revelation of mercy (9:15), and not to a "naked sovereignty"; here Barth is on the same wavelength with Calvin's protest against "naked majesty."

Kuyper, in 1880, characterized sovereignty as the "authority that contains all right within itself, . . . and exercises power to . . . destroy every resistance to his will." He added that the original, absolute sovereignty is fitting only for the "majesty of God as the only absolute sovereign, the only planner, creator, ordainer, and determiner of all things." Reading Kuyper now we see that he fails to make it clear how all this is any different from an arbitrary determination of an "absolute might." To question Kuyper's language is not to question what the church has always confessed about the sovereignty of God, nor is it done with a desire to re-place determinism with an indeterminism. But it does have to do with the irrefutable fact that the knowledge of divine sovereignty is possible only within knowledge of the God in whom there is no arbitrariness.

Words like "sovereignty" ought not be approached abstractly via a formal concept; this can only create the impression that we are capturing our *own* understanding or words in transparent definitions and then applying them directly to God without deeper consideration, as though he naturally fits the definition garnered from human experience. Not surprisingly, this abstract notion of sovereignty has a profound effect when theologians apply it to Paul's view of God (especially with reference to Romans 9) and to such parables as the laborers in the vineyard. The Lord had said to the protesting employees: "Am I not free to do what I choose with what belongs to me?" (Matthew 20:15). The word our Lord uses *(exousia)* seemed to clarify everything by its indication of "that absolute possibility for action that God possesses, over against which every question about the relationship between power and justice with respect to this *exousia* is pointless" (W. Foerster, in G. Kittel and G. Friedrich, eds., *Theological Dictionary of the New Testament*, II, pp. 566f.). But is anything made clear by phrases like "incontestable freedom" and this "absolute possibility"?

In the Canons of Dordt absolute sovereignty and freedom are deployed over against those who murmur "at the free grace of election and the just severity of reprobation" (I/18). "Am I not free. . . ?" And is this freedom perhaps the deepest background of double predestination? It is wise to consider that the laborers' protest is aimed against the goodness of God, and that, in response, his freedom is meant as the sign of his goodness. ("Is your eye evil because I am good?" 20:15.) If we do not reckon with this, we are likely (just as with Romans 9) to con-clude — via a logical parallel — that God's freedom refers to his absolute disposing of all those many who are called and the few who are chosen. Many and few (Mark 22:14), the first and the last (Matthew 20:16) — do these phrases find their home in the "absolute might"? Or is there validity to the almost unanimous construction of these crucial words that points, not to a factual appointment of people to their individual destinies, but rather to a summons to conversion?

It is alarming and shocking that anyone should move from an abstract notion of sovereignty to a serious consideration of the *number* of the chosen — a statistical research into the population of the two groups, the many and the few. In 1772, the cardinals of the Congregation of the Index put Gravina's "optimism" under censure, for suggesting that the number of the "chosen" was much larger than that of the merely "called." It reminds us of a bit of study into which Kuyper was seduced in connection with children who die very early. He assumed that dogmatics was obliged to take account of statistics, in view of the confidence that the Canons gave to believing parents about children who die very young (*Gemeene Gratie*, II, pp. 654ff.). But waving the banner of *absolute* divine autonomy does not dam up anguishing questions, and is certainly not likely to lead to praise.

If divine freedom explains everything, and if revelation is only a window in which absolute sovereignty is displayed, one asks how it is possible that Paul, in those tremendous chapters of Romans 9—11 — after his words about the clay and the potter, and his rejection of any and every complaint against God — does not end with a reasoned conclusion that the destiny of everything and everyone is sealed from eternity. Why does he, rather, end with a breathtaking doxology: O the depth of the riches and wisdom and knowledge of God! How unsearchable are his judgments and how inscrutable his ways! (Romans 11:33)?

From whence this hymn of praise with its "astonishing exclamations!" (Käsemann) in response to the depths of God, and how does it enter our horizon as an insight into the ways of God? When Calvin read this "summons to praise" he accepted it as a bridle for our discussions of God's eternal counsel; he wanted our sober discussions to end with "speechless astonishment." The doxology comes out of the discovery of the ways of election. On these ways, the Word of God proclaims the elective intentions of God, "not because of works, but because of his call" (Romans 9:11). In Paul's doxology election is still decisive. It sounds in the citation from Isaiah 40:13, which says the Lord has had no counsellor, and denies that forgiveness is a reward for human achievement. In this hymn there is no hint of bending the knee before a power that has no defining content, a power that we might conceive of outside of the knowledge of *the* God (an "absolute might"). Here there is perspective into depths that are other than those which we often meet in the history of theology, other, too, than what we evoke from our own hearts. Here the doxology arises, not out of shock at the mystery, but rather (as with Henri de Lubac) from the consciousness of the resourcefulness of God's mercy, a mercy without arbitrariness. From the depth of this richness the controversy against God becomes meaningless and, for that matter, totally illegitimate.

As I review many discussions that took place in churchly and theological circles, discussions in which I too participated with both questions and doubts, I recall not only important signals that came from Luther and Calvin — in spite of some unfortunate definitions — but also an article written by O. Noordmans in which various motifs came forward that appeared again later (O. Noordmans, "Predestination" in *Geestelijke perspectieven*, 1930). Noordmans was fascinated by the "mystical delight" in which Paul concluded Romans 11. Here, he said, there is nothing of "the inexplicable arbitrariness of power that moves one to put his fingers to his lips." There are only positive accents, accents which the church unfortunately took over only with hesitation. Very often, he said, we felt in God's sovereign election only arbitrariness and power, without the experience of expanded life-space in our thinking. And so we were struck with predestination as a concept caught in the principle of sheer power. The church "seldom was able to follow Paul to the climax of his contemplation."

These words are in tune with the real human situation, or at least they were during a time when the questions of dogma still captured the hearts of believing people who wanted to understand their meaning. Noordmans discerned a joyful election in the Gospels as well as in Paul. The Gospels "vibrate with predestination" in a most powerful "re-valuation of all values," especially in their concentration on the Lord's love for sinners and publicans and in their rejection of moralism. Prior to Barth, Noordmans pleaded for an understanding of "election in Christ" so that election could be freed from the shackles of logical deduction. This, he thought, would set divine election apart from abstractions culled from a barren concept of sovereignty as such. There is a "pre-," but it is the divine *pre*ference for sinners, in support of which we can quote half of the Gospels. This is the preference we find in 1 Corinthians 1. It is a "pre-" of divine desire, not of logical determinism. Noordmans was ahead of his time with respect to understanding what the heart of the church involved.

Not surprisingly, Noordmans had great sympathy for H. F. Kohlbrügge. He discerned, at crucial points, a significant congeniality between Kohlbrügge and Barth. Barth, in his fierce criticism of nineteenth-century subjectivism, had said that Kohlbrügge was an exception in view of his insight into prevenient grace. Kohlbrügge, said Barth, had on this point "attained the profundity of Calvin" and in a sense excelled him. When Kohlbrügge thought about the Reformed Church's doctrine of election, he put a question to the Synod of Dordt. He asked why the fathers had "let themselves be outwitted and led away from the righteousness of Christ to the notion of predestination . . . when in fact they could have had the Arminians on the run simply by preaching the righteousness of God and of Christ, and so could have closed the mouths of future critics" (this in a letter to Reumen).

I once called Kohlbrügge's criticism unfair because the Canons' doctrine of election made it clear that "the sovereignty of grace was opposed to all human pretensions of merit." I still think that this was the real intention of the fathers of Dordt. But I now believe that this does not really respond to what troubled Kohlbrügge. For this "pre-" is set in a construction that does not let the grace of election come to its own, in spite of all the warnings against misunderstanding that the Epilogue contains. Grace takes a back seat because of the double focus of the divine decree, a dual focus that the fathers of Dordt thought necessary in order to secure the "pre-" aspect of election. Is the "pre-" dimension secured only through double predestination? Or is there something in John 3:17 that suggests a holy reserve in Scripture?

It is striking that the other way of seeing this "pre-" — the way we find in Noordmans, Kohlbrügge, Barth, Otto Weber, H. N. Ridderbos, and many others — does not compel us to force predestination into harmony with the preaching of the gospel, since this harmony — as Bavinck so explicitly insisted — was *a priori* clear within the meaning of election. This harmony is created in the mystery of election *in grace* (Romans 11:5) which occurs — revealingly and liberatingly — as an election "not on the basis of works. . . ."

All this is still very much part of the animated discussions of our own time. Some fear that absolute sovereignty will not be given its due if we make election a "general rule" in which a bona fide selective action of God disappears. The result may be, it is thought, that the moderate orthodoxy of the Arminians will still prevail. The danger is that the "selective" aspect of election would make way for a general election, with election only a quality of God's free action. That this criticism (directed at me, as well as at Herman Ridderbos and others) is unconvincing is clear from the way Jesus speaks of the good pleasure of God (the *eudokia* in Matthew 11:25 and Luke 10:21) that is hidden from the wise and revealed to the children. One could speak of a "rule" here, but not of an "abstract rule." Much rather, here is a divine *act* of hiding and revealing — for which Christ *thanks* the Father (Matthew 11:25). Here we do not have living human beings exchanged for "qualities" (humility and self-conceit) which form the deeper ground of election and reprobation. Rather, we meet here the way in which God's elective actions are indicated — God's good pleasure not looming from a dark hinterland, in which the real decisions were made, but from his grace in Christ toward actual people.

To be grasped by this thought in our reflections on God's good pleasure has nothing to do with a devaluation of divine sovereignty. It is not motivated by respect for the autonomy of the free man. It does help reveal the meaning of election without creating tension between election and preaching. This act of hiding and revealing is something wholly different from a "formal arbitrariness" (Bavinck) that leaves us without a word to speak. This is why we ought not be seduced into thinking — in view of election — of two separate groups of people. With some justification E. Schlink has written that we are lured out of this abstract reflection "as we hasten to move from his word of judgment to his word of grace and, then again, from the grace we have received to the grace that he will give to others" (*Der theologische Syllogismus als Problem der Prädestinationslehre, Einsicht und Glaube*, 1962, p. 317). Drawing conclusions from our concept of God's eternal being is forbidden us, among other reasons, because the Bible does not present us with two classes of people, but only one, the sinners who are called to salvation. Historically, we could say that the church always drew back from dividing the human race into the selected and rejected ones. The Council of Valentine in 855 confessed a predestination unto life *and* unto death, but it was an exception. Even here the parallel lines were broken by saying that while the mercy of God was prior to human merit, the sin of man was prior to judgment. This indeed is the point at which hesitation always arises in the face of theoretical and deductive ways of working with predestination. The New Testament speaks of merciful election in a way that brings us up short with our logical tools. Wherever one experiences this mercy, he finds it impossible to come to a "theoretical reflection that is cut loose from the act of receiving, thanking, and witnessing" because in this way "God's decree of love is transformed into a vulgar formula of predestination that is cut loose from God's saving acts in Jesus Christ" (Schlink, *op. cit.*, p. 304). It also loads us with all the conclusions that are drawn from this formula as to predestined of sin and the order of decrees, conclusions which, it is supposed, we cannot avoid. This awareness of a terrible danger forms the basic reason for all protests against the predestined parallel lines on which the select and the reprobate walk toward their destinies. It forms the background of the warnings issued by the Canons of Dordt (the "not in the same manner" of the Epilogue) and of the repeated resistance to logicism, even when the resistance is not able to come up with a clear formulation of its own. When Kuyper spoke of reprobation as running parallel with election, he intended this as a response to the biblical witness, not as a logical deduction. But for many it is precisely that biblical witness which not only militates against logicism but testifies to the *gracious* election of God.

Understandably, Romans 9–11 always came back into the discussion, and Romans 9:6 in particular. Here Paul writes that the Word of God did not fail inasmuch as "not all who are descended from Israel belong to Israel." In discussions that took place between 1940 and 1945 this text was the focus of much debate. Appeal was made to it in various publications in order to show that we must speak of the covenant, and of the baptism that is contained within it, with all caution, and must guard against "objectifying" because the covenant has its limits in God's election. (Not all who are *in* the covenant are *of* the covenant.) The Word of God has not failed — the thought went — because the "genuine" covenant was defined by election as the great proviso for all our thinking about the covenant. We must always keep this "proviso" in mind; the authentic Word of God as an *unconditional* promise was given to the limited number of authentic children of the covenant — and thus the promise cannot fail. Others, grieved by this problematic use of predestination as the background of the covenant, saw this way of thinking as an attack against the "objectivity" and integrity of the covenant and of baptism. It led, they thought, to the conclusion that when people are baptized and do not come to faith, they had only an *apparent* baptism. Looking back on this dispute, we ought to begin by recognizing that Paul in Romans 9:6 was not working with the problem of a background. The problem that busied Paul was whether the promise was rendered void by Israel's unbelief. He denied this in Romans 3:5, where he wrote that our unrighteousness only underscores God's righteousness; and this is what he is concerned to say in Romans 9:6. But this does not mean a limitation set by a hidden background; there is indeed an unmistakable limit, but it is set by the fact that the promise 'is not given as a reward on the basis of which one could, as the children of Israel did, glorify oneself. The promise of God is not a handy means for us to claim a *character indelebilis* "which cannot be undone even by false reactions of the elect" (H. Wildberger, in *Theologisches Handwörterbuch zum Alten Testament*, ed. Jenni-Westermann, I, 1971, p. 886). It is not a guarantee that entails a claim on God. What Paul writes is limiting in this sense, that it "eliminates the confidence of an Israel that boasts of its own selection." And it is in this way that the question of the true Israel becomes urgent. The covenant is not made uncertain. Rather, the perspective is fastened to the faithfulness of God and to the certainty that the gospel gives. This became evident for Paul in the history of Jews and Gentiles out of which, in the clearest light, the way of the elective purpose of God appears.

At this point we can enter upon the gravamina that have been brought within the Gereformeerde Kerken during the last twenty years against certain expressions in the Canons of Dordt. Before we do, however, we should pause to consider the backgrounds that formed the impetus for this gravamina. I wish to do this partly because of the various reproaches and criticisms that have brought me into close connection with them. Anyone in touch with the tradition of the doctrine of election will recognize a persistent longing for greater clarity that has been part of the tradition. And in that longing for clarity, various contrived solutions are deployed that one gradually discerns as unacceptable and impossible when one keeps his eye on the gospel. In confrontations, we have not only the danger of polarization, but also the possibility of a helpful and healing experience. We can be shocked by the caricatures that are drawn in controversy, and the caricatures signal ways that are untraversable, even though the right way is not yet clear to us.

For me personally — and everyone has his own experiences — the unquestionably sharp theological thought of the American theologian Herman Hoeksema played an important role. He wrote a spate of journal articles centering on the confession of election, especially in connection with a conflict he had within the Christian Reformed Church about common grace. After his death in 1965, his *Reformed Dogmatics* were published (1966). In them the sovereignty of God was set centrally over against all relativizing of it, a sovereignty he typified as "complete and absolute" (p. 158). Hoeksema accepted all the implications of it as seen in the supralapsarian position, which he called "the scriptural and the only consistent presentation of the decree of God's predestination" (p. 164). When I met Hoeksema in 1952 I was impressed anew that his manner of thinking about election was impossible. It has been said that I made it easy for myself by choosing Hoeksema as a dialogue partner because he allowed himself to be seduced by supralapsarianism into highly questionable positions concerning the place of reprobation within preaching. I would reply that I have seldom met a theologian who reasoned through so consistently from his original standpoint; he never wavered from his starting point. He was one of the few who dared draw implications from reprobation for the task of preaching the gospel to all men. In view of the *a priori* decree of election and reprobation, universal proclamation is not possible, so long as the seriousness and genuinely intended offer of grace is concerned. The offer of grace could not be directed to people who were excluded from salvation by God's decree. If the gospel is universally preached, it is possible and meaningful only in the sense that no one knows who the elect are, "head for head and soul for soul." The "joyful" message, the good news, can really be addressed only to the elect as to the authentic addressees. For Hoeksema this was so clear because, in his judgment, the Bible everywhere speaks of election and reprobation, and teaches that there can only be an "eternal, sovereign hate" for the nonelect. The logical implications could not be denied, he believed, and he drew and maintained them without hesitation in the face of those who viewed them with shock and deep disturbance. I did not, in fact, select Hoeksema as a partner in dialogue; he simply came along my path and, indirectly, helped me to move further along the path that he himself thought was impassable and against which he warned me and others urgently. The power of suggestion within his arguments forced itself on everyone who looked at them seriously.

I do not believe that he came to his excessive formulations by way of his special supralapsarianism. I think they resulted from his having set his thought processes within his vision of double predestination. The problems were sharply illuminated by the position that Schilder took within the dispute. It would not be accurate to identify Schilder's views with those of Hoeksema; nor would it be accurate to suggest that, in their frequent associations and in their shared objections to the doctrine of common grace, Schilder allowed Hoeksema to speak for him. They touched each other, not only in the context of common grace and their common opposition to Kuyper, but also with respect to what for Hoeksema was a central issue, namely his vision of the universal offer of salvation. With respect to the latter, Schilder came to a different conclusion than Hoeksema did. Hoeksema tied the universal offer of salvation to the possibility of knowing who was elect and who was reprobate. Schilder rightly saw that Hoeksema's explanation of the Canons of Dordt (with respect to Christ being offered in the gospel) could not be supported. He maintained the offer, given to all, as a summons to faith and conversion, a summons that goes out to all men. But in this view he left one question unanswered: To what ought and to what *could* faith be directed? There was talk of an "offer" of Christ, but this was not an offer in the sense of authentic inviting. It lacked the sincerity of the Canons, which bind the offer with "what is pleasing to God, namely that the called come to him." Hoeksema's denial of the universal offer of salvation and Schilder's subtle analysis of the concept "offer" (with his distinction between the "offer of Christ" and the "offer of grace") hardly are contradictory, since Schilder's analysis also stands under the heavy burden of double predestination (love and hate), from which the way to the proclamation of the gospel is very hard to find. (Cf. A.C. De Jong, *The Well-Meant Gospel Offer. The Views of H. Hoeksema and K. Schilder,* 1954, dissertation.)

The unresolved tensions evoked increasing objections to the aprioristic double decree with its two groups of human beings, each of which was the "object" of one decision within the twofold decree. The two groups were the elect and reprobate, which, in A.D.R. Polman's phrase, were "two groups, shut off from each other by a static objectification." The universal proclamation of the gospel could be accommodated to this notion of "two groups of human beings" only via a contrived dogma. Awareness of this and of the fact that in this way pastoral work was often made fruitless motivated many objections to the doctrine of the double decree. No matter how emphatically it was claimed that the gospel could still be preached, the background loomed as a decision made by a God who remained hidden from us within an irresolvable dialectic of revelation and hiddenness. Against this background, preaching had to be confined to other things that did not have to be kept in the shadows; but even these things stood in the shadow of the final mystery that enveloped the elect and reprobate, a mystery very different from the mystery that has been revealed, the mystery of which Paul writes and from out of which he sees the way open to the proclamation of the gospel to all peoples (Romans 16:26). Anyone taking refuge in another mystery can never fully comprehend — as Bavinck put it — that election itself is a motive for proclamation. Nor can he escape the thought that has so often intersected the comfort of the gospel, the thought that in spite of all subtle reassurances the inscrutable decree sets the proclamation of the gospel under a tremendous question mark.

Against the background of such discussions I, not without hesitation and persistent questions, published my book *Divine Election*, in 1955 (E.T. 1960). Here I travelled other routes than those taken by such as Hoeksema and Schilder. Wary, not of logic, but of certain logical consequences that had been drawn, consequences that are hardly recognizable as the "good consequences" of which the Westminster Confession speaks, I came to the question of Scripture's own speech. Here, in the Bible's radical and open character, I found a way of speaking that is not defined by some darksome eternal background, but by the way of history that led Paul to his remarkable doxologies. In this connection I cannot but recall how, before my book appeared, I enjoyed some probing theological conversations with Herman Ridderbos, who had just at that time written a monograph on *Israel in the New Testament, According to Romans 9–11* (Dutch, 1955). We had never talked about this together, and it was natural that a theologian, seeing his own questions multiply before him, would be intensely interested in the exegesis by a New Testament scholar like Ridderbos of those chapters in Romans which had held me captive for so long and which I, in spite of Calvin and Barth and others, found so difficult that I went for lengthy periods without preaching from them. Our discussion was supportive for me in my conviction that my rejection of consistent views like Hoeksema's and others need not lead me into a fruitless polarization; I did not have to posit indeterminism over against determinism.

Ridderbos once lectured on predestination to a ministers' conference and offered this thesis: "The New Testament does not recognize a *problem* of predestination; it has only a predestination *gospel*." This releases the predestination question from the tension between determinism and indeterminism. It avoids a dialectic between divine freedom and human freedom. Ridderbos wanted to set predestination within the message of the New Testament. God's salvation is not tied to a "number clause" and is not defined in terms of an *object* that is determined. It is wholly linked to God's own sovereign *grace*. This was Ridderbos' view, and he read Romans 9 as supporting it. The "beforehand" texts of the New Testament (knowing beforehand, accepting beforehand, etc.) are not pointers to a hidden background. "The meaning of these 'beforehand' clauses does not lie in a general predetermination, which, in turn, is the logical implication of an abstract idea of God; it lies in the advent of God's unique plan of salvation (*the* mystery) that was revealed in Christ. All the 'beforehand' concepts are, at bottom, categories of salvation, and they point to the fulness of God's virtue as the origin and the power of his saving acts in Christ."

Without identifying Ridderbos' view with Barth's, we can notice a congeniality with the way Barth began his doctrine of election, at least on one point. "The doctrine of election is the sum of the gospel." A comparison between Barth's *Shorter Commentary on Romans (Kurze Erklärung*, 1956, E.T. 1959) and Ridderbos' own commentary on Romans in 1959 (along with his great work, *Paulus*) shows that this same motif runs through their exegesis of Romans 11:5 (the election of grace). It also is present in their views of the *ekloge* as the "firm principle" by which God deals with his people and in the light of which Israel has to be understood "according to her election" (Ridderbos, commentary on Romans, *in loco*). In this "predestination gospel" we encounter a view totally different from that which has played — particularly in connection with Romans 9 — so great a role in traditional predestination doctrines.

Ridderbos also asks whether the Bible justifies our penchant for considering predestination as a problem of election versus human responsibility. He thinks not. Paul does not set human freedom and responsibility in the shadow of divine predestination; rather, says Ridderbos, he "maintains the freedom of God's grace over against all human complaints or merits." In view of this, Ridderbos did not interpret Paul's words about Jacob and Esau as teaching double predestination. Indeed, the notion of double predestination is "an arbitrary and radical distortion of the original intention of the biblical words." The word "radical" is not an exaggeration. Ridderbos sees election connected, not with a definite number of people, but with Christ. This newer exegesis operates in another climate than did the older exegesis, and it implies another kind of pastoral opportunity as well. Ridderbos fails to find anywhere in the development of Paul's thought "the hidden decree" that might function as "the background or explanation of the separation (between people) that comes about by the preaching of the gospel . . ." (*Paul, An Outline of His Theology*, E.T. 1975, p. 352). Preaching, for Paul, creates a meaningful open situation; his argument does not move toward "twofold destinies and twofold futures, but to the . . . way of faith as the only way of salvation in view of God's liberating grace." Here the motif and pattern of God's *action* are opposed to arbitrariness.

Thus the reconsideration of election has tended for several years, not in the direction of a double decree that merely waits to be executed, but in the direction of grace as the nature, the character of election. Election is seen precisely as *not* arbitrary; and this tendency is not merely an intuitive protest — however needed — against the notion of "absolute might," but one that moves from a new recognition of the character of election itself. It arises from an awareness that anyone who expects salvation from grace rather than from works is set immediately within the sphere of election; but he need not encounter alongside or over election in grace a decision that was made in a *hidden* decree. I cannot help noting that this shift within the firm tradition of the election doctrine has gained an encouraging consensus, supporting my own efforts to understand the meaning of the confession of election, and to discover in it anew the possibility for a celebration of the depths and riches of grace.

In all this the significance of history, and of the seriousness of preaching, comes to fuller expression. The confession of election has often borne the overtones of eternity, the effect of digesting the "beforehand" statements of various New Testament texts into a system of God's aprioristic eternal decrees.

Remarkably, the same danger of eternalizing the confession was often seen in earlier times. We may recall Kuyper's talk about our tendency to fit God's work into our human conceptions, and how he quoted, in connection with our election "from before the foundations of the world," an expression from Dijk, that it is better "not to speak of *another* decree that lies *behind* the gracious choice that is in Christ," lest we cut election loose from Jesus Christ. Indeed, this sensitivity to caricatures of election (in the forms of determinism and eternalizing of the confession) is hardly new at all. Calvin, for instance, warned against speculation and curiosity. And others reacted against the idea of the counsel of God as a "program" that is merely played out, "point for point," in history. Schilder, for example, disparaged the image of the divine decree as an "unmovable petrifact," and he added that God's decree "occurs each instant over again." He did distinguish between the decree and its execution, but he said that "there is no essential difference" between them.

But this legitimate search for the biblical connections between election and gospel preaching can be truly meaningful only if it is not a now and then thing, incidentally thrown out into discussion. It must be given content by *constant* attention to the biblical teaching of grace — the direct opposite of arbitrary and hidden decrees — so that the way to authentic pastoral comfort is made clear. It must bring to reality the seriousness of Bavinck's complaint against the doctrine of election "as it is often preached," offending instead of inviting people to the riches of God's grace in Christ.

Bavinck could say that the doctrine of election is an "inexpressible comfort" for both the believer and the nonbeliever since it proclaims that there is hope for the "most miserable of men." He thought that pelagianism was mercilessly hard because, in its demand for meritorious virtue, the poor publican has no chance. Here, in snippets, without being worked out further, is the suggestion of a positive view of election, one that does not reason in terms of two groups of people eternally separated from each other by the decree, but of a single humanity made up of sinners, in the light of him who justifies the godless without respect to works. This is a thought that is a scandal for the moralism which always sees the election of grace as an offense.

That gravamina should be brought against the Canons of Dordt should not be surprising what with all this theological reflection going on. The first gravamen was addressed to the Hervormde synod by A. Duetz, a Reformed minister, under the suggestive title, *The Heart of God, the Heart of the Church* (Dutch, 1953). It was directed against the first canon. Duetz objected, first of all, to the canon's use of scriptural proof: Matthew 11:25,26, which was used to support reprobation, and Matthew 20:15 and Romans 11:33-36, which, he said, were taken out of context. Further, the gravamen objected to certain deterministic tendencies in the Canons and to the division of the human race into two groups, some elect and some reprobate. The gravamen concentrated on some of the same objections that had been playing a role in the theology of our time. The Hervormde church formulated, in response to the gravamen, some guidelines for dealing with the doctrine of election. These were adopted in 1961. The guidelines dealt critically with the Canons' appeal to Scripture and with abstract theories of divine sovereignty; this was accompanied by an accent on election in Jesus Christ, in a gesture toward Calvin's insight into Christ as the "manifestation of election." The publication of the guidelines provoked a renewed consideration of the deepest intentions of the Arminians of the seventeenth century: their fear of the thought that God would be the author of sin and their fear of determinism.

The same problems came to expression in the gravamen that B. J. Brouwer, a physician, addressed to the Gereformeerde synod. Brouwer was concerned about the morality of signing a subscription to the creeds (which he was obliged, as an elder of the church, to do) while he objected to certain expressions in the Canons of Dordt, particularly their teaching of reprobation in I/6, 15 and I/8 (Rejection of Errors). The gravity of his objections is clear in the question he asked about the Canons' statement on the decree of reprobation: he asked whether the authors — unwittingly — were guilty of blasphemy, a question, he said, that he himself could not answer negatively.

The delegates at the synod were unanimous in their understanding of the central thrust and intentions of the Canons: the unmerited sovereign grace of God. But the question was raised as to whether this fundamental intention had not been forced into the category of the "universal causality" of God. They pointed out that Brouwer's objections were directed at the doctrine of double predestination and, therewith, against the "eternal decree of reprobation." Most deeply, then, the gravamen touched on the question of the character of God and on his manner of relating to the human race. A synodical study commission concluded that the disputed sections of the Canons did not rest on the scriptural passages they cited, but were products of another source— namely the philosophical-theological concept of the all-causative God. "They are rooted in the doctrine of double predestination, of which election and reprobation are aspects of the unchangeable and eternal divine decree, a decree that is realized in time." But the commission also had to deal with the question of blasphemy that Brouwer raised. It acknowledged the real intention of the Canons — to put all possible emphasis on the sovereignty of God's love and grace for guilty and lost mankind, with which Brouwer agreed. But then it added that the disputed passages do "not speak in a correct way of the Lord God." The synod then concluded that it was justifiable to "entertain and to publicize such objections as Dr. Brouwer brought against the passages in the Canons of Dordt."

With this, a far-reaching decision was made. It did not spell the end of the discussion of the deep questions that revolve about this confession. It also occasioned several accusations that the synod had sacrificed the confession of the "absolute sovereignty of God." But I am convinced that this accusation does not really touch the motives and the arguments that had led to this profound shift within the confessional life of the Reformed (Gereformeerde) churches. In any case, the ongoing discussion will have to concentrate on the question of whether this criticism of the Canons is indeed truly responsive to the manner in which the gospel speaks about the sovereign freedom of God's gracious election. The growing theological (and exegetical) consensus on this point does not in itself guarantee the truth of the criticism. But the content and motives of this consensus have led many of us to think that the freedom of God in his works is recognized and honored only in terms of grace. For herein the way is opened, not to a theoretical answer to the question: Who is God? nor to a clear view into the "unapproachable light" within which God dwells, but certainly to a better understanding of the prophetic translation of God's freedom and sovereignty, a translation which formed the pendant of Paul's doxology in Romans 11: "Who is a God like thee, pardoning iniquity and passing over transgression. . . ? . . . because he delights in steadfast love" (Micah 7:18).

5

The Authority of Scripture

AT EVERY STAGE ALONG THE WAY THROUGH THE LAST HALF-CENTURY
of theology we encounter the issue of Holy Scripture, its authority
and its trustworthiness. It is an issue of abiding, normative, and
direction-giving importance for both the church and its theology.
This is true, incidentally, not only for Reformation churches but
for the Roman Catholic Church as well. Concern for Scripture is
natural for the Reformation churches in view of their accent on
the *sola Scriptura* principle and their conviction that Scripture
is its own interpreter *(sacra Scriptura sui ipsius interpres)*. Its own
interpreter: with this, the Reformation rejected every other standard including, most particularly, the church as the single authoritative interpreter of the Bible and tradition as a "second source" of
revelation. *Sola Scriptura* implied a subjection to the Bible, free
from *a priori* dogmas and free from predetermined categories in
which Scripture must be understood. So it is understandable that
whenever, in later times, questions arose about the authority of
Scripture a sensitive nerve was touched. Questions about Scripture
touch a deep conviction regarding the decisive and fundamental
standard of truth for the church. This also meant that when Scripture was going through the fires of historical criticism, it was not
possible to fall back on tradition and so to trust the church
serenely to follow its course. One felt a sense of "to be or not to
be" in many of the discussions about the Scriptures during the
last half-century. Its very subjection to the Scriptures alone meant
that when Scripture was in crisis, the church was in crisis.

But there has been an intensive concern for the scriptural
question in the Roman Catholic Church as well. Though Trent
spoke of tradition alongside of Scripture, it also spoke about the
inspiration of the Old and New Testament, and this meant that
criticisms of the Bible could not leave Roman Catholicism untouched; its belief in the inspiration of Scripture prevented Rome

from taking refuge from higher criticism into the safety of tradition. It is true that the stress on tradition "alongside" Scripture has had a dampening effect on biblical criticism; and the dogma of papal infallibility tended to cushion unrest and make biblical criticism less threatening in principle. But this could not last over the long term; the questions that arose regarding the authority of Scripture sooner or later forced themselves on the attention of Roman Catholics. Tradition could not provide the secure refuge that it once did. The question arose whether the church did not have to recognize the Bible's priority and whether the church did not have to realize that tradition itself contained many problems. Moreover, Catholics became alert to the danger that the Word of God could be fossilized within churchly dogma. There arose a tendency to think of tradition as the "complement" to Holy Scripture, and to think of tradition not so much as an additional revelation as an interpretive guide to Holy Scripture.

Naturally, such a shift had consequences. The question of whether there are two sources or only one source of revelation (a matter that occupied Vatican II in a profound way) had to influence how one thought of Scripture, especially as the sense of its primary significance grew. I recall participating in a conversation between Protestants and Catholics with respect to the ascension of Mary; a Catholic theologian remarked that, though Scripture did not speak of it, Rome had access to another source of revelation, namely tradition. But this conversation took place in 1940 (the dogma of Mary's ascension was declared in 1950). And since then much has changed so far as such uncritical reference to two sources of revelation is concerned.

Increasing attention was given to the question of how the Bible could function freely as long as tradition was coordinate with it. Many Catholics had problems with the schematizing of Scripture within fixed categories, and this uneasiness grew as biblical studies raised questions that could not be dealt with within the categories of established tradition. At the beginning of the century, when the biblical questions became intense — in connection with exegetical problems that modernism put on the agenda — the Pontifical Biblical Commission, established in 1902, tried to hold the line by making various *ad hoc* decisions, which in the light of later research were seen to be untenable. The warnings issued in the famous encyclicals (1893 and 1920) about Bible study, with their strong apologetic flavor, could not halt the increasing critical concentration on the written Word. Trent itself had appealed for Bible study, and when the appeal was answered students of the Bible encountered exegetical questions that could not be answered by way of a simple word from tradition. We recall the influence that M. Lagrange (d. 1938) had on scriptural studies; his conclusions unsettled tradition-minded Catholics so much only a special papal action kept him from getting into serious trouble. The last word against biblical research could no longer be: "It is dangerous." For a conviction was loose in the church that serious, unhampered biblical study was implicitly necessary; and thus a steadily stronger concern was born for the human character of Scripture (though without devaluing its divine character), for the so-called organic character of inspiration, and for historical and psychological involvement in the birth of Scripture.

We meet expressions like these (familiar to readers of Bavinck and Kuyper) in the famous encyclical *Divino Afflante Spiritu* issued by Pope Pius XII in 1943. Here was a Pope, in the midst of World War II, when Italy was being invaded from the south, issuing an encyclical about the mystical body of Christ in which he also addressed profound biblical questions. The Scripture question had to be dealt with in view of the fact that the biblical authors were "organs" — feeling and reasoning instruments — of the Holy Spirit. He must have been deeply concerned about the continuity of the church to have chosen that time for his encyclical. In any case, a measured freedom for biblical research was opened up by this encyclical, more freedom than was ever given before. Now scholars could inquire into the times of the biblical author, the sources he had used and the literary styles he had appropriated. All sorts of questions protruded, questions about literal and poetic style, of historiographic standards in the recording of events, and many others. The questions were accepted, not in fear of attacks against the inspiration of Scripture, but out of respect for inspiration.

If scholars were previously conscience-bound to restrict their findings to the dictates of the biblical commission, now they had a great deal more freedom. Five years after the encyclical of 1943, questions relating to the Pentateuch and Genesis 1–11 were in the spotlight. Scholars became publicly sensitive to the fact that, in spite of all the earlier positiveness about the infallibility of the Bible, the questions could not thus be answered and they had to be subject to further theological study. The encyclical of 1943 stressed the literal meaning of the text; but it also granted that this literal sense had to be discerned with the help of all available intellectual tools. The challenge was accepted with great élan and it had considerable influence in Catholic scholarship (albeit in close association with the church). This happened amid keenly felt tensions, especially as the specter was raised that the new freedom could jeopardize the life of the church, by undermining the authority of both Scripture and dogma.

During the Second Vatican Council, according to one Catholic theologian, a movement was started to recall the encyclical of 1943 — an almost incredible occurrence. But it indicates the depth of tension at the time. These are the same tensions that we meet everywhere in the church, tensions that arise with doubts about the legitimacy of the ways scholars deal with Scripture. It is an ecumenical problem, and it creates a sense of estrangement in people when Scripture is at stake. The problem is roughly epitomized in the furor raised by the historical-critical method which was adopted in nineteenth-century Protestant theology and which the Catholic Lagrange introduced to Roman Catholic circles in his 1902 study, *The Historical Method (La méthode historique).*

Discussions about historical-critical research give occasion to the question: How can we speak clearly and honestly about the authority of Scripture when it is turned into an object of scientific study? Is not the sphere of science wholly different from that of faith? Faith listens and obeys; science masters and controls. The question goes deeper than is supposed by those who answer it with talk about "organic inspiration." For, while it is true that "organic inspiration" does not undermine the authority of Scripture, it is also true that the problems are not removed, but only restated by it. This fact comes out in the question of whether scientific study is truly unbiased and free from prejudgment. Also the question remains whether the Word of God does not establish its *own* limits as to how far research can go with it. Ought students of the Bible be neutral, approaching the Bible without knowing beforehand where one may come out?

We come against such questions constantly. Sometimes they are answered with great care, sometimes in a fearless plunge into research. Moreover, we meet all sorts of hesitation whenever the "Abrahamic adventure" (Hebrews 11:8) of scriptural criticism confronts and challenges dogma and tradition. Here, "neutral research" often comes to a halt. And with this we encounter a striking facet of the relation between research and dogma. For the halt does not seem to be caused by any reason implicit in the research itself. And the question is asked: Has the brake on research been pressed by dogmas that negotiate the results beforehand and thus prevent acceptance of the radical results of research?

In the nineteenth century P. A. de Génestet hurled a lance-like criticism against inconsistent study of Scripture. "Criticism may tackle anything, for her arena is unlimited; it extends even to the content of the sacred books — except when things get *too* critical." He had in mind the halt in the process that occurs whenever things get too dangerous and whenever the method seems to lead to results that cast doubt on what the church has always confessed as God's truth. Is the "standstill" in scholarship — and this is what De Génestet was getting at — not an inconsistency, one that is neither honest nor authentic? Can a route that is taken by choosing a method that is thought to be legitimate simply be abandoned when it proves risky? Others too, in a less popular vein, attacked inconsistency in biblical study. Once one concludes that the Bible is fair game for objective research, there is no turning back — Troeltsch argued this. He was sure, as were many others, that the historical-critical method of biblical study had brought about a radical change in our approach to Scripture, and that once we had begun with it there was no stopping point. "He who offers his finger has to give his whole hand." For Troeltsch, historical-critical research began an unavoidable revolution: what the church confesses as the Word of the Living God now becomes an "object" of scientific research. Ebeling, too, saw here an about-face and thus much more than a minor adjustment of the reformational position. The unbiased historical-critical research of the Bible belongs to the essential thrust of modern Protestantism. Ebeling chooses a relatively easy target when he cites what he calls the "astonishing thesis" that "Any exegesis that does not agree with the confessions of the evangelical Lutheran church is *a priori* untrue" (H. Echternach). But his talk of a great turnabout — since the Enlightenment and the advent of historical-critical studies — goes much deeper than a criticism of Lutheran confessionalism. It touches the concerns of many others who do not want to resolve all problems by making a confession the absolute norm for scriptural study. Here too — precisely here! — very real questions arise from the bosom of the church's confession and from the relationship between historical research and faith.

This question has plagued the last half-century whenever scholars were sensitive to the uncertainties that grew out of the consequences of historical-critical research. Troeltsch tried to be reassuring. When he talked about accepting the consequences of an approved method, he did not mean to minimize faith. Much rather, in his judgment, honest research liberates us from apologetic anxiety. When this happens, we will be able to "see the glory of God in history without hindrance." In any case, we can say that the ongoing discussions of the time show how far-reaching (and how ecumenical) the consequences of historical-critical study of the Bible — and the uninhibited acceptance of them — are for the life of the church.

The validity of the historical-critical method was questioned in an illuminating way by Karl Barth. He wrote his commentary on Romans without the use of historical criticism, working with the text as though Paul's authority was unquestioned. He was criticized from several sides for working too uncritically with the scriptural words. A. Jülicher and Bultmann, who in many ways were of the same mind as Barth, joined the criticism. Bultmann said that the question had to be raised as to whether Paul always spoke out of the Spirit of Christ or whether perhaps other spirits were not implicated in Paul's writing at times. Does not the task of interpreting Paul imply that we "sometimes understand him better than he understood himself?" Bultmann asked. This led him to wonder whether Barth's exegesis did not conceal a new dogma of inspiration.

Barth responded at length to these criticisms, all of which were related to the historical-critical method. He was no enemy of scientific study of the Bible, he said, and in fact thought it necessary. But he repudiated the notion that one could be satisfied with an analysis of Greek words and word-groups, as though philological and archeological research could get at the truth of the Word. He wanted more, and what he wanted was theological exegesis, an exegesis that listened for the Word of God within the many words. This is what he missed in many commentaries, and what brought him to say: "We must be more critical than historical-critical." Recalling that criticism (krinein) implies judgment, he insisted that being critical meant to plow through to the real matter, the gospel. True criticism lets the words bring us to where the gospel can be preached as the "new world of the Bible." We must not linger at the *pre*-labors, necessary as they are. That they are necessary goes without saying. The validity of higher criticism "is an insight proclaimed these days in all tongues and believed everywhere." This door we need not close again; this fight has had its day. What is now imperative is that we focus, not just on the background, the local color, literary genre, and the cultural environment of the text, but on the significance, the meaning, and the intention of "what is written." With this, we can zero in on that which "the Word points to," namely the message of the gospel. Barth was not embarrassed to appeal to Calvin on the matter. Calvin had said that the Scriptures have full authority for believers "when men regard them as having sprung from heaven, as if there the living words of God were heard" (*Institutes*, I/7/4). Further, the highest proof of the truth of Scripture "derives in general from the fact that God in person speaks in it" *(ibid.)*.

But this only increased suspicions about Barth. And suspicions were not relieved when, in his answer to A. Schlatter and Bultmann, Barth said that he considered Calvin's inspiration doctrine at least worthy of consideration. Barth insisted that the real conversation with the Bible begins only "on the other side of our insight into its human, historical-psychological character." What did this mean? Was there in this "other side" a sort of dualism, perhaps a docetism, that could not fully respect the textuality of the Bible (with all its problems) in a historical-critical sense?

One thing was clear. Barth has always rejected an approach to the Bible that side-steps the actual problems; his exegetical work demonstrates this fully. He did not choose the way of spiritualists ("I am no *Pneumatiker*"); he was never inclined even to join the discussions that were going on about "spiritualist exegesis" (cf. his foreword to the *Philippians* commentary, 1928, E.T. 1962). For him, being occupied with the Scriptures was to be grasped by the message, and to be open to totally unique assumptions in the witness of the apostles and prophets. It was to walk a path full of surprises. Barth was not interested in disturbing the scientific scholars — the experts with their legitimate concern for the human aspects of the Scriptures. But he wanted to reach for an understanding of the message to which this human witness itself points. He spoke regretfully of the alienation between historical and theological exegesis (cf. his foreword to *The Resurrection of the*

Dead, E.T. 1933). He was willing to wait for "the great man who would overcome this situation," but meanwhile, conscious of his own "limited historical-philological equipment," he felt compelled to say that we have not understood the Scriptures if we have not heard the *message* of the living Word of God for all times.

We need not be surprised that the questions circling around the authority of Scripture continually pre-empted a high priority on the theological agenda. This fact is tied in with the conviction that, for a correct understanding of Scripture, we cannot side-step the disclosure of historical facets of the Bible that have come under scrutiny during the last centuries. We need think only of the history of the canon, the cultural environment of the Old and New Testaments, the historical transmission of the text, and the organic connections between the Bible and the world around it. The question was raised as to whether, in the thinking inspired by all this, it was still possible to point to the Bible as *the* book of the church. Could historical criticism support the church's dependence on the Bible as the Word of God, not a critical, but an obedient, believing, listening dependence?

This raised the problem of impartiality. Is impartiality the only proper posture to take vis-à-vis the authority of Scripture? The word "impartial" suggests open-ended investigation, and it has played a fundamental role in discussions about the Scriptures. One can espouse impartiality as the only proper attitude without using the word as such. For instance, when the Reformation rejected dogmatic exegesis and other so-called "keys" to the Bible it did so because the "keys" closed the door on new discoveries of the meaning and mystery of Scripture. Dogmatic exegesis had become a "canon" for an understanding which was in fact alien to understanding. So the Reformers, in their way, demanded impartial reading. Impartiality in exegesis was a relationship of openness, of attentive listening in contrast to dogmatic manipulation of the texts. Now, in everyday speech, impartiality suggests neutrality, fairness, being unbiased, and in this sense the Reformers were not unambiguously impartial. But if it is set within the context of trusting, in contrast to skepticism or mistrust, it is readily understandable that impartiality is a virtue in reading Scripture. In the history of theology in our century, we hear a call to this kind of impartial listening. It is the spirit of the young Samuel: "Speak, Lord, for your servant hears" (1 Samuel 3:1).

Childlikeness is the model. Jesus' words about becoming like a little child are apropos; the only attitude with which one can enter the kingdom is the attitude of the child (Matthew 18:3). And the key to understanding the Scriptures is the same childlike, uncritical openness. There is a unique relationship between children and revelation (Matthew 11:25) that is in contrast to those who have become biased in their *own* wisdom and so miss the opportunity to hear the Word of God. The Scriptures praise simplicity (Psalm 116), the simple of heart (Ephesians 6:15), and recommend that we be simple as doves (Matthew 10:16). Have we come upon the hermeneutical key in this simplicity (in the sense of impartiality)? But, alas, we soon discover that "simplicity" is not all that simple.

The word comes to play in respect to God, too; the Confession speaks of him as a "unique and *simple* essence." When K. H. Miskotte delivered his inaugural lecture at Leiden, in 1945, he spoke of the "practical significance of the simplicity of God." He sought to underscore what divine simplicity meant for his people, for the world, for us. But he saw something in this confession quite different from a speculation about the *Oneness* of God. Much rather, divine simplicity reflects the *faithfulness* and *trustworthiness* of God in Jesus Christ. Miskotte warned that we should not assume "we already know precisely what 'simplicity' is, and then paste our notion on God as an explanation of him." Applying our "pre-understanding" of simplicity to God could, indeed, oversimplify him. God's simplicity is not without depth, unfathomableness, and incomprehensibleness (cf. Article I of the Belgic Confession). We hear that the Spirit searches out all things, even the *depths* of God (1 Corinthians 2:10), the depths of him who dwells in unapproachable light (1 Timothy 6:16). So, whatever else it means, simplicity cannot mean shallowness.

What then, in our human experience, answers to the simplicity of God? Miskotte reminded us that faith is not "the crown of a simplicity of mind that is psychologically construed – the uncomplicated soul, disposition, character, or life-style." Simplicity, in our context, is not a superficial understanding that achieves clarity by avoiding all deeper reflection that might stir up and trouble our minds. We recall Barth's fine expression, quoted by Miskotte, in which he says that God "may permit and require both human complexity and human simplicity" (*CD* II/1, p. 458). The gospel can make the deepest profundities seem ridiculously

simple and it can get down to our level so that no one is disquali-
fied by its depth and its wisdom.

All this should commend care in turning the notion of simplicity into a key to the understanding of Scripture. In fact, the
Word of God has often been distorted by an appeal to simplicity.
The appeal to simplicity has sometimes blocked the way to further investigation of the Scriptures, to the harm of the church.
Miskotte tried to protect the biblical stress on simplicity — as holding to the one thing necessary in the service of God — against
any notion of simplicity that would rule out "an honest confrontation with the complexity of reality." Simplicity, he said, "is not the
beginning, but the ending, not the start, but the ripe harvest of
much spiritual struggle" (Miskotte, *Om de waarheid te zeggen,*
1971, p. 49). All this is accented by the fact that Holy Scripture is
given in words that cry out for intensive research.

The danger of cheap simplicity was discerned by Schilder as
well as by Barth and Miskotte. Schilder did not mean to reserve
deep faith for an elite group of intellectuals who were competent
to cope with complexity, and thus were promoted above the simple believers within the church. But he did mean to put his finger
on a form of naive childlikeness that is nothing more than stupid-
ity. He recalled how Peter, on the mountain of transfiguration, had
an immediate proposition, "a fickle proposal without style, without confession, and without prophecy." Cheap simplicity can be
anybody's posture; but Christ had to learn through suffering
(Hebrews 5:8). There is a naiveté that has to be "won through a
sturdy, intensive and extensive working of the Spirit of Prophecy."
Obedience to Christ — in the Word — is not to be pressed into
the mold of our need for a simplicity that will lift the load from
our shoulders. There are yokes that we ought to carry; and the
church that is ready to carry them — including the yoke of study
— is praised (Acts 17:11).

And yet the question keeps coming back. Is there not an
important truth in the appeal to a simplicity of understanding?
All sorts of New Testament illustrations come to mind. For instance, there is that Johannine model of a church that does not
need anyone to teach her since she has been anointed (1 John
2:27). Anyone who reads Calvin sympathetically recalls how he
loathes the fanatics who confuse the faith of the church by
means of science. K. J. Popma has tirelessly warned us against
this danger, particularly with regard to theology (K. J. Popma,

Evangelie en geschiedenis, 1972). Convinced that the Bible itself is clear and understandable, he is very wary of "persons called theologians who clothe themselves in almost supernatural official-dom." He has in mind anyone who struts as an authority, the expert with a "religious authority" invested in theologians only by the pagans who thought of theology as "the speaking of divine language." This sharp criticism of "professional theism" is not a raw plea for simplicity as a substitute for hard reflection about Scripture. Popma is too versed in the history of thought to steer us into the mist of an arbitrary, be it simple, exposition of Scripture, with doors closed to further discussion of it. He reminds us that the Bible was, in the first instance, given to the *church*, while the church thankfully makes use of the "services of theology or biblical philology." But the church must be mature and selective in its use of the "services" offered to it. We can have too many teachers, as James warns us (James 3:1). And problems always seem to arise between the church's intuitive and mature grasp of the truth and the "help" that scientific theology wants to offer the church. Popma's willingness to throw the church back into a false simplicity points again to the unavoidableness of the problem. We are not in the pagan sphere of oracles who speak with religious authority; we are talking about the ministry, the help, that theology can and must offer. And the church ought to accept the ministry in order to avoid the arbitrary interpretations of Scripture which the Scriptures themselves warn us about (2 Peter 1:20).

The church has been aware of the enormous influence of biblical research in the eighteenth and nineteenth centuries. But it has had to decide whether the research really brought about a better and deeper understanding of the Word of God. And if modern scholarship did change things so much, what is the church to think of all the study of the Scriptures that went on before this new scholarship?

When Harnack stressed the *scientific* theology of the modern period, Barth asked Harnack whether Luther and Calvin were then to be classified as unscientific. And, for that matter, how did Paul rate? Barth said he knew students of the Bible who had not travelled the route blazed by the eighteenth century and whose scholarship (defined as a serious effort to understand the material) he could not doubt.

Clearly, we need to recognize the power of the Word of God
within the church of *all* ages, and therewith the continuity of the
church's life in the midst of all its changes and processes. Respect
for this continuity does not imply a minimizing of ongoing research into the Bible, but it does deny that scientific scholarship
caused a revolution that sets us face to face with a "totally new"
situation. Even if we concede that modern research has deepened
our insight into the Scriptures (their background, structure, and
style), we need not disqualify the labors of previous times. How
can we explain the fact that Barth, fifty years ago, was disillusioned with all sorts of biblical commentaries which, in spite of
their baggages of scientific material, could not help him with the
task of preaching for his time? And how was it that lights went on
for him from other times in which the vaunted historical research
had not even begun? What is the background of Luther's influence
on exegesis; what was there about pre-scientific Luther's exegesis
that led Karl Holl to speak of Luther's "grand style" and of the
"depths he had uncovered"? Must we attribute to Luther a special
charisma? We certainly cannot do so if charisma refers to a
"spiritual" approach that transcends the text itself, along with the
labor of understanding the text. After all, it was Luther who so
emphatically referred to the "words" as the scabbard for the
Sword of the Spirit. There is no way to knowledge outside of the
"external word"; we must concentrate on the Scripture itself as
its own expositor. For this reason, Luther could not abide the
notion of an officialdom of expertise that could speak with a
religious authority to which ordinary readers of the text had to
bow. Holl saw in Luther's "emphasis on the intrinsic claim of the
documents themselves" an "event for the whole of the spiritual
sciences." What is decisive here is not whether Luther always suc-
ceeded in getting at the correct exegesis of the texts; this after
all is not claimed by anyone. But his difficulties were raised by
the words of Scripture itself. And if Luther saw nuances within
the significance of the Gospels (John versus the Synoptics, for instance) and used standards of value judgment in preferring one
book above another, he was still occupied with the texts themselves and with the questions that differences in the text provoked. He testified to his relationship with the text during his
debate with Zwingli: "I am a captive; I cannot escape. The text
is too strong for me; the words will not let me avoid their meaning." Out of this method of understanding, lights were turned on

that illumined the meaning of the text, even though Luther's understanding is not normative for all times.

The approachability of Scripture excludes discrimination against older methods and insights, especially as we note how often the gospel has broken through in unexpected ways. The approachability of Scripture does not render modern discoveries irrelevant either, as though they are all born only of a rationalism impervious to the mystery of the Scriptures. But it does set up parameters, then and now, within which the Word of God must be sought and understood.

There is such a thing as a "spiritual" dimension for our understanding, and to be alert to charismatic insights does not necessarily commit us to a spiritualism which guarantees the continuity of the church within a certified pure understanding of Scripture.

Holl pointed out that Luther's concern for the word (*die Sprache*) *and* for the Spirit created a kind of circle of thought. But it was not a vicious circle; rather it was a circle within which everything was laid out, and within which all spiritual understanding unavoidably moved. And it was clear, precisely here, how definitely Luther was disposed to set spiritual understanding within the mandate that came to him from the words of the Bible itself. In this mandate the decisive element is present to withstand a spiritualism that transcends — spiritualistically — what is written (1 Corinthians 4:6).

Rudolf Smend, in an article written for a Festschrift honoring Barth's eightieth birthday (*Parrhesia*), raised questions that hover around the tension between reflectiveness and simplicity with respect to Holy Scripture. His article was titled: "Post-critical Exegesis of Scripture." The word post-critical suggests that a stage can be reached in which we leave criticism behind us. Here he moves in Barth's direction; for Barth above all — in spite of his refusal to turn against historical-critical research — was concerned with that understanding which receptively, rather than critically, listens to what the Scriptures say. Barth once remarked that if he had to choose between historical-critical research and the dogma of inspiration, he would surely choose the latter; "it has the larger and deeper validity" as a pointer to the voice of God. Barth's comment was not celebrated with thanks; it was in fact interpreted as a fall back into rigid fundamentalism, no matter how much Barth protested to the contrary. (Cf. Barth, *Die Schrift und die Kirche,* 1947.) But there lies in his preference a desire, after all the research into the details, the distinctions, the backgrounds, and the methods has been done, to go back to the whole Bible, to read it "as the text itself invited us" and to do that "with a tested and critical naiveté" (*CD* IV/2, p. 479).

All this may sound a little paradoxical, perhaps even dualistic, but the intention is clear. After its affair with critical methodology, scholarship must begin to consider again the *content* of Scripture that is mediated through human language, and thus finally to adopt a post-critical approach. This is not to be taken as a chronological sequence as though particular phases are passed through at particular times. But it does mean a continuous renewal of concern for an understanding of the *message* of Scripture; one must turn before long to an attentive listening to it, so that God's word can actually be heard through the witness of the human word. It then can be understood that this Word of God is not an "object" of our sovereign research, but is the sovereign Word of the living God himself.

Whenever objective research and attentive listening do not exclude each other, and do more than merely succeed each other as distinct phases of scriptural study, theology will encounter questions raised by objective research. For many, this raises doubt and temptation, for scriptural research must follow certain methods that are linked with scientific study, and this sometimes seems to compete with believing listening. The tension is illustrated in the study of the origins of the Gospels. Here research impinges on the believing congregation very directly.

The congregation lives by its confession of the Jesus Christ who comes to us in those Gospels. The church is aware that research into the gospel records is not a faithless and illegitimate undertaking; it knows that there is every reason to look into the differences between the Gospel writers with the purpose of finding out, as far as that is possible, how the Gospels came to be written. Slowly but surely the conviction has grown that the various evangelists went about composing their Gospels each in his own peculiar way, and that each did it with a special purpose in mind. We may recall John's statement that the gospel story was written down so that "you may believe that Jesus is the Christ, the Son of God, and that believing you may have life in his name" (John 20:31). The Gospels, it was discerned, were not cool reports of facts, but reports in which the purpose of writing played and sounded through the story in all sorts of ways. Thus we could speak of a "religious pragmatic," an expression that has been used in reference to the way the historical accounts of the Old Testament were influenced by the purpose for which they were written. Awareness that the gospel records were portraits of Jesus Christ rather than ordinary historical reporting, witness rather than journalism, proclamation rather than photographic chronicling did not mean that the Gospels had to be "dehistoricized." Nor was there a contrast between what was preached and what actually took place. But there was a sense that closer attention had to be paid to the purpose of the Gospel writers in and through which they interpreted the facts they reported.

As scholars occupy themselves with the specific characteristics of each evangelist, questions are provoked as to whether the Gospels are, after all, historically reliable. Do they give us an exact account of what actually happened? These questions came to our attention during my student days in the form of warnings against the so-called *Gemeinde* theology (the theology of the believing community). Even at that time, there was much talk about the form-critical method. F. W. Grosheide warned us against letting the form prevail above the content, but he did not say that the form was insignificant. Thus plenty of room was left for detailed study of the form in which the content was given. Grosheide had a theory about the Synoptic Gospels that laid much more emphasis on proclamation stereotypes than on their dependence on sources. His objection to the two-sources hypothesis was related to his concern about *Gemeinde* theology's theory of subjective input into the Gospels by the early church. He did not deny that each Gospel writer put together the gospel stories in his own manner. What he opposed was the notion that these were the *creation* of the early church. If the latter were true, we would have a subsequent human vision, a creation by the original community, a projection from the hearts and minds of later believers rather than a revelation about Christ and his work. This is why Grosheide labelled *Gemeinde* theology a subjective theology.

His concerns were not new. They were present in Roman Catholic opposition to a modernism that had capitulated to the notion of the "pious fraud" and thus had given up on the trustworthiness of the Gospels. The notion of a "pious fraud" was condemned by the Pontifical Biblical Commission as a threat to the historicity of the Gospels, especially with regard to John's

Gospel. In 1960, a report came from a biblical conference in Padua rejecting the traditional exegesis of the Lateran University; it fell like a bombshell on Rome. So in 1961 a "monitum" (an admonition) was issued by the Holy Office, and in 1964 an instruction was issued by the Biblical Commission "Concerning the Historical Truth of the Gospels." In it, the right of "form-critical" exegesis was stoutly affirmed, but with this admonition: it had to rid itself of all philosophical prejudices. Moreover, it pointed to the danger of exaggerating the creative contribution of the early church *(creaticem potentiam huius communitatis extollunt)*. Scholars could reckon with the various facets of tradition within the Gospels as they presented the life and teachings of Jesus. That each Gospel writer had his own purpose, and selected and arranged the material in keeping with his purpose, was recognized. Besides, it was admitted that the writers wrote with an eye to the situation in the churches. Thus, the Gospels were not bound to a literal recording of sequences of events. But the scholars had to work on the assumption that the writers brought us the truth which is the foundation of the church. This was a thesis which was reaffirmed at the Second Vatican Council. Every element of interpretation given by the Gospel writers was intended to express the truth in that particular manner; this was the case even where they took into account the later situation of the church. The Council declared: the church "affirms without hesitation the historicity of the Gospels."

Here we meet a solution whose intention is clear enough, but which only kept the door open to many new questions. Accepting the possibility of later interpretations was bound to raise questions about the nature and extent of these interpretations as they appear within the Gospels. Many gratefully received the church's statement as an encouragement of freedom in exegesis. They were thankful that at least the point of view held by Cardinal Ruffini of Palermo (a member of the Pontifical Biblical Commission) did not prevail; Ruffini had written an article which was dogmatically opposed to any concessions to the notion that the Gospel writers interpreted as they reported, and he had sent the article to all Italian seminarians and published it in several American journals. In this article he went so far as to suggest that statements by Pope Pius XXI (in the encyclical *Divino Afflante Spiritu*) were absurd. But the admonition made an end to the confusion created by Ruffini, while leaving many questions open in spite of its insistence on the "historicity" of the gospel record (cf. J. A. Fitzmyer, *Die Wahrheit der Evangelien*, 1965).

But clearly we are not talking about a problem that is unique to the Roman Catholic Church. There are clear parallels between what was going on in Rome and what was keeping Reformed exegetes occupied. Among others, there was the question of the Gospel writers' own input (which is, in scholarly circles, called a "theology") or their special purposes in view of later situations in the church. There was some difference, for example, in the way that Luke reported Jesus' speech about the last things (Luke 21) from that of Matthew and Mark, a difference that was explained in view of the later situation (specifically, the situation of Jerusalem having been occupied by Rome). Thus we have to take account of the historical standpoint of the Gospel writer (H. N. Ridderbos). This approach is different from the one in which an exact reporting of facts, without any interpretation or influence by historical situations, is considered the only legitimate assumption about the gospel writings.

Further discussions about the "trustworthiness" of the Gospels revealed a persistent fear that by following this approach we would end up with the notion that the writers projected something into the account. We would, it was feared, conclude that the subjective vision of the early community was inserted into the record, a vision that could be different from the actual truth of the matter. The notion of a "projection" does play a role in New Testament research; and it summons the same questions again and again, questions that have not yet been satisfyingly answered. What is the concrete significance of Käsemann's expression that the Gospel of John is a "projection backward from the Christ-presence" within the early community? (Cf. E. Käsemann, *The Testament of Jesus*, E.T. 1968.) Käsemann emphatically places the authority of John's Gospel on the block and declares that — as historical fact — the church erred when it "declared orthodox" this "fascinating and dangerous theology of John." Yet, Käsemann affirms nonetheless that John brings us the only and last will of the earthly Jesus, and points us to his glory. Other discussions likewise kept embroidering on the theme of projection. W. Marxsen proposed a theory that the resurrection was an "interpolation" arising from the continuing "Jesus affair." G. Friedrich wrote in reply: "What the Pope is to the Catholic, the early community *(Gemeinde)* is for Marxsen; it is the substitute for Jesus Christ."

Friedrich here is contending against the notion of projection and invention, and pleads for concentration on what the biblical message testifies as to the real Jesus. We hear in this reverberations of former discussions. We can almost hear Kuyper speaking from another day about the possibility of a biography of Jesus that would, in fact, leave embarrassing gaps in the three years of Jesus' ministry on earth. The purpose of the Gospel writers, said Kuyper, was to show us the *significance* of Jesus' life and work. (Cf. A. Kuyper, *Encyclopedie der Heilige Godgeleerdheid*, III, pp. 163f.) This rejection of the concept of journalistic literalism, and this acceptance of the possibility that each writer employed his own technique and composition, leaves us with old questions still pressing. They are always relevant because the New Testament is the book of the church, the book with the message of its Lord.

Growing criticism of the so-called "quest for the historical Jesus" is part of the background of current discussions about the New Testament kerygma. In the liberal "historical Jesus" quest, it was thought that we could make a portrait of the real Jesus by means of historical science, and this was thought to be the only way of getting at the truth of the matter. The counter-movement was begun when Albert Schweitzer tore up the foundations of the whole historical effort (cf. his *The Quest of the Historical Jesus*, originally published in 1906, E.T. 1910). But Troeltsch spoke in 1911 about the "Importance of the Historicity of Jesus for Faith" and he was still (Schweitzer notwithstanding) convinced that the route of historical research could be followed without radical skepticism. For Troeltsch it seemed likely that "the sensational denials (of the gospel) will disappear once we get to work on these matters in a professional way." (Pannenberg cited these words later as a "famous prediction.") But many were not appeased by Troeltsch's confidence, and they kept asking questions about historical certitude. The undeniably tentative results of historical studies did not solve the problem of certainty. Resistance to the possibility of historical verification only increased. Bultmann claimed that no one was served by insisting that "the fruits of the historical-critical theology are still useful for faith" (1924). He was on Barth's side here, over against Harnack's thesis that faith is dependent on historical research, a thesis that Bultmann found "frightening."

Martin Kähler had considerable influence in this discussion. He lanced against liberal theology with its historical Jesus. He refused to believe that Christian faith was dependent on "the learned patter of historians." Barth testified to his agreement with this rejection of the liberal "quest for the historical Jesus" when he spoke of the tragic "colossus" of the "life of Jesus quest," whether it was conservative or skeptical. For Kähler there was only one way, that of the "historical-biblical Christ"; researching into a Jesus who presumably lurked behind the biblical report was abortive. This did not mean that he opted for an "idealistic christology" (i.e., Christ as an idea); he did mean that we should not rest the certainty of faith on a scientific foundation. On this point, there was strong affinity between Kähler and W. Herrmann. Herrmann wanted to let certainty rest in the "inner life of Jesus" that shines through the Gospels. He did not mean the same thing that is ordinarily indicated by inwardness, but, as Barth characterized it, "the transparent, irresistible, illuminating Light" that shines through the critically or uncritically evaluated tradition. If faith's certainty depends on historical research, then, as many would say in echo of Barth's words, faith hangs on a thin thread and this would be "obviously a very disturbing fact" (CD IV/1, p. 288).

The tensions involved in this problematic are revealed instructively in the surprising attention given in our time to Lessing's famous question of how accidental truths of history could be the basis for "necessary truths" (G. E. Lessing, *The Proofs of the Spirit and the Power*, 1777). His formulation bears the imprint of the Enlightenment; but we can see in it the same questions that Herrmann, Kähler, Barth, and Bultmann were busy with, directly or indirectly — the relation between faith and historical research. It was the problem of historicism as it bore on our certainty regarding the unique events of the past. Lessing was convinced: "The only passage from an historical report to the foundation of eternal blessedness is the way of a leap." He talked of the "yawning chasm" which "I cannot get across, however often and however earnestly I have tried to make the leap. If anyone can help me over it, I beg him, I adjure him. He will deserve a divine reward from me." Understandably, the Lessing question came back on center stage in later times, especially wherever people were struggling against the tendency to place faith within the grasp of historicism with its relativizing of certainty. It returned especially wherever people wanted to preserve the link between salvation and history. Over against "idealism" as a devaluation of history by way of the eternal idea, the im-

portance of the historical question was stressed; for whenever
the history to which faith is tied becomes an illusion, there faith
falls away. "If Arthur Drews were right with his claim that Jesus
never lived, but was only a floating image of a mythical fantasy,
then every christology would be but a speculative apparition" (H.
Grass). The questions surrounding Jesus' resurrection (for instance,
the empty tomb) were especially relevant here. (H. von Campen-
hausen particularly put this on the agenda as of utmost seriousness and importance.)

Lessing's problem came back via Kierkegaard, who, with
respect to the "distance" between us and Jesus, was unwilling to
flee into the authority of the church in order to overcome the
distance, but who resolved the problem by means of the category of the "contemporaneity" of later believers with the original
eyewitnesses. It is our contemporaneity that faces us with the
same personal decision about Jesus that his disciples faced.

The problem resurfaced in dialectical theology's early attack
on historicism. (Cf. F. Gogarten, "Der Historismus," in *Zwischen
den Zeiten*, 1924.) But it was W. Pannenberg who brought Lessing's question to life recently when he placed the question of
historicity on the table again, and did so emphatically. He considered the inquiry behind the New Testament kerygma to be
unavoidable. Theology, as it stands before the texts, needs this
"detour" so that it can pierce through to the historical realities.
The substance of faith, according to Pannenberg, cannot be set
loose from historical research, at least so long as we are convinced
that the acts of God really are involved in the history of Jesus
Christ. We cannot and must not dissociate ourselves from historical
research in order to flee to a storm-free area in which we need
have no bother with criticism. Pannenberg discerns such a flight
in Kähler's "transhistorical kerygmatic theology" and Barth's concept of *Urgeschichte* (pre-history). He thought Troeltsch performed a genuine service; at a time when the historical ground
of faith was being sacrificed, Troeltsch tried to establish the
historical Jesus once again as the ground of faith. "Why did no
one try to step in to fill the breach left after Troeltsch?" And
why did we capitulate before historical relativism with all its extreme consequences — with everything left uncertain by miscon-
ceived historical researches? Why, asked Pannenberg, did so few
have an eye for Troeltsch's "famous prediction" of 1911: "The
sensational denials will disappear once we get to work on these

matters in a professional way." We must, he says, get on with the "inquiry"; we must go back to historical verification with respect to the ground of faith because it is clear that the essence of our faith "is not to be found in the texts themselves, but must be uncovered behind them." The mistake of kerygmatic theology is, in his view, that it declared the texts, in their witness character, to be binding. The appeal to the Word of God then became a weapon "to skewer opponents."

"We have begun these days to see that this is no solution," said Pannenberg. We must, if Christian faith is linked to history, go back to that history itself. Too often, we have concentrated exclusively on the New Testament problematics when dealing with the problem of the kerygma, especially with respect to the "single event," namely the resurrection of Jesus, instead of using the Old Testament and its witness of "the history employed by Yahweh" (*Basic Questions in Theology*, I, E.T. 1970, p. 56). He sees Gerhard von Rad's theology as a corrective to kerygmatic theology, even though others see von Rad as teaching a kerygmatic theology himself, since he lays strong emphasis on Israel's *understanding* of history in distinction from the "historical-critical view of history." Pannenberg considers that the historical picture of Israel's history is assumed by von Rad. In any case, the incarnation tells us that God's redemptive act does not occur in a redemptive-historical ghetto or in a "pre-history" that sets quotation marks around ordinary history. Thus, historical verification is urgent along the way of historical-critical research.

Pannenberg's thrust seemed challenging and promising, and in the beginning he was, in some American circles, heralded as the advocate of an orthodox way of looking at redemptive history. But what was overlooked was what Pannenberg said about the "unique way": "If after two thousand years, we ask whether a certain event was established or not, faith cannot provide us with certainty about it; only historical inquiry can do that." He is aware that Kähler and Herrmann discern in this a total dependence of faith on historical science and consider this ruinous; the results of historical research "have only a probability character and therewith can offer no sufficient basis for the certainty of faith" (*ibid.*, p. 54). But Pannenberg insists that there is no storm-free territory, and that we cannot avoid the risks of history if history is indeed a serious matter for us. Pannenberg is himself not insensitive to the questions of historical certainty that are set on the agenda here, for he adds: *"in so far as* certainty is possible with respect to these things at all" (emphasis added); and, in respect to the resurrection of Christ, he speaks of "at least an approximate certainty" and says the resurrection is "historically probable" (*Jesus — God and Man*, E.T. 1968, pp. 99, 102).

Pannenberg does not offer a conclusive answer to the problem which occupied Lessing and Kierkegaard, since *certainty* and not more or less *probability* is the issue. Clearly, Pannenberg's criticism does not blaze a new trail for us, especially in view of his agreement that "not every Christian" needs to undertake this task (*Basic Questions*, II, p. 33). The average Christian is willing to "trust the hypothesis that the ground of his faith will be shown to be well placed." This sets the reliability of the Christian tradition in the foreground. Along this way, Pannenberg seeks to overcome the problem of the complete dependence of faith on historical verification. Faith can trust "that its ground will stand firm against all critical tests." But this was not what Kähler was concerned about; it was the *verification* which Pannenberg wanted in preference to an appeal to the Spirit or to the texts themselves. Pannenberg warned us against flight into the storm-free territory of texts and witnesses; but, suggestive as the warning is, it cannot of itself solve the problem.

Barth's way of dealing with Lessing's problem is especially interesting. Pannenberg contended that dialectical theology used Lessing's "leap" as star witness for the way to establish the historical. But it is better to listen to Barth's own explanation. Barth had to deal with Lessing's question, given his rejection of historicism and his confrontation with Harnack. So he begins by pointing out that the distance (Lessing's "yawning chasm") between the life of Jesus and our life is central in Lessing's question and central for our (certain) knowledge. Can this "past time" come to us other than historically, mediately, namely through "report, tradition, and proclamation. . ."? Is it not bound to "middlemen" and thus to their credibility and truthfulness? Can such a mediation ever be the unshakable basis that guarantees faith? And can we ever, via this route, get further than an historical faith?

Barth gives a remarkable answer to these and similar questions. In his view, we have too long been fascinated by the problem of the "then and now," by the distance that has to be bridged, as if therein the real difficulty, the real *skandalon*, lay for our thinking. The new Protestantism has forced this "very interesting problem" on us as a technical problem of thought, as a problem of method, formal, tentative, and without concrete content: but historical mediation in its uncertainty and relativity can never offer a real bridge over the "yawning chasm." According to Barth, the *skandalon* lies elsewhere, not in the "problem" of the relation between then and now, but only in the material content of the gospel itself.

With this, Barth arrives at a totally different approach to the problem. Another sort of "distance" problem interests him, the kind that comes out in words like those of Peter: "Lord, depart (distance yourself) from me, for I am a sinful man" (Luke 5:8). Here we are faced with the presence of Jesus in the same space and in the same time with Peter. Similarly we see the presence of Yahweh with Isaiah at the time of his calling, yet very distant from him (Isaiah 6). The eyewitnesses spoke as men who were overcome and confronted with a present reality; there was no place at all for the technical problem of historical distance. If we now turn the problem into one of a distance between the original times and the present (the "yawning chasm") we act as though we are living pre-Christian, as though Christ had not come and as though he does not really keep coming to be with us. Accepting the problem as Lessing posed it we would be able to excuse ourselves for lack of faith in view of the difficult questions centering around our certainty and the "historical approach": "all thanks to the existence of Lessing's question!" (Barth, *CD* IV/1, p. 292).

One could exploit Lessing's question, too, in a desire similar to that of Adam and Eve in Paradise — to hide oneself from Jesus Christ, who makes himself present and who mediates his own presence with us. Clearly, Barth is refusing to deal with the problem of distance as a problem in its own right, as if one could move from the theoretical possibility of bridging the gap to the reality. Nowhere, it seems to me, is it clearer how zealously Barth determined to think about reality rather than about possibilities. It is "the presence of Christ" that provides the starting point for considering the distance problem — that it was "others" who really *saw and heard* him while we only hear and read *about* him. "The impact of it on us is too powerful, too decisive." Lessing's question is certainly a real one; there are those 1900 years between Christ and us, and there is a problem with respect to the transmission of the message through the years. Still, it is only a problem for us if we flee from its solution. Lessing's problem can not be anything else than a problem of flight; it is a serious question insofar as we create the problem by fleeing from its given answer. In another context, Barth recalled Abel Burckhardt, Basel pastor of a century ago, whose children's books were Barth's first lessons in theology (*CD* IV/2, p. 113). Here he was first deeply impressed with the reality of the redemptive events. This reality was a present one: "Lessing's 'yawning chasm' did not exist, Kierkegaard's 'contemporaneity' was no problem, and the Savior himself was manifestly the same, yesterday and today." It is as though Barth anticipated what the New Testament scholars would say about the impressions of youth and the impact of childhood hymns, for he added:

> Is it all very naive, and not worth mentioning at all in academic circles? Yes, it was very naive, but perhaps in the very naivete lay the deepest wisdom and greatest power, so that once grasped, it was calculated to carry me unscathed — although not of course untempted or unassailed — through all the serried ranks of historicism and anti-historicism, mysticism and rationalism, orthodoxy, liberation, and existentialism, and to bring one back some day to the matter itself. (*Ibid.*)

Barth is not opting for an irrational leap, for one or another kind of spiritualism, as a way to skirt around the Word of God. This is really the way of discovery in which the prophetic-apostolic witness is of decisive significance for Barth, in particular the New Testament witnesses to Christ. It is not a matter of subjective experience, of vague impressions, but of an "event" in one's encounter with the witness of the Scriptures.

This forms the background of Barth's rejection of the quest for the historical Jesus. It does not imply that he was disinterested in Jesus of Nazareth. But it does indicate this denial of the possibility that we can get a firm clue to the mystery of Jesus through what can be learned by poking behind "the so-called Sources, and thus without reference to the witness of the New Testament as such" (thus Barth in a conversation with David Friedrich Strauss). One can appreciate that Barth's response to Lessing's question would strike many as odd. His reference to Luke 5:8 prompted H. Diem to say: "For Barth, Lessing's question has become Peter's problem." What, it was asked, did Barth mean by referring to the improper "technical" problem of distance? (Cf. K. Schwarzwäller, *Theologie oder Phänomenologie*, 1966, pp. 190ff.) Was Barth answering Lessing by way of a sermon (about Christ's presence with us) instead of by argument? Compared to Barth, was not Pannenberg at least trying to bridge the "yawning chasm" — and did he not therefore deserve the divine "reward" more than Barth?

In fact, Barth did not escape Lessing's problem by preaching a sermon. It is important to remember that Lessing was not really interested in a solution to his own problem. Even though he claimed that he often and earnestly had sought the way to leap over the chasm, he was utterly convinced that there was no way. His nice words about the "divine reward" were pure irony. He had no faith at all that the truths of reason could be established by reports about history; he was really telling us that this kind of historical apologetics was invalid.

Barth saw this clearly when he said that Lessing was pointing to an entirely different proof — the proof of the power and the spirit. Human spirituality was his proof, and it eliminated the need for a "leap" or a "bridge." Barth, with good reason, called attention to Lessing's passionate resistance to any undertaking that would hang "nothing less than all eternity" from "the thread of a spinning wheel." The historical approach had, for Lessing, done more damage to religion than all the scholastic dogmas; and yet men have tried to erect the "edifice of faith" on such a foundation. From this we can grasp the point of Lessing's story about the occupants of a palace into whose hands several blueprints from the hand of the original architect fell. But the blueprints contradicted each other, and the occupants went on endlessly arguing about which was the genuine sketch. There were a few who declined to enter the argument. They were glad enough to live in the palace no matter which sketch was the authentic one. So it was with Lessing: he was glad enough to live in the palace of the human spirit no matter which religion testifies accurately to its creator. Lessing was deeply persuaded that no certainty was possible through historical investigation, and he would have been confirmed in his opinion had he had a chance to know of Pannenberg's efforts.

Barth too was convinced that faith is not dependent on science — in this case, historical science. Barth was concentrating on the material itself, on the reality that gets its validity through the biblical witnesses. "Seeking to understand, I must advance to that point where I stand before nothing but the mystery of the matter itself and not the mystery of the documents." This is not a retreat from the text, but an intense concentration precisely on the deep content of the text. Lessing's story about the palace and the occupants who did not take part in the dispute about the genuine sketch has a certain affinity with Barth's preference for reality over possibility. But Barth's "dwelling" in reality is set in the context of authentic witnesses who guide us into the path of discovery and provide perspective along the way. This is why Pannenberg's method could not be acceptable to Barth. We must see, in Barth's way of pointing to the reality within which the technical problem of reason evaporates, that the word "event" which he so frequently used went much deeper than a subjective experience.

Still the question is asked whether Barth's response to the Lessing question does not contain a failure to recognize the existence of an unavoidable dilemma: either the route of historical-critical research (to find certainty) or the route of a pneumatic, irrational, and unverifiable (and thus, irrefutable) experience. Barth stoutly rejected this dilemma. He appealed to a concrete focus on the New Testament witness. This was not to take flight into "pre-history" or "trans-history" where the storms of dispute can never reach; but it was a way of rejecting any route that leaves us outside of the witness of Scripture.

In the late thirties some of us did speak of the kerygma as the "way out" of the problems of uncertainty. But later the accent on the kerygma was meant, not as a "way out," but as *the* way in which the witness employs its power. Speaking of the way in which we come to know Jesus of Nazareth, Luther once said: "Suppose that Jesus walked into our church; we would not recognize him. But now he comes to us through the gospel, and that is much better." Here we are not plagued with a dilemma; and this is not a flight from problems. We should remember this as we hear Pannenberg telling us that kerygmatic theology is a flight from skepticism and historical relativism.

How the front has shifted is suggested by a remark Pannenberg is reported to have made in his lectures on revelation and history: "the whole of theology during the past thirty years is a mistake." When individuals are impressed with the newness of their own insights, they often see their moment as a break with the recent past. But usually this stems from an oversimplification of what has been going on in the past; a new insight blinds one to the motives that were at play in other efforts to understand the gospel. This, I think, happened with Pannenberg in his critique of the theology of the Word; he saw a dilemma between "events" and preaching. But it is precisely the connection between event and preaching within the history of tradition that shows how Pannenberg misses the mark. Kerygmatic theology *can* be born of a radical skepticism. This was definitely not the case with Kähler (and Pannenberg recognized this in his note that Kähler's was not "kerygmatic theology in the modern sense"), since he was not interested in a contrast between "pre-history" *(Geschichte)* and "history" *(Historie)*. What concerned Kähler was the independence of faith from historical sciences, without meaning to be radically critical of science. The kerygma, he insisted, was not a flight, nor was it a compensation. The kerygma is established in the substance of the gospel. But Bultmann's kerygmatic theology *is* locked into historical skepticism with respect to the historical Jesus. Bultmann uses 2 Corinthians 5:16 ("We no longer know Jesus after the flesh") to indicate the kerygmatic disinterest in the historical, earthly Jesus. ". . . The 'Christ after the flesh' is no concern of ours. How things looked in the heart of Jesus I do not know and do not want to know" (*Faith and Understanding*, E.T. 1969, p. 132).

Cullmann took another tack; he, like Kähler and Barth, refused to ignore the Jesus of history (O. Cullmann, *Salvation in History*, E.T. 1967). Barth too was anti-docetic, and took quite a different view from Bultmann's with respect to the earthly Jesus. We may recall how important he thought the phrase "suffered under Pontius Pilate" was as a way of confessing the concrete, historical event. He did indeed reject the "historical Jesus" as construed in modern Protestantism, namely as a way of evading his divinity. But there is no opposition between the decisive significance of the witness and a concentrated attention on Jesus the "Royal Man" or Jesus "the Conqueror." There is no opposition here, such as that which Bultmann poses, between *Geschichte* (revelation-history) and *Historie* (history). This is a wholly different viewpoint from that in which a personally significant encounter with the kerygma is divorced from events that occur on the plane of history with their objective facts.

134 A HALF CENTURY OF THEOLOGY

134   A HALF CENTURY OF THEOLOGY

Bultmann created the impression that he was totally unconcerned about history: "What Jesus means to me is not exhausted
by, indeed does not even come to expression in what he appears to be in the historical-critical view. He is not to be found
in his historical appearance; his real significance is first apparent
only when we stop asking questions about his history." But the
whole truth about Bultmann's attitude toward the historical
Jesus is not told here. He himself insisted that the notion of his
complete disinterest in the earthly Jesus was untrue. Were he
to "discount the historical cross as an event of the past" he
would have to give up the kerygma — and this "is in no sense
my intention." His concern is with "the historical (as revelation-
history) *significance* of the unique historical (as ordinary history)
events." The encounter with Jesus in the kerygma is not an
encounter with an idea or a symbol. Bultmann spurned the
suggestion that he was trying to rescue some last thin element
of the gospel out of the fires of criticism. It was the conservatives,
he thought, who were doing the anxious rescue work. "I calmly
let the fire burn, for I see that what is consumed is only the
fanciful portraits of Life-of-Jesus theology . . ." *(Faith and Understanding,* p. 132). But this helps explain why some of his
disciples thought that the historical Jesus had no importance for
Bultmann; he could be critically radical because he was unconcerned about the outcome for the Jesus of history.

Some of Bultmann's disciples began to argue the legitimacy
of concern for the historical Jesus, partly in criticism of their
teacher. E. Käsemann became a conspicuous example of this
when, in 1954, he wrote an article, which became rather famous,
in which he focused on the kerygma's dependence on the historical Jesus. According to Käsemann, we cannot avoid historical
research. Enormous difficulties present themselves whenever we
seek a criterion for recognizing the "authentic Jesus material."
This he admitted. He wrote in response to Joachim Jeremias,
who minimized these difficulties, that he thought it would be
"easier to run blindfold through a minefield." To seek verification
for the kerygma along this way is for Käsemann absurd, even
blasphemous (E. Käsemann, *New Testament Questions of Today,*
E.T. 1969, p. 47). But there is no reason, nonetheless, for
"disengagement from the historical Jesus," no reason for resigna-
tion and skepticism. He thought Bultmann's historical skepticism exaggerated.

Thus, a new problem arose. People began to talk of a schizophrenic streak in Bultmann's theology. They had reference to the radical division he created between historical and substantive continuity, between Jesus and early Christian preaching. E. Fuchs saw this, and distanced himself from Bultmann on the matter of form-historical inquiry: the kerygma itself brings us in touch with the earthly Jesus, the kerygma accepts him as the criterion. This is why it is no longer possible — as Bultmann thought — to consider history as such empty of theological significance. We are not dealing with a futile search for historical guarantees through historical research. We are dealing with the concrete content of the kerygma, and therewith very much, if not everything, stands or falls: "the earthly Jesus must therefore secure the proclaimed Christ . . . lest he be twisted into a projection of an existential self-understanding or to an image of religious ideology" (Käsemann). And so Käsemann, at the decisive point, says that the mystery of the earthly Jesus cannot be solved by the historian, but only by the kerygma itself. This is not a leap into irrationality in Käsemann's view; it is a discovery of authenticity which must be recognized whenever the theologian is tempted to be an historian. In the kerygma's involvement with the earthly Jesus we keep our focus on the faith of the church, without making it dependent on scientific verification. Not a kerygma "as such," but a kerygma filled to the brim with content. Not a truth as such, but a truth *about* Jesus. This kerygma and this truth blaze the trail to confession, in spite of and in the midst of all kinds of questions that arise in scientific inquiry. Faith cannot avoid the problems that arise when we relate Jesus of Nazareth to the Christ of proclamation, the earthly Jesus and the living Lord. Faith cannot escape the question of how the One who proclaimed became the proclaimed One and of how Jesus who taught us faith becomes the object of our faith. Everything is concentrated on our interest in the historical Jesus. And here the ways part again: on one hand attention is riveted on Jesus as the "subject matter" and on the other the continuity between pre- and post-Easter events is located in the faith people had in Jesus. E. Schillebeeckx proposes that the new problematics (the so-called "new quest") sets a very real problem on the agenda, of great importance for Christian faith. He says that Christian faith implies "not only the personal, living presence of the glorified Jesus, but also a bond with his earthly life." He is thinking of the continuity between the earthly Jesus and the Christ of faith, a continuity which has always been the assumption of the church's confession. In this context it is a very positive word, a decision: "Therefore Christianity and the kerygma without the historical Jesus of Nazareth would, for me, be without content; certainly there would be no Christianity" (Schillebeeckx).

So, after all the New Testament research, the quest for the historical Jesus and the criticisms levelled against it, after weighing many methods for unlocking the mystery of the New Testament, we finally come back via kerygmatic theology to the important question posed by the New Testament itself: Who really is the Son of Man (Matthew 16)? If the quest for the historical Jesus was motivated by doubt about the dogmatic Christ, now the legitimate attention given to the earthly Jesus raises again the central question of the New Testament. At the same time, we stand before the problem of whether it can be maintained seriously and with good conscience that the Scripture is, after all, its own interpreter. This Reformational starting point had credibility when posed against tradition as the second source of revelation and as the authoritative interpreter of the Scriptures. But now this canon comes back into what many view as a crisis because of our questions about method. The question is then asked if "the historical-critical exegesis has a place in the self-interpretation of Holy Scripture" (O. Weber, *Die Treue Gottes und die Kontinuität der menschlichen Existenz*, 1967, pp. 68f.). The question is pertinent especially since this method "in many circles is seen as unbelieving and anti-church." Weber refuses to let these difficulties force him to remove Scripture, as a holy book, from the arena of serious research. This, he knows, would be "the death of exegesis."

Aversion to biblical docetism poses all sorts of questions precisely because it is justified. And the questions give people a feeling of crisis, for the methods of biblical research (form-historical, redaction-historical, tradition-historical) touch on far more than formal questions of composition; they involve the content of the gospel itself. Several hypotheses play a role here, and this too creates the impression that we are shifting ground, that something is happening to undermine our certainty regarding the witness of the gospel. The question received new urgency when we asked what it means to speak of the authority of Scripture. We had been persuaded for some time that the Bible did not fall "from heaven in the form of a printed book." What must we understand, not in the abstract, but in the concrete, by "biblical faith"? Once, such a term seemed clear and definite, charged with calling and urgency; but later it became clear that the phrase "biblical faith" is not a label that guarantees a proper use of Scripture. The label takes on authenticity only in the *actual* subjection of ourselves to Scripture, a subjection that shows respect to Scripture for what it really is. It is this respect that has led to the question of correct understanding, not an understanding that is content to capture all the familiar echoes, but an understanding that grows from total involvement with the categories and the structures of the entire Word of God. With this, we stand before the question of what it means to appeal to the witness of Scripture in our situation, and to appeal in a way that calls for a high and final decision of great clarity and simplicity: "It stands written."

These words have functioned in countless discussions as the final word, a word that lands us on a niveau of great decisions. But the important question has steadily become more pressing: Does this appeal really settle things, or does it not merely give rise to a plethora of interpretations that hardly create the impression that the Bible itself speaks the decisive word for everyone and eliminates the need for further discussion? How does it stand now, after centuries of confessional struggle and continuous biblical research, with this simple appeal to the written word? It is not to be denied that the fact that "it is written" does not automatically clarify the mystery of Scripture once and for all. And we must also face the fact that theology, with all its problems and hesitations, has helped create this doubt.

The decisive character of this appeal — "It stands written" — had made a powerful impact on me at the time (1938) I wrote *Het Probleem der Schriftkritiek* (The Problem of Biblical Criticism). Shortly before this book was published, I had spoken at a minister's conference on "The Isolation of Reformed Views on Scripture." In this speech I said that the Reformed view of Scripture was isolated because of its radical commitment to the fact that "It stands written," and I set this commitment in contrast to all sorts of other views which posited other criteria for our life and faith, such as science, for instance. I recall that one preacher remarked that another dimension should be added to this theme, namely the work of the Holy Spirit in connection with scriptural authority and scriptural faith. Later I thought about the intuitive insight, and perhaps under the impression of it I remarked in the book that the confession of the authority of Scripture is "indissolubly bound with the confession of the Holy Spirit." This certainly agrees with the Reformed confession of the Word and the Spirit, namely that true obedience to the Holy Scriptures is possible only through the Holy Spirit, and that therefore the motto "It stands written" cannot and ought not be a principle to be used as if it were a simple and self-evident technique that we have at our disposal. At any rate, the minister's remark had more to it than I realized when I first heard it, though I certainly was ready then to admit its truth.

It reminds us of the fact that, in understanding the Scripture — or in appealing to its authority — we are not dealing with a formal principle but with a deep spiritual witness to Jesus Christ to whom the Spirit testifies. The Spirit is he who leads us into understanding, not an understanding of a contingent legal document to which all alike can appeal, but an understanding of a *witness* in its depth and perspective. Therefore, the phrase "It stands written" has a profound presupposition, namely that this appeal to Scripture can never be separated from a right understanding of Scripture. Lessing's remark in this connection is often cited: "Religion is not true because the evangelists and apostles teach it, but they teach it because it is true." Lessing's quip offers only an apparent solution to the question, since what is written is written because the writers were faithful and true to what they saw and heard, and thus people can be comforted and encouraged simply by the written words, full of authority (cf. Revelation 21:5). But we cannot take refuge in a formal authority-principle as though what is "true" is determined simply by a word invested with authority, without any immediate connection with its *content* as the truth of God.

We touch here on dangers that simple appeals to the authority of Scripture have always had for the church. The Scriptures can be approached as a blank reality in which the challenge of understanding need play no role, and which can be used like a code book whose articles are perfectly transparent and wanting only to be applied to practical instances. We can, thus, fail to recognize the kind of reality that Scripture is. We can appeal to Scripture in a way that overlooks the very character of Scripture, and so turn our appeal into an easy technique without variations and without genuine perspective. Bavinck noted that theology has sometimes condemned science, not in the name of Scripture, but in the name of a wrong interpretation of it (*Gereformeerde Dogmatiek*, II, p. 459). Anyone who does not take account of the fact that the reality of Scripture may be something other than what is deduced from a certain theory of inspiration is almost certainly going to cry "It stands written" and still come out with something that misses the truth and power of Scripture.

As I reread my book of 1938, I sense that the difference between then and now is not that I was at that time impressed with "It stands written" and that later, in my volume on the Scriptures, I was less committed to it. I still wish to stand, attentively and devoutly, by that appeal, made by Christ — in the uttermost loneliness of the wilderness — with which he withstood the tempter. He put between him and Satan the "wall of the Word of God." And thereupon the devil left him and, see, the angels came and served him.

The fact that Satan himself cited Psalm 91 in his temptations shows how close the connection is between the appeal to the written word and the right understanding of it. The words themselves, as isolated and unrelated things, can be used as pawns in a game of interpretations. Christ's appeal has the background of his own relationship with the Father, his ministry in the business of his Father; it has nothing to do with a formal declaration of authority or with a blind faith. Much rather, it is an obedient and witnessing subjection to the leading of God which he had learned to recognize and respect within the written words. The demonic appeal to Scripture discloses a problematic, not of the Word of God, but of any or all formalism in which the question of the right understanding of Scripture is ignored. In contrast, Jesus walked the way . . . to the depths . . . and decisions . . . in the *act* of obedience.

Only in this way can the slogan "It stands written" have an abiding power within the church. We could shout our appeals to "It stands written" while in fact the key to understanding had been removed from us (Luke 11:52). And it is possible to know the Scriptures and yet understand neither them nor the power of God (Matthew 22). The Bible itself warns against a simple identification between reading and understanding. One can read without understanding, see and hear without really seeing and hearing, just as the disciples saw the "loaves of bread" and still did not see what had happened (Mark 6:52).

The impression is sometimes created that the appeal to Scripture is a simple and massively effective matter, concerning which profound reflection is quite needless and for which attention to the specific situation to which the Word was directed is of no real account. The genuine functioning of "It stands written" is threatened thereby. The result has often been that the Bible underwent a huge shrinkage, and could hardly function as the Word of God in certain instances where certain words seemed crystal clear to those who used them and yet caused deep divisions in the church.

The possibility of a direct and simple employment of Scripture has always had an intense fascination. And this has been intensified by legitimate rejection of autonomy and self-will. The universality of the scriptural appeal was thus defended against the so-called dualistic theory of inspiration. I have myself in times past seen hardly anything else in various Roman Catholic distinctions than a capitulation to a dualism that undermines every appeal to Scripture. I have criticized the notion that the Bible writers received no new scientific orientation, but used their own level of understanding for their own purposes; I mistakenly attributed this view to a dualistic effort to synthesize the inerrancy of Scripture with science. Where are the limits to be drawn, I asked, "if inspiration is to be harmonized with all sorts of scientific errors that were part and parcel of the level of knowledge reached at the time the writers lived?"

To speak of *errors* when we deal with previous levels of knowledge is to speak out of an unhistorical approach. Bavinck not only was convinced that the Bible used the language of ordinary experience (a much used device for harmonizing scriptural faith with the results of science), but also recognized "without hesitation, that the Bible writers' world-views were no different from those which were generally held at the time" — for example the antiquated notion of how the heavenly bodies moved in the sky. Bavinck sometimes used the distinction between historical and normative authority of Scripture; thus, with respect to the thought patterns that the Bible writers shared with their contemporaries, he could say: "They in no way bind us in any normative sense" (Bavinck, *Kennis en Leven*, 1922, p. 196). Bavinck was looking for a solution that avoided dualism and maintained respect for the meaning and depth of what it was that stood written. We can understand why Bavinck could write that "the dogma of Scripture is not nearly completed with regard to these matters; a great deal of study is still ahead of us."

In 1938, I tried to draw a comparison between the Roman Catholic doctrine of the Pope's infallibility and the Protestant doctrine of the Bible's infallibility. The comparison is frequently drawn, and both are often attributed to a need for a tangible and manageable guarantee of certainty. The need is for a firm standard with which everything else can be measured and which would relieve us of the need to bother with problems of interpretation. This is why Lessing called the Protestant Bible the "paper pope"; the shift from Pope to Bible was only a shift from one guarantee to another. Orthodoxy derived its view of Scripture, Kähler complained, from a need it felt for a reliable transmission of revelation; it had the need so it postulated a view of infalliblity that met the need. The same explanation is given to the Roman view of papal infallibility. But it has become clear, through a process that has been difficult for many, that this parallel is not true to the facts. In Roman Catholic theology, awareness has grown that there are deep problems connected with specific infallible decisions, decisions that are clouded by historical problems of interpretation common to all human words. And on the Reformation side, the understanding has grown that an appeal to a final word ("It stands written") is not a magic wand that can be waved to eliminate all problems, but is workable only along with insight into the full riches of the biblical witness. But many have seen this as an undesirable complication that takes the edge off the effectiveness of any final court of appeal. In fact, it tends to eliminate the final word. We discern a certain homesickness for earlier clarity, for a direct and final decision-giving power that can remove any confusion and uncertainty that threaten the faith.

There is a fear lest theology be turned into hermeneutics, a hermeneutics that waters down the authority of Scripture in the solvent of sophisticated interpretation. The knives are always being sharpened, but never used for cutting. The word seems to be removed a distance from the congregation — not in space, but in the secret regions of research with all of its uncertain interpretations. This leads to a feeling of uncertainty and doubt within the church; the people seem no longer able to find refuge within the clear Word that is close at hand (Deuteronomy 30 and Romans 10). Indeed, the uncertainty is not confined to the congregation. It is evident in theology itself. Helmut Thielicke, for instance, while conceding the legitimacy of hermeneutical questions, says that he "cannot avoid the impression that the present preoccupation with questions of method signals that theology has gotten tired out." And while theology recuperates, we have to settle for a diversity of interpretations that together offer no authentic help to the church as it makes its confession. This is why we sense a homesickness for an uncomplicated and unproblematic approach in which we can declare with certainty: "It stands written." Homesickness can lead to impatience; and this can provoke the church into cutting through the maze with authoritative declarations that, in fact, sweep under the rug many real questions that arise from the very Scripture whose authority we want to uphold. The result is that the Reformational confidence in the "Holy Scripture as its own interpreter" is undermined.

We have seen that every method by which Scripture is studied is in turbulence. We have also seen that there is no way to avoid turbulence. This is why so much tension is felt in this area. This need not happen just because much attention is given to details, as though looking at the trees will leave us without a vision of the forest. Details are part of the witness of the Scripture itself and so they belong to the task of research (cf. H. N. Ridderbos, "Tradition and Editorship in the Synoptic Gospels" in *Jerusalem and Athens*, 1971, pp. 244f.). We cannot neglect the details. But we can strive to overcome any gap between our efforts to understand the Scriptures and the proclamation of its riches, riches that make the Word of God an actual lamp to our feet and a real light to our path (Psalm 119).

A New Testament scholar of our time has remarked that, at the present time, for every exegetical question there are contradictory answers, and that those who are responsible for the preaching of the church have a feeling of frustration and weakness. This is truly a shocking observation. We hear about the "current misery of New Testament scholarship," a misery of having too many methods, each of which claims to be *the* way to go. We would be misguided, however, were we to let ourselves be led by empathy with such complaints to turn against all hermeneutical questions. But Käsemann's complaint is that the historical scholarship devoted to the New Testament is "today without any systematic leadership and has resigned itself to carrying on without theological partners to the discussion." And he adds that "if no one else will, dogmatics must lead exegesis to its task" (*Das Neue Testament als Kanon,* 1970, p. 372). Theologians would be badly advised to rush too fast to reclaim the "queen of sciences" title. But we do face a real issue. We must make sure we do not lose our vision for the "It stands written." We must not resign ourselves to a new sort of skepticism. We must keep looking for ways to reassure the church that we are not merely looking for problems, that we have indeed heard the answer and intend to keep hearing it, and that we know the answer transcends our questions and problems in a way that keeps them from becoming the main theme. Herein lies the right perspective in our conversation with the Scripture. And here is where our attention is recalled to what we, in our discussion about authority, sometimes forget, namely to the positive purpose of the Scriptures. The purpose gives to our preoccupation with Scripture an ever renewed relevance. For the purpose of the "divinely breathed" Scripture is not to give us problems to solve, but to "furnish us unto all good works" (2 Timothy 3:17). *That* stands written.

6

Faith and Reasonableness

CAN WE FIND GROUNDS FOR CHRISTIAN FAITH THAT NOT ONLY ARE meaningful for believers, but can be, at least to some extent, convincing to nonbelievers? This possibility has intrigued theology throughout its history. We touch a problem here that comes to life whenever people come into contact with each other, respect each other, but then, at the threshold of this one area, faith, part company. Must we ascribe this estrangement to an inexplicable, irrational, and alienating appearance among men of a thing called faith? Or can the estrangement be overcome? The question is alive in a world that prizes "communication" and esteems a "reasonableness" that we all share in our thinking and working together; for here, at the point of faith, communication seems to break down. The impression is given that at this point we enter a totally foreign world of thought and hopes, a reality that is viewed as real only by some and as unreal by others.

In our time, people have come to feel that we cannot accept this impasse, that we have to plow through to a place where we can meet one another responsibly, so that genuine human contact is created and maintained. We are all responsible, it is said, for the one world which we share, a world torn apart, threatened, and in desperate need of our common help. The world has been compared to a ship that is floundering with four billion people aboard and that at any moment, because of conflict between the crewmen, can sink. As Roger Garaudy, a Marxist, put it, we must move away from excommunication and into dialogue.

Pope Paul VI makes a plea (in the encyclical *Ecclesiam suam*) for contact, not only with other Christians, but with all others. He asks for something more than the mere appearance of dialogue which actually is dominated by the pretensions of each side and finally comes down to a monologue, in which each side assumes the rightness of its view and expects victory for its own

144

principles, a monologue that really has the purpose of demonstrating one's own superiority and power. We are reminded also
of numerous dialogues between Christians and Marxists in which
the terrain is studiously scouted together, dialogues motivated
by a common concern for this world and, in that connection, for
the meaning of the future. Attempts are made in these dialogues
to make an end to caricatures that have accentuated the differences in the past, and thus to open the way, in mutual understanding, to a communication in common responsibility for humanity, for actual human beings in this world. (Cf. J. M. Lohse,
Menschlich sein — mit oder ohne Gott, 1969.) Can we overcome
our isolated blocks of conviction, isolated ideologies, or will it
appear, after all, that there can be no genuine dialogue?

In one discussion between Christians and humanists, in
Zurich in 1950, both parties tried for ten days to understand each
other. Barth reported that the discussions occurred "without the
discernible emergence of a helpful vision from either side, a
vision that was clear and compelling for all the participants, to say
nothing of the contemporary world." There are those who, on
the basis of their experience, conclude that dialogue is impossible,
that when it is tried it is usually a phoney maneuver. Further,
they say, this impasse is predictable because faith is a personal
matter, a conviction not given to rational argument, and can only
be witnessed to. The experience of faith — conversion to faith —
must be described in terms of the man born blind who did not
know much about the Lord, but did know that, whereas he once
was blind, he now could see (John 9). Once he was able to see,
he was in the arena of fact, of irrefutable fact that lay beyond all
doubt and discussion. Is it so, that at the one point of faith all
valuable communication is stopped?

As is well known, the answer to this question is not always
affirmative. Over and over again, someone rises to demonstrate
that faith is reasonable — or at least is not unreasonable. The
proofs for God's existence have always loomed large in this scene.
The conviction behind these proofs is that believing men do not
have to be content with a "Here I stand, I cannot do otherwise."
There are evidences, arguments that can be cogent for any
reasonable thinker. The arguments, or proofs, have for the most
part been taken from what is observable by anyone in our world;
their ingredients have been culled from the life and experience
that all men share. Thus the notion of causality is used to demon-

strate God as the first cause, the notion of movement to demonstrate the need for a First Mover, the notion of design to show the need for a Designer. To this is added the "proof" of the universality of religion. Now, the cogency of these proofs has impressed fewer and fewer people in our century. This has happened, not only because the arguments seem unconvincing to the atheistic world, but also because people are preoccupied with urgent problems of evil and suffering in our real world rather than with abstract problems of causality and the like. As Nicholas Berdyaev put it, the only serious concern of atheism today is its problem with the existence of a powerful and good God alongside a world of suffering and evil.

In 1870, the First Vatican Council declared that it was possible to know God via worldly reality. This was after Bautain (in 1840) was condemned when he refused to confess that God's existence could be proved with certainty. Vatican I then said that it was possible to know God via the created world through the natural light of reason. In the anti-modernist oath, this possibility of knowing became "proof" for God's existence. Roman Catholicism has kept this conviction intact since then; it came out in the encyclical *Humani Generis* of 1950 and was reaffirmed by Vatican II.

But while the position is not changed, there has been a notable silence about it. While the powers of reason were not denied, a shift of interest has taken place. Rational apologetics gradually lost its attractiveness. Indeed, there has been talk of a crisis in apologetics, both in Roman Catholic and Protestant circles. There has been a growing sense that an abstract element filtered through the proofs, that they were really about being and existence and not about the living God or Christian faith. Once the existence of a "God" was demonstrated, one could define him further, in whatever way one was personally inclined. A shift in interest occurred as men turned to experience within the world and wondered whether *human experience* contained a hint of God, a point of contact for faith and reason. With this we are back at the basic question of whether there exists a motive for faith present within and not outside of human life, or whether faith is a leap that can be recognized only by those who, in a similar wonderful experience, have also taken the leap: "Thou art stronger than I, and thou hast prevailed" (Jeremiah 20:7).

That there is no way to validate the Christian message through reason is a conviction that has taken deep root. When Bavinck warned against putting too much stock in proofs for God's existence, he also cautioned against dissociating ourselves from rational argument. But the problem for him was not strictly the problem of reason as such; he simply was not persuaded that the traditional arguments were convincing. Besides, if we relied on arguments, we would give the impression that faith is "a poor faith that needs to wait for God to be proven before it dares pray to him." Thus, it appeared as if the only way was the way of mystery, the way of "the leap," the way of irrationality — the enigma that has no rational basis. "Understanding always leads astray; only faith can show the way."

If we are to speak of a ground for believing, our only recourse is divine revelation. Faith is fixed on that revelation. *This* faith does not arise from man's rational thought; it can be only a work of God's Holy Spirit. After all, one could recall Ephesians 2:8 ("through faith; and this is not your own doing, it is the gift of God"). Faith has its origins in that which transcends human wisdom. Over against the unspiritual person who does not grasp the gift of the Spirit (1 Corinthians 2:13f.), the believing person knows that he has "the mind of Christ" (1 Corinthians 2:16).

In this view one senses how certain biblical expressions have taken hold. Jesus, for example said: "No one can come to me unless the Father who sent me draws him" (John 6:44). Or, consider his response to Peter's confession: "For flesh and blood has not revealed this to you, but my father who is in heaven" (Matthew 16:17). Concentrating on words like these, one lets the rationality of faith slip to the background. Why should anyone bother too much about the human motives and the rational preparations for faith when faith arises as a person is *overcome* by that which conquers reason (Jeremiah 20:7)?

Faith, it would be pointed out, is not *against* reason, though it is *above* reason. From the perspective of its transcendent origins, faith becomes defenseless, in a sense. It has no defenses for itself; it has no *apologia*, maybe no way of giving answers — except private ones. This could be like the person who, finding himself among God-deniers, responded by saying that he had just talked with God that morning. This "defense" is not a rational answer, but an answer from private experience, an answer that really closes the door on open discussion. Here we can only speak of personal surrender, without further analysis; here we are in the sphere of faith "in spite of" everything that could count against it. One is reminded of Habakkuk, caught in a hopeless situation — the fig tree without blossom, the vine without fruit, the fields without food, the stalls without herds — and saying, "*yet* I will rejoice in the Lord" (Habakkuk 3:18).

This way of looking at faith and reason has played a large role in modern theology. It appears in a conscious choice of the "in spite of" motif as an inscrutable mystery, and it comes out in the questions that are raised about faith in the face of this point of view. Almost all the problems that it provokes focus on the notion of *mystery*. Mystery — the totally incomprehensible, the enigmatic, the hidden! Faith in its uniqueness can easily be interpreted as an acceptance of the incomprehensible mystery, not open to any counter-explanations. Bonaventura's word about the eucharist is an example. (Paul VI quoted Bonaventura in his encyclical *Mysterium Fidei*, 1965, against novel views of transubstantiation.) He spoke about the difficulty — the *maxima difficultas* — of supposing that Christ is really present in the sacrament as well as in heaven; and he added: "this is why it is of highest merit to *believe* it."

The problematics of this point of view have not gone unnoticed. For it puts faith and reason in severe tension, a tension relieved by holding that faith gets its significance precisely from its being " in spite of" all difficulties in the way. Theology today enjoys a consensus that this way of thinking about mystery is not the biblical concept of mystery. For the Bible's mystery, though long maintained, is now a secret that has been revealed (Romans 16:25). Hence, the biblical mystery is not one that arises amid abstract problems of theoretical knowledge.

Bavinck was right when he branded the identification of mystery with enigma as a flattening out of the mystery of faith. It is interesting that Barth praised Bavinck precisely for his insight into the incomprehensibility of God. "In the newer literature I know of only one, the Dutch theologian H. Bavinck, who seems to have perceived this . . ." (*CD* II/1, p. 186). Bavinck, said Barth, saw it clearly as opposed to those for whom "it was not finally clear whether they really wanted to understand the incomprehensibility of God from Plato and Plotinus, or from Psalm 139, and from Paul, and therefore as an article of faith confirming the revelation of God as such" (*ibid.*). We find

Bavinck's critique in Karl Rahner, too, who rejects scholastic theology's tendency to define the mystery negatively, as something not understood by reason — with the consequence that, instead of *the* mystery, we get many mysteries that are believed without any connection with insight or thought (cf. "The Concept of Mystery in Catholic Theology" in *Theological Investigations*, IV, E.T. 1966, pp. 36ff.).

Even the *absurd* might find a place within mystery; indeed, it can even be canonized (cf. J. Ratzinger). Now and then, this possibility is made explicit, and someone exults in the break between faith and thought: "I believe *because* it is absurd." It was Leo Shestov who revived this motto, noting that he had ample models in the history of theology — Tertullian, Pascal, and Kierkegaard, to mention a few, men who consciously grasped the divorce between faith and thought, accepted it, and tolerated no compromise.

We will not make a general judgment here on paradoxes like Tertullian's thesis that the crucifixion of the Son of God is credible *because* it is absurd, and his resurrection certain *because* it is impossible. One should make a distinction here between a respect for Paul's awareness of the foolishness and weakness of God in 1 Corinthians 1 and a positing of absurdity as the essential content of faith — something that neither Pascal nor Kierkegaard did. One should not always read the whole abstract problem of theoretical knowledge into every striking expression of the contrast between faith and the conclusions of reason. One should recall the one mystery: "God revealed in the flesh" (1 Timothy 3:16) and "The Word was made flesh" (John 1:14).

This was doubtless what Luther was doing with his putdown of that "whore, reason." Luther scholars have reached a fair consensus about Luther's antithesis being motivated, not by irrationalism, but by his "theology of the cross" (cf. B. Lohse, *Ratio und Fides*, 1958). Even when Luther expressed a kind of "vicious pleasure" in his rejection of reason, he was concerned to underscore Paul's claim that "I did not receive it from man" (Galatians 1:11) and not to postulate a mystery that is wholly impervious to human reflection.

When the motto, "I believe because it is absurd" is declined, the problem of faith's connections with reason remains. The way of faith is not the route of argument and deductive reason, to be sure. But the question, then, is whether faith is something other than a blind submission to an "exterior" revelation, or an "exterior" authority. More, is there in the process of persuasion no human motivation at all, is there no connection between faith and one's own experience and insight?

Experiential theology in particular scored orthodoxy for talking about faith as though when people believed they did something that had no contact with their own humanity. Faith, said the theologians of experience, was an encounter with Christ in an experience that was very different from blind faith or blind obedience. What does happen when a person is persuaded to believe and what sort of human motives are present? How is the subjective experience of coming to faith related to faith's being given by God? Bavinck insisted that experiential theology did not mean to locate the origins of faith *within* man. It wanted, rather, to indicate how man himself was involved as he was confronted by revelation, and how he came to entrust himself to this revelation. Bavinck admitted that the question was of prime importance (*Gereformeerde Dogmatiek*, I, p. 494). Must we, finally, say that faith is an irrational leap without any point of contact in ordinary human experience, and is it, therefore, in the last analysis in conflict with all human reasoning and rational demonstration?

In the period of theology we have in our sights, this sort of question persistently demands attention. We grope for connections between Christian faith and human experience, just as we need to respect what comes to us in the gospel as an "offense," as the refutation of human wisdom (1 Corinthians 1:6f.) and as that which transcends all that the eye and the ear and the heart of man can grasp (1 Corinthians 1:9). The question arises in recognition of the *paradoxical* aspect of faith.

A little time spent in modern discussions of paradox reveals a wide variation in understanding of what paradox is. Indeed, we can speak of widespread confusion. Sometimes – in theological as well as in popular writing – "paradox" is used in the sense given it by Luke 5:26, where the crowd, on seeing the healing of the paralytic, calls out: "We have seen strange things today." Paradox, then, refers to something out of the ordinary. What is novel and surprising, what causes amazement, what comes as something different from anything yet experienced – this is paradox. We hear it in the words of the people: "What sort of man is this, that even winds and sea obey him?" (Matthew 8:27).

Obviously, this sort of "paradox" cannot be turned into a
religious theory of knowledge. It surely cannot be ground
for branding religious knowledge as the acceptance of self-
contradicting notions. When our experience provokes a sense of
wonder because it transcends anything we have experienced
before, we must not rush words like "contradiction" into the
scene. Here we are only talking about that which surprises us,
and when hearing about it (rather than experiencing it) we
may think it incredible. We may recall Paul's questions to Agrippa:
"Why is it thought incredible by any of you that God raises the
dead?" (Acts 26:8).

Nonetheless, it has been common to typify the paradox, not
as something that transcends our (limited) experience, but as a
contradiction, as that which logic cannot tolerate.

There are, indeed, several New Testament words that, on
first hearing, give the impression of a contradiction. For example,
the Bible speaks about losing and gaining life (Mark 8:35);
and, in the case of Paul, it says: "as dying, and behold we live . . .
as sorrowful, yet always rejoicing; . . . as having nothing, and
yet possessing everything" (2 Corinthians 6:9,10). But such expressions as these, while they are striking and point to the fact
that there is more to Christian life than meets the eye, have
nothing at all to do with a theoretical problem or with logical
contradiction. These striking phrases are used to tell of the wonderful things that have happened, as is the case when Paul talks
about the wisdom and foolishness, and the power and weakness,
of God (1 Corinthians 1:25).

We may recall what we have called the "strangeness" of the
gospel in terms of our human *presuppositions*. (This is the reason
for talking about "offense" and "foolishness.") In this sense, Bultmann often uses the word "paradox" for what he calls "the strang-
est aspect of the Christian faith, that it should reckon an historical,
an inner-temporal event, as the eschatological event." Bultmann,
in this case, is not thinking of an offense against reason or a
theoretical problem. Indeed, he denies that the gospel is something "anti-rational, a demand for a sacrifice of the intellect."

But we arrive on a different track whenever "paradox" is
meant to indicate a logical contradiction. Haitjema's introduction
of Barth to the Netherlands (in 1926) is an illustration. For
Haitjema, the paradoxical element lies in the object itself; it is
not an apparent paradox that lies only in our thinking. The para-

dox of scriptural teaching is rooted in reality. And it was within this conviction that he greeted Barth's theology as the beginning of a new and important period in Dutch theology.

My own impression was that Barth's theology was not paradoxical in the sense meant by Haitjema (cf. my *Karl Barth*, 1936, p. 250). But Barth, nonetheless, was introduced in Holland as the theologian of paradox. This stimulated Schilder to open a discussion about the knowledge of faith, in which he suggested that revelation breaks through our laws of thought. Schilder aimed his critique at Haitjema, Barth, and Kierkegaard as one (cf. K. Schilder, *Tusschen ja en neen*, 1929). When Haitjema cited a phrase from Calvin — a phrase he took over from Peter Brunner, who had translated it as "a paradox that runs straight against reason" — Schilder responded by saying that Calvin did not mean that God broke our rules for thought, but only that revelation seemed nonsense to the *natural* man.

It is clear, in any case, that paradox as a problem of thought, in and of itself, was of no great interest to Barth — even though he did use the term. In an address given in 1925 ("Church and Theology") he stressed that all our knowledge is incomplete and inadequate. We cannot create a finished synthesis which gathers everything within a single concept; we must talk about things in their place, about creation and providence, about a visible and an invisible church, about justification and sanctification, about faith and obedience, and about Word and Spirit. From this we see that Barth was not working with logical paradoxes in the sense of things that contradicted each other. He wanted to acknowledge that we cannot say all that needs to be said within one word. The formula of Chalcedon was, for him, a prime example.

The early Barth certainly had a flair for striking phrases that smacked strongly of offense, paradox, and even the absurd. He once wrote: "The sending of God's Son can be described only in strongest negations, proclaimed only as paradox, understood only as the absurd. . . ." But even here Barth was not working with a theoretical problem of understanding, for he concluded, "because it is the divine reaction against sin."

In 1932, Barth wrote that we ought to be intensely serious about the *offense* of the gospel in 1 Corinthians 1:18–2:10 (*CD* I/1, p. 190). Taking the offense seriously is not the same as positing a theory of paradox. When he began his *Church Dog-*

matics, Barth said that the word *paradox* had done its bit of service and that we might well -- in view of the confusion surrounding it -- use it more sparingly. And when we did use it, he thought, we might best use it as illuminated by the first chapter of 1 Corinthians, where we hear, not of a logical paradox, but of breaking through the wisdom of the world.

Schilder, who first saw Barth's theology in terms of logical paradox, noted this and spoke of a "remarkable, be it somewhat laconic, announcement of a change of view." But the change was not really that remarkable, for Barth was never really concerned with paradox as a problem of thought. Back in 1925, he had said that what confronts us first as a paradox is resolved for the faith that rests on the Word.

Much later, in his doctrine of reconciliation and in connection with the incarnation, Barth wrote: "In him there is no paradox, no antinomies, no contradiction, no disloyalty to himself, indeed no possibility for it." From this it appears how Barth was distancing himself increasingly from Kierkegaard. He remarked once, in a lecture at Copenhagen, that every theologian ought to go through Kierkegaard's school, but ought not to stay in it too long and, once through it, should not go back to it.

Schilder saw Barth as if he had stayed in Kierkegaard's school. Kierkegaard's theology created a confrontation between paradox and reason, not an apparent paradox that was resolved in faith, but an absolute paradox that could not be resolved. And, for Schilder, Barth's theology was on the same track. But Barth's own words give little support to the notion.

The relationship between Barth and Kierkegaard has long been a popular subject for scholars. In one such study, A. McKinnon wrote that Barth had never gone beyond Kierkegaard, precisely because Kierkegaard himself had not taught an objective paradox. He cited this sentence in support: "It is naturally understandable that the faithful in no way find the material of faith to be absurd." McKinnon concluded that Barth later dissociated himself from a nonexistent Kierkegaard, a "phantom-Kierkegaard" whom we meet only in those, like E. Brunner and H. Diem, who have twisted Kierkegaard into an irrationalist and a fideist. (Later, Diem told McKinnon that he could make no sense out of his view.)

We cannot go into the problem of Kierkegaard interpretation, but if McKinnon is right the difference between Barth and Kierkegaard -- on this point -- would evaporate, as would that between

Schilder and both Barth and Kierkegaard. All of them would be concerned about something other than the theoretical possibilities of reason or about logical contradictions that offend the intellect with absurd miracles which can be accepted only if the intellect is sacrificed on the altar of credulity. For all of them, the "paradox" would involve only the tension that the New Testament underscores, namely the opposition between God's truth and human wisdom. They are not concerned with one or another human faculty — reason, in this case — but with natural man *en toto,* confronted with God's wisdom and foolishness, the scandal of the cross and the mystery that it reveals. The conflict is not an anthropological, but a religious one. Not logical contradiction, but the revolt of the wise and intelligent human beings for whom the mystery stays hid though it is revealed to children (Matthew 11).

There is still another fascinating aspect of the discussions about paradox. Barth, as we have seen, was not interested in paradox as a problem of reason (in the sense of paradox as contradiction). This is generally agreed. But it is nonetheless claimed that he still went the route of conflict between faith and intellect and gradually came to a sacrifice of the intellect in this sense: he posited faith (as assent) in mysterious, supernatural *truths.* The *Church Dogmatics* in particular was seen as a return to rigid orthodoxy. The basis for Barth's concept of faith was seen in his strong accent on "God has spoken" and on the divine revelation as being prior to everything else said about theology. Man was called only to put himself under this revelation.

The original dynamic of Barth's theology, some said, gradually hardened into the rigid structure of a number of truths, in objectivism. In spite of his outbursts against Rome, Barth settled for a home in the vicinity of the Vatican and the climate of the First Vatican Council, at least in regard to one point. That point was not natural theology, of course, but the Roman Catholic concept of God's hidden mysteries as set out for us to believe: man is totally dependent on God, totally subject to the uncreated truths, and so is duty bound to believe that whatever is revealed is true. We are obligated to believe, not by our own insight into the truth, but by the authority of the God who reveals these things. All this is from Vatican I (cf. Denzinger, 1789).

The same authoritarian spirit, it is claimed, reappears in Barth. Brunner expressed concern about Barth's development;

for example, when Barth made a case for the confession of the virgin birth — in the first volume of his *Dogmatics* — Brunner saw it as a classic example of faith as a belief *about* external matters. Barth seemed to be turning faith into acceptance of a super-natural fact made known to us by revelation, which on this authority was required to be believed. Brunner further saw Barth throwing aside all the warnings sounded by the Reformers when he spent hundreds of pages expounding the mystery of the trinity.

We might summarize Brunner's concern in this way: the legitimate protest against nineteenth-century subjectivism ran its course into an unreformed objectivism, which closed out on the existential understanding of faith and revelation, giving up on "Truth as Encounter."

Brunner's concerns were present in Bavinck's protest against the Roman Catholic view of faith which, as he understood it, made of faith an agreement *(assensus)* with a list of revealed truths, a list that grows as time goes on. For the Reformation, faith was different. The grace of God in Jesus Christ was its ob-ject. A sum of truths could not be what faith was centered on, for faith was a personal relation of trust between a man and God (*Gereformeerde Dogmatiek*, I, p. 583). Brunner thus delivers to Barth's address the same message Bavinck sent to Rome.

But Brunner was not alone. Bonhoeffer spoke about Barth's "revelation positivism." What Bonhoeffer meant by positivism has been debated in many discussions of Barth's theology. The phrase appears in the *Letters and Papers from Prison*, where Bonhoeffer characterizes it this way: Barth's "positivist doctrine of revelation . . . says, in effect, 'Like it or lump it': virgin birth, Trinity, or anything else; each is an equally significant and necessary part of the whole, which must simply be swallowed as a whole or not at all. That isn't biblical" (*Letters and Papers from Prison*, E.T. 1971, p. 286). The *gift*, the pure gift from Christ, is squeezed into a *law* of faith, and runs the risk of losing its connections with the world. So Bonhoeffer is not talking about the philosophical positivism of the nineteenth century when he labels Barth's doctrine of revelation as positivist. It is Barth's accent on the given, the revealed truths which we are obligated to accept.

This sort of objection to "revealed truths" is reminiscent of Wilhelm Herrmann's criticism of "heteronomy," of things that are thrust on faith from outside, of a law that obligates one to believe things. Actually, Bonhoeffer is thinking about *blind* obedience. He knew that Barth would have no sympathy for this kind of obedience, but he saw a trace of it in him and feared it was giving rise to a new orthodoxy. It has been suggested that Bonhoeffer had in view particularly Barth's volume on election, but this does not clarify anything. Barth (in 1968) told Bonhoeffer's biographer, Eberhard Bethge, that the phrase "revelation positivism" had never made any sense to him. What Barth probably heard in it was a fear of some sort of fundamentalism. But lurking in the aborted exchange was the same problem about *motives* for believing, about ways in which a person is convinced of the truth, and about the role of one's own experience in faith.

Bonhoeffer's criticism seemed as sharp as it did because it not only rejected an authoritarian view of faith, but discerned in it a break in the believer's contact with the world. If we establish a "law of faith," Bonhoeffer thought, we imply that "the world is in some degree made to depend on itself and left to its own devices, and that's the mistake" (*Letters and Papers*, p. 286).

The focus here is on the dangers of an "authoritarian" view of faith. At issue is the notion of faith as an assent to certain truths. One could say: we are dealing with a concept of faith that makes the object of faith heteronomous, foreign to man's nature, and remaining foreign while one keeps believing. Further, faith would lose its dynamic because it would impose on us an alien, dictatorial (revealing!) law that would keep us from true freedom. There is here a fear of a blind, servile obedience without any authentic insight and personal decision, lacking a liberating and releasing "eventfulness" — in short, faith on the basis of *authority*.

That Barth never accepted the indictment of "revelation positivism" is clear from the way he wrote about "the nature of faith" in 1950. He answers Bonhoeffer's objection, as I see it, in a way that discloses the problematics in terms of what he rejects. We may dismiss, he says, "the idea that faith is a blind subjection to a law imposed upon the will and understanding from without . . ." (*CD*, III/3, p. 247). Certainly, Barth agrees, faith is "an arrest and commitment in which man is set free from his own caprices and acquires a Lord whom he must follow. It is a new and strange light shining upon man from above." This light "not only shines upon human life . . . from without, but it also illuminates it from within. It does not close our eyes, but opens them. It does not destroy our intellect . . . but it sets it free . . ." *(ibid.).*

In Barth's response, we get a sharp picture of the entire debate concerning "faith on the basis of authority," and can recognize it as one of the most profound questions that cluster around Christian believing.

The notion of an *external* authority is used — and this is striking — to indicate a reality that is alien to us compelling us to subject ourselves to revelation. When we encounter the label "external authority," then, it is as though the argument is finished, as though everyone will agree that it is unacceptable.

During the last few centuries — since the Enlightenment — we have become hypersensitive lest someone believe on the basis of authority. Since Kant, we are often told, the assumption is that man is mature and free, and therefore is dishonored by any authoritarian obligation to believe anything. The traditional Roman Catholic view of churchly authority is especially in the crucible.

Yet, we meet the same genre of problems much earlier, whenever faith and authority are set in the same picture. Calvin wrestled with it; he spoke of the unique character of faith, but had no mind for *blind* faith. Faith, for Calvin, was not a leap in the dark; it was a form of knowledge, the knowledge of God's benevolence toward us. It was not an assent to something pressed on us, nor a mere believing *that* something is true; it was a personal trust that negates blind obedience (cf. *Institutes,* III/II/1, 2).

Faith, for Calvin, expressly does not consist in "respect for the church" (*Institutes,* III/II/3) and therefore is not an "implicit faith" that leads one into a labyrinth of unknown truths. Implicit faith can lead us to accept any and all errors in the name of the church's authority. Faith is not ignorance; it is always in touch with what one knows, as the Bible everywhere tells us (*Institutes,* III/II/3). Staying in tune with the Reformation, the church was convinced that faith was never blind, that it received the truth with eyes open. And in the measure that this conviction grew, resistance to any sacrifice of intellect, in which thinking was dissociated from faith, grew as well.

Theological thought achieved a consensus of sorts in its critical stance toward any suggestion that in order to believe one had to set his intellect on the shelf. We may recall Bavinck's characterization of faith as a "healthy intellect." We may also

mention Ebeling's critique of the sort of servile subjection to
authority that is content with hazy faith rather than earnest with
clear truth. Bultmann, too, in his way, rejects the sacrifice of
intellect as the price of faith (*Theology of the New Testament,*
I, E.T. 1951). Dorothee Sölle launched out against a formal notion
of authority that leaves no room for personal responsibility and
insight, a kind of "an order is an order" mentality. She opts for
"seeing obedience" and rejects "blind obedience." The latter, she
says, is an obedience based on what others know and experience,
and an obedience that discounts the question of *how* one personally experiences and assimilates the authority one affirms. We
could go on to mention many others.

Considering what we have seen in modern times of blind
obedience in our world, it is understandable that the issue of
authority is treated gingerly for fear of its misuse. We have seen
in the Roman Catholic Church, where authority has always been
crucial, several critical responses to its authority. Hans Küng's
discussions of infallibility and the structures of the church are
only very visible tokens of a widespread critical attitude. The
growing Catholic, as well as Protestant, consensus appears to have
solid New Testament support. For it warns against heavy burdens
that are hard to bear, and forbids calling anyone on earth father
or master or rabbi since "you have one master, the Christ"
(Matthew 23:4,8-10). The New Testament will have nothing of
having burdens laid on us as heavy yokes; it offers a yoke that
is easy and commands that are not burdensome (1 John 5). Paul's
own use of his apostolic authority is very reserved; he refuses to
"lord it over" the congregation and wants instead to be co-worker
"with you for your joy" (2 Corinthians 1:24). We discern something of this conviction everywhere in the theology of our time,
and in it all there is a sense that it bears on the relationship
between faith and authority.

Authority, real as it is, cannot be a darksome power that
compels us to subject ourselves without reason. It is rather a
reality "over against" us that offers perspective, joy, and hope.
"Over against" — this is a key phrase. The biblical notion of authority does not relativize the radical character of this reality.
Nor does it tone down the call to obedience (cf. 2 Corinthians
10:5). There is an authentic subjection and obedience (Acts
26:19). There is an "intervention and supervention" (Barth) from

above, an apriority that cannot be denied; but this is another sort
of "other" than is usually meant by "external authority."

We can, in fear of rationalism and intellectual arrogance, refuse to take account of *how* the gospel takes hold of a human
life. But this is a treacherous route. Something happens in revelation that is totally different from the way the authorities on earth
coerce people into servile obedience. And the difference begins
with the *content* of that which is "over against" us. Authority
may be asserted in the mere identity of the speaker: "I am the
Lord." But when he commands, he reveals what is truly good:
"He has showed you, O man, what is good; and what does the
Lord require of you, but to do justice, and to love kindness, and
to walk humbly with your God" (Micah 6:8). This "classic catechism of the prophetic ethos" has no trace of arbitrary authoritarianism; it is rather a clear marking of the route for life's journey.
What comes to us "over against" us does take the form of command, and sometimes of many demands (Luke 12:48). It comes
as an address from the Lord (Luke 6:46). But the demands and
the address have this in common, that none of them asks for
blind obedience.

Our task, in the light of the unique sort of "over against" us
that we find in the Bible, is to let the discussions about faith and
authority lead us into the nature of faith. And to do this, we must
not get caught up in an emotional reaction against such phrases
as "believing on authority." Everything depends on the character
of the authority and the character of believing.

No one has focussed the problem of the sacrifice of intellect
more sharply than Wolfhart Pannenberg. He has concentrated on
several concepts of authority that used to prevail, but sees all of
them as unacceptable. The authority of Holy Scripture, as it was
accepted in the church as a way to cut off all objections to faith,
gets his special attention. During the last few centuries, we have
experienced a crisis in the principle of biblical authority. Once,
the believer simply accepted the authority of the Bible with no
heed to what secular sciences had to say about matters in the
Scriptures. As long as scientists were willing to affirm the Bible
and the teachings of the church, crisis was averted. But as the
sciences developed a wall was gradually erected between them,
as secular specialties, and sacred theology. From the side of
science critical questions were put to theology which, in turn,
relied on special revelation as a distinct and decisive authority.

For Pannenberg, this protective use of authority has brought about a "crisis of fundamentals" for modern evangelical theology. By concentrating on the Bible as the source and norm of truth, theology lost its broad perspective of universal truth. Theology landed in a ghetto where it closed itself to the results of other sciences. It worked with its supernatural knowledge, and found itself unable to defend it against the arguments from natural knowledge. This posture was given legitimacy by the absolute authority of the Holy Scriptures; but historical and critical research made the stance clearly problematical, by demonstrating that it is not possible to assume the unity and harmony of Scripture. If the unity and harmony of the Bible is not assumed, one vital ingredient of its claim to authority has been sheared off. No longer is it possible to posit a special place for supernatural knowledge, a place where natural knowledge cannot stake any claims for itself. As a result, Protestant theology finds itself in an entirely new situation, with which it must come to terms.

First on the agenda, says Pannenberg, is the long tradition of scriptural authority, held as an unproblematic assumption and seen as an isolated guarantee of truth. Here we have belief in revelation on the basis of authority, a belief in the other world as a form of obedience. It is a *blind* faith, a *blind* trust, a sacrifice of the intellect that bids us ignore our ordinary ways of seeing and hearing and thereby loses its touch with all that we come to know by natural means.

Pannenberg is deeply struck by the dangers of a faith rooted in authority. He mistrusts Bultmann's definition of faith as obedience. He probably agrees with Metz's accusation that the church and its theology have "repulsed and betrayed" the inheritance offered by man's movement into emancipation. Once all of society and spirituality was stamped by authority; but now, says Pannenberg, we must ask whether the very roots of our Christian experience of God are not cut off from the old authoritarian structure. He talks, in this connection, of a program of "de-positivizing" Christianity. And he wants to apply this to the authoritarian traits in the Old and New Testaments as well as of the Christian tradition. For authoritarianism rules out our own judgment by giving priority to hearing over seeing, and this brings us, not to a real insight nor to an authentic persuasion, but only to subjection to an alien authority.

Pannenberg faults the Reformation for "positivistic" thinking in its identification of human proclamation with the Word of God. With Luther as his prime example, he labels the unity of human proclamation and divine word as one with "all authoritarian forms of tradition." Both Luther and Calvin opposed the authoritative structure of the church, but they failed to see the full implications of their own position. As a result they were locked in the circle of authoritarianism.

We confront a very critical issue here, if only because the reformers did in fact engage themselves with the function of humanity *within* the divine "over againstness" of revelation. They did not, therefore, dismiss all the "authority structures" in the Old and New Testaments as if they were obsolete; rather the reformers saw them as essential to the church and faith all along the route of history. When they reflected on the human medium of revelation, they were busy with the same basic issue that later came up as the cultural conditionedness of revelation, or as Barth put it, the "worldliness" of revelation. The point is that revelation does not fall from heaven untouched by human hands, but is mediated through men who performed a definite function in it.

Their awareness of man's function in revelation led the reformers to their own view of authority. The authority of the Bible is mediated through men; and sensitivity to this fact did not tempt the reformers to return to authoritarian structures such as those they had rejected in the Roman Catholic form. They accepted the consequences of the "worldliness" of revelation, and included it in their respect for its authority. They saw authority as part of God's regard for our needs, as "when from among men he takes some to serve as his ambassadors in the world, to be interpreters of his secret will and, in short, to represent his person" (Calvin, *Institutes*, IV/III/1).

Calvin was acutely aware of the dangers of a *simple* identification of human with divine authority, and he refused to invest human beings with an authority they could wield on their own, as if it were somehow their private property. He recalled the profanity that Stephen warned about (Acts 7:48, where Stephen reminded his listeners that the Holy One cannot be contained in temples made by human hands). But, in that very regard, Calvin could say that Xerxes acted "rashly" when he destroyed the Greek temples on the grounds that the gods, "who ought to have free access to all things," could not be shut up "within walls and roofs." For Calvin, Xerxes betrayed a failure to see the "worldliness" of revelation or the human accomplices in it. "As if it were not in God's power somehow to come down to us, in order to be near us." Were God to speak from heaven, we would be confounded by his splendor. But "when a puny man risen from the dust speaks in God's name," we show ourselves teachable if we listen. Calvin is trying to come to terms with the phenomenon of divine treasures within earthen vessels. It is not strange that Barth was so impressed with this motif that he built his whole homiletic around it.

In this way, the human factor is enlisted in the service of the gospel, which alone has authority. The service of man does not create an unambiguous identification of the human with the divine. Pannenberg has no reason for complaint at this point. The tension that lies in the task of holding the Word of God intact is present especially in the human proclamation of the Word. Paul lived in this tension, and if it is not allowable in Paul, "it is certainly not allowable today" (Calvin). But still the authentic gospel — along with its authority — comes through. The Galatians received Paul at first as an angel of God, as Jesus Christ even, and were pleased to do so. They changed their minds, though, and prompted Paul to ask: "What has become of the satisfaction you felt" (Galatians 4:15)? In 2 Corinthians 5:20, too, we meet that same profound association: "God making his appeal through us." It is not "as if" God were speaking through Paul; rather, it is that human Paul was being made a servant of reconciliation. For the apostle this was basic, though not self-evident, which is why he expressed thanks when people like the Thessalonians received his word as the Word of God (1 Thessalonians 2:13).

G. Bornkamm speaks (with reference to 2 Corinthians 5) of an officially authoritative character within proclamation. But he means something different from that bristling authoritarianism that one always finds irritating. Human proclamation is not that of an apostolate in glory. It is more a matter of being in the service of a calling, and so quite the opposite of an impressive, self-styled authority in a formal sense. This authority enlists men as witnesses, it summons them to "open-eyed" obedience, and is experienced as blessing and liberation.

Anyone who proclaims the gospel as though he were waving a scepter of office, deluded with official importance, might remember that a vain trumpeter on a pulpit is no closer to the kingdom of God than is a knicknack on a shelf (Gunning). Who would not be suspicious of authoritarianism when men pretend to carry authority in vestments? Indeed, to chuck this kind of authoritarian pretense is the *sine qua non* of the Reformation principle. But this, too, is why it is sad to see an anti-authoritarian reaction lead to a critique of the Reformation on this score; it was the reformers' business to liberate the gospel authority from all pretentious authoritarianism. They did this, but not by way of Pannenberg's "de-positivizing" of revelation. Rather, they brought a new view of a positivity which appeared in "worldly" form, and with which men can converse only in "fear and trembling."

The mystery appears in these contours, and the way to recognize its authority is to accept it within its human mediation, full of tensions and even of dangers. Bonhoeffer, as suspicious of authoritarianism as any theologian of our time, was dealing with the human dimensions of the Word as it comes to us when he said: "I listen to another person, a mere man, preach the gospel; he reaches the sacrament to me, and he says, 'You are forgiven.' " This is the secret of the authority that Metz recognizes when he, while spurning authoritarianism in the shape of fumbling formulas, pleads for the positivity and unavoidableness of the Word that comes "over against" us, really confronting us within the world, but with a power that blesses, that liberates even as it limits us.

Pannenberg's "de-positivizing" of revelation is close to the heart of the matter, as he sees it. This comes out in the discussion he has with Barth in his *Wissenschaftstheorie und Theologie* of 1973. In the chapter on "The Positivity of Revelation in Karl Barth" he attacks the isolation of theology that takes place when we set its contents outside the sphere where they might be verified. Theology, he contends, is mistaken when it rejects the postulate of verifiability. In Barth, this happens by construing faith as a "gamble of wholly unsecured obedience." Pannenberg thinks that one cannot say anything meaningful about the truth or falseness of such a gamble. He notes, interestingly enough, that Barth later rejected the notion of faith as a gamble: "faith is definitely no such venture as that which Satan, for instance, suggested to the Lord on the pinnacle of the temple (Luke 4:9-12). It is, instead, a sober as well as a brave appropriation of a firm and certain promise" (K. Barth, *Evangelical Theology: An Introduction*, E.T. 1963, p. 102). Even so, the risk of faith does not mean putting up with uncertainty and absence of security; it does mean that faith is not made secure by outside agencies. But Pannenberg sees in the phrase nothing but an irrational and uncertain risk, a gamble, a dangerous experiment, a leap. And this, he contends, is an unacceptable alternative to subjectivism; far more likely, it is the extreme form of subjectivism.

So, Barth is now accused not of objectivism (as by Brunner) but of subjectivism. The reason is that he proceeds from revelation, *positing* it in an act of "irrational subjectivity," an act of "subjective arbitrariness." He makes of faith an "arbitrary gamble" or a "self-projection" of one's own subjectivity. These labels all point to what theology ought not and cannot do, namely set itself loose from the demands of logic. If one begins with the apriority of revelation one can only be involved in a "rootless postulation of theological consciousness." We cannot rest with this "naked existentialistic certainty that allows no ground or argument to support it." There must be a connection that we can discern between faith and human experience, a connection that can verify faith. What we believe must not hang in the air; what we need is faith that has connections with the real world, with *present* experience (*ibid.*, p. 348). If faith has no such connections, it is indeed a gamble, a leap from and into the revelation which we ourselves postulate.

From this we can understand Pannenberg's interest in the anthropological question (cf. *What Is Man?* E.T. 1970). He wants to lead faith out of its ghetto and theology out of its isolation. If they are not brought off their island, they will become defenseless, subjective feelings that cannot meet their responsibility to the world. This leads to the question of whether there is in fact a point of contact between faith and our experienced world. In the old rationalist apologetic, theologians tried to demonstrate God's existence from evidences within the world. It was assumed that knowledge of God could be reached by the natural light of reason, by arguing from abstract notions without getting involved in real man and his experience. This drew limits around the knowledge of God reached by argument; the God so demonstrated looked like an abstraction, a first cause and a first mover. Knowledge, so gained, was naturally inadequate and incomplete, and needed the complement of the knowledge of God as revealed in Jesus Christ. But it did have some significance as an answer to atheism and agnosticism.

· In this older apologetics there is certainly no place for the nineteenth-century notion, crystallized in Gottschick's aphorism: "Without Christ I would be an atheist." A Christocentric view like this has no place for the abstractions of natural theology, for a knowledge of God as "the unconditional" (Tillich) or the "first cause" or "absolute being." Obviously, this Christocentric thinking could have no interest in Pannenberg's "Reality that determines everything." Such a concept could shed no more light than any of the other God-concepts that have arisen from natural theology. Yet the phrase is very important in Pannenberg's thought, precisely as the key to the "scientific rationality of theology" (*ibid.*, p. 335).

Pannenberg's characterization of God as the "Reality that determines everything" does not, of course, stand by itself. Nor is it the conclusion of an argument in the spirit of classic natural theology. Rather, it is linked to man's experience of existence within this world. The focus is not on the abstraction called "existence" or "meaning" of things as the starting point for an argument for God. The focus is on man himself, his questioning nature, his realm of experience with its limits and boundaries. Here we meet the problem of the bridge between revelation and experience, and here lies the distinction between Pannenberg's concern and that of the points of view that begin with the *fact* of revelation, the "God has spoken" syndrome. Pannenberg sees everything concentrated on "the problem of God" and he is sure that theology has often brought confusion into the problem. We cannot, he admits, extract the answer out of the problem; if we did, revelation would be no more than the echo of the human question. Tillich saw this, even though he began theology by considering the human question: "the existential question is not the source for the revelatory answer" (*Systematic Theology*, II, 1957, p. 13). On the other hand, revelation would have no point "if there is no question to which it is the answer." Revelation's meaning and significance must come from its response to the problem of human experience.

Pannenberg is on this same track. The answer prevails over the question, but without making the questioning of human existence less important. On the face of it, there is nothing remarkable about bringing faith within the dialogue of human questions and divine answers. We meet the same dynamic in the Bible almost constantly; man's relationship with God is one of seeking and asking and finding. We see Paul, for instance, noting the altar to the unknown god in Athens, preaching *the* unknown God as the answer to the Greeks' question. We know the history of debate as to what Paul was really doing here, whether he was really assuming a point of contact between the question of the Greeks and the answer of revelation. After all, Paul does end his speech with a summons to conversion. Still, Paul's words are not trivial gimmickry, neither here nor in his references to the pagan poets and their reflections on man. In any case, it is clear that revelation does not fall into an empty space, but into a space filled with human searching. To call attention to this is useful, if only to say that Pannenberg's concentration on the human question is not a capitulation to anthropology, as though he were reducing theology to a study of man.

Scripture gives account of the human quest, but what is striking is that it shows that the question reveals where the deepest initiative lies. Zacchaeus' quest, for instance, ends with Zacchaeus not finding, but being found (Luke 19:10). This is what the Reformation stressed. Moreover, the apriority of revelation is manifest as taking precedence over man's seeking and asking. "I was ready to be sought by those who did not ask for me; I was ready to be found by those who did not seek me" (Isaiah 65:1). Paul, we may recall, says that Isaiah *dared* to say this (Romans 10:20). But what Isaiah says about being ready to be found does not negate the importance of seeking. The Psalms speak of a time when God will let himself be found, and then, when he is close at hand, he incites us to look for him: "Thou hast said, 'Seek ye my face.' My heart says to thee, 'Thy face, Lord, do I seek.' Hide not thy face from me" (Psalm 27:8,9).

When Pannenberg speaks of the "questioningness" *(Fraglichkeit)* of man, he means to say that man's very nature is to question, a fact that has to have large importance for theology. He is doing a lot more than writing comments on such words as: "Seek and you shall find" (Matthew 7:7). He asks, rather, whether the questioning nature of man is so deep that it must, if man is to be man, go without an answer. Is it possible that we must opt for nihilism: man doomed to question but never to have an answer? Pannenberg rejects the nihilist conclusion. To ask implies the anticipation of an answer. Asking implies that one expects to receive the answer. Analysis of the human situation suggests "an openness to the world," an eccentricity in the form of an orientation toward God, and God as Person at that. This is denied by many, to be sure, but on the other hand, "as a question it is also always open to the reality it seeks as something different from itself and before which it stands to be tested" (*Basic Questions in Theology*, E.T. 1971, II, p. 224).

One might ask whether the availability of an answer is really implicit in the question-asking, or whether the confidence that there is an answer stems from a prior faith that the answer has been given. But Pannenberg employs the question-answer correlation for apologetic purposes. He wants to show that the answer corresponds to the question, that it does not confront man as an erratic and alien word that falls into his experience from the outside. He wants to show that the answer is woven into our experience of existence in a way that verifies the truth of faith.

At this point, man's tendency to focus on the future gets theological significance; it becomes the starting point for dialogue on the meaning-horizon of life. This explains Pannenberg's interest in Ernst Bloch and his concern for the openness and the power of the future. Bloch does not draw the same conclusions that Pannenberg does from man's openness to the future. Pannenberg himself admits that his interpretation of the power of the future as being God's future is "the most difficult problem" (*ibid.*, p. 224). Still, he does not hesitate to take the step, and to contend that there is verification for Christian faith's answer to the question that is implied in existence. The truth is verified; but it is not verified *by* human existence, rather *in* it. For now existence is recognized as a "witness to the truth of revelation" (*ibid.*, p. 209). At least it is clear that Pannenberg is not dealing with a message that is basically alien to man's life, and that can come to him only in an authoritarian demand for belief.

We see here the contours of a dynamic apologetic theology against the background of an anthropological analysis of the "meaning experience" in human existence. Similar motifs are present in current theology elsewhere, and wherever they are present they focus on the same correlation between the questioning of human existence and the answer of faith. I have the impression, however, that there are distinct variations, as, for instance, between Pannenberg and Moltmann and between Pannenberg and Schillebeeckx; and the differences are related to Pannenberg's radical desire to "de-positivize" the theology of revelation.

Pannenberg criticizes all kerygmatic theology that works out of an *a priori* and "that permits no questioning of the truth of the kerygma itself" (*ibid.*, p. 66). The longer theology continues in this train, "the greater will be the devastation it will meet when it awakens from its kerygmatic dream." We must be interested, then, in how Pannenberg hopes to avoid the devastation. We get a clear hint from his view of how the Christian religion is related to other religions. He again rejects the *a priori* approach of revelational theology which looks at all other religions "as if seen through Christian glasses" (*ibid.*, p. 117). And he proposes instead an unbiased analysis of the history of religions, without a theological "boasting about the claim of a revelatory word . . ." (*ibid.*, p. 68).

Should we ask whether Pannenberg manages to get beyond Troeltsch's relativism, we would have to say that, in spite of his enormous admiration of Troeltsch's work, he intends not to be relativistic. He seeks to avoid relativism by way of what he calls "a preliminary anthropology of religious experience" (*ibid.*, pp. 77f.). When we deal with the question of truth, it becomes clear that we cannot get our bearings from the "feel for reality" that is present in the world's religions. To move from a "feel for reality" to the truth about reality would be to put all religions on the same level, to say nothing of making a logical *faux pas*. Not even the orientation of man toward the transcendent is a proof for the reality of the transcendent. The proof can only be found if anthropology should demonstrate that "the idea of God or — to put it impersonally — of a mysterious ground of all reality transcending one's own and all other finite existence, is so implied in the movement of human existence beyond everything finite that man finds himself referred to as this transcendent mystery" (*ibid.*, p. 102).

This quotation is long, but it is decisive for Pannenberg's whole vision as it focusses on the conviction that God is implicit within human experience of existence. The eccentric character of human nature is not a fact that witnesses to nothing beyond itself. It points, as a "transcending movement of its existence," to the reality of the divine mystery. Pannenberg uses in this connection a word that we find very often in Barth: event (*Widerfahrnis*). But Pannenberg is not thinking of a leap into revelation. Rather, this event by which "the gods or god prove their reality" (*ibid.*, p. 104) leads us back into the history of religion. And if one asks how the truth (in the "reality-reference") can be found, the answer has to do with Christian perspective and the differences between religions in terms of Israel and its special experience with God. Once again, however, he does not mean to go back to "some sort of construction developed from the standpoint of Christian dogmatics" (ibid., p. 117), but rather "in working with an unprejudiced openness to create space in the history of religions for the appearing of the divine mystery" (ibid.).

It appears that a decision is made somewhere along the line. For the possibility of the intervention of a definitive power cannot be ruled out, on methodological grounds, even in the "study of non-Christian religions" (ibid., p. 116). One cannot suppress the question whether, in the unprejudiced interest in the total development of religions, a kind of apriority is injected. For is there not a decision one makes with respect to the Christian understanding of God, a decision that is not all that different from that which Pannenberg criticizes in others, a decision concerning an "intellectually nonobligatory, merely subjectively accepted supernaturalistic standpoint" (ibid., p. 69)? Pannenberg thinks his own view is nonetheless different from the others, and the difference lies in his intense analysis of the religious experience. The notion of God as "the reality that determines everything" must be kept in touch with our experience of the reality of the world and man. If this is done, then we can say that "the process demonstrates itself as a form of the ontological argument for God's existence, considered as the self-demonstration of God."

In his small book on anthropology, he found implicit aspects of human experience that were important for theology. This was particularly evident in man's hope for something beyond death. Not only does man feel a constraint to think beyond the world to the God who is over against us (which could be an illusion, after all), but the reality of God lies implicitly within the experience of life. And in this, Pannenberg finds a point of contact with the Christian hope of resurrection. "For the Christian, the resurrection of the dead is much more than a mere imaging of human longings." And it certainly is more than a "merely unspecified future." But here we observe unmistakable signs of an *a priori* creeping into Pannenberg's thought, and his own criticism of revelational theology now is seen in an odd light. As he judges Barth to have finished off Feuerbach's critique of religion too easily, we can ask whether he does not have the same problem on his hands in his own view of the correlation between human experience of existence and the reality of God. Indeed, is the problem not even more intense?

Pannenberg takes any occasion he can to attack the theological ghetto and the sacrifice of intellect. (In this respect he continues a valuable tradition in theology.) So we are not surprised to find that he has enormous interest in the relationship between theology and the other sciences. Theology and science parted ways, as he sees it, because of the crisis of authority. The result has been that theology has tended to be on its own, off by itself, with its special, supernatural revelation, and has lost contact with the natural knowledge that we gain through other sciences.

When theology is cut off from other sources of knowledge, a dualism is created that can be acceptable to no one for long. The impression is given that natural sciences give us the authentic reality, while theology speaks of "truth" that can be recognized only by faith. So theology, while not anti-reason, surely seems to be para-reason. How, then, can there be any communication?

Moltmann used the phrase "cool schism" to characterize the relationship between theology and other sciences (J. Moltmann, *Hope and Planning*, E.T. 1971, p. 201). Moltmann would like to see the schism healed, but not by setting limits to science by means of Bible texts that happen, incidentally, to deal with natural reality. (The classic example would be the use of Judges 10 to limit the work of Galileo.) He wants rather to break through the stalemate in which conflict is stifled, where theology and the other sciences have no word for each other — as is the case, in his view, with the theology of Barth and Bultmann. Moltmann considers it urgent to break the silence between theology and the sciences, not so much because there are particular conclusions of one that need correction by the other, but because the modern developments in science have brought us all to an unprecedented responsibility for the whole world. He is concerned about the goals of science and with their breathtaking successes, some of which endanger the very existence of mankind.

Now anyone who does theology must deal in some way with the relationship of his study to that of other sciences. When Karl Barth published his doctrine of creation in 1945 (*CD* III/1), he said he expected to be asked why he had "not tackled the obvious scientific question posed in this context." And so he answered: "It was my original belief that this would be necessary, but I later saw there can be no scientific problems, objections, or aids in relation to what Holy Scripture and the Christian Church understand by the divine work of creation" (CD III/1, Preface ix). He wanted to fasten his attention to the witness of Scripture without getting engulfed in dilettantism, as he would have had he gone the other route. Perhaps he was thinking of the complicated arguments that seduced Bavinck when he wrote his doctrine of creation. In any case, we can understand what Barth meant by avoiding dilettantism. He wanted to stick to his own last, doing his theological work, and leave "free scope for natural science beyond what theology describes as the work of the creator" (ibid., p. x).

Moltmann and Pannenberg see in this only a continuation of the "cool schism." Pannenberg, while he feels for Moltmann's concern for the purpose and threats of science, is mostly concerned with the issue of apologetics. Theology must venture out of its isolation and meet the substantial challenges of the sciences, even in those instances where they have had the pretensions of liberating reasonable men from faith in God. He does not want theology to flee into an unreachable island where it can be safe from all criticism. Its confession of God as the Creator will be empty as long as "it cannot be claimed with good reason that nature, as it is viewed by natural science, has something to do with this God." For this reason alone, we must seek out a "common ground" for the problematics of natural science and theology.

Pannenberg, for this reason, involves himself conscientiously with the work of current natural science; and he finds this common ground indicated by natural science itself, for the natural sciences have given up the old deterministic world-view, with its ironclad laws, and have opened themselves to the contingencies of natural occurrences. This does not reintroduce the possibility of a Deus ex machina which Bonhoeffer inveighed against, a notion that only provides "apparent solution of insoluble problems" (Letters and Papers from Prison, E.T. 1971, p. 281). But it does mean that Pannenberg works on the hypothesis that modern natural sciences are not incompatible with faith in God.

The connection between contingency and constancy in natural events is best illuminated by way of God's action. For God's actions display these aspects too, since only God remains the same within the contingent succession of events. Pannenberg's remarks take on the look of a new proof for God's existence when he concludes that "the reestablishment of the connections between events through an ever renewed backward reach from later events into earlier events bears the mark of a personal power." Along this way, Pannenberg tries to lead theology out of its ghetto and to heal the schism.

We should note how the necessary relationship between faith and reason leads him to his attack on the concept of faith that demands a sacrifice of the intellect. If a man on the way to faith is asked to sacrifice his intellect for the sake of faith, he has nothing left to do but make a *decision* to submit himself to the authority of revelation. This would not be an act motivated by an understanding of the issues, but an unreasoned choice made in the air. There is no experience of being convinced, no being seized by an insight, no act of recognition. A man believes and that is all, which is to say he gets the word and agrees with it.

There will be no change in this as long as believing is explained simply as a work of the Holy Spirit who gives man faith as a gift. Pannenberg rejects the familiar thesis that the truth of faith cannot be recognized by reason but only is given by illumination through the Holy Spirit. He thinks that this view seduces our attention away from what a man does when he believes, since the focus is entirely on the transcendent origin of faith. Faith then becomes a mechanical and miraculous link between man and revelation, with the result that revelation itself loses its revealing function. He is suspicious when people refer to the Holy Spirit as a mysterious power which validates everything. In this way, the Spirit takes over where Christian proclamation fails, and becomes "a kind of supernatural key to a Christian message which has meanwhile become incomprehensible" (*The Apostles' Creed in the Light of Today's Questions*, E.T. 1972, p. 133). When this happens, everything seems to be explained. We compensate for our inability to understand by injecting the miracle of the Spirit. And so the "incomprehensible, indeed even the absurd, is nevertheless to be legitimated" (*ibid.*, p. 130).

Pannenberg thinks this tendency to use the Spirit to validate what we do not understand is really a modern phenomenon. Earlier, people were expected to be convinced of Christian truth by its contents. Put on the defensive, however, later theologians made a virtue of their inadequacy by appealing to the Spirit, who offered a transcendent protection against all the problems raised by "the critical thought of modernity." Christian faith was thus immunized against critique, so Christian thinkers no longer needed to take criticism seriously. A priori, faith was set transcendently above all human criticism. Certainty was assured — it was a gift of the Spirit independent of any and all human efforts to show that what we are certain of is plausible.

This is what Pannenberg calls "Spirit-subjectivity." It is of a piece, he thinks, with the enthusiasm of the anabaptists and their pietistic heirs. It should be said that Pannenberg does not think that the Spirit's work of illumination is superfluous. It is a rather "banal fact" that not everyone recognizes the connection between faith and understanding, and, further, that people can blind themselves to reality; for these the work of the Spirit is needed. But the Spirit moves with the Word. When these are separated, the believer loses his contact with human experience, and all he can do is counter every No with a dogmatic Yes.

We can grasp his criticism of Gollwitzer in this light. Gollwitzer talks about revelation as having the "power of self-attestation" and as being an "event." But Pannenberg sees this "event" as happening out in the stratosphere. The Christian, experiencing it, cannot defend its validity; "all he can do is protest and witness." Christianity loses its missionary vitality this way, because in it faith is given by a power from above that disregards all the human components. Moreover, it demands that the believer set his intellect aside, sacrificing it on the altar of transcendence. The connection between revelation and human experience is sheared. Revelation is accepted as an alien truth that need not be understood to be believed. The question of whether what we believe is really true can be answered only by pointing to the miracle of the Spirit. To this, Pannenberg answers: no, the question of truth can be answered only in reference to the content of what is believed (Basic Questions in Theology, II, p. 35).

At this point, we are back to a question we discussed earlier: If faith is related to history, must we know what actually happened (in a fides historica plus the notitia historica — that is, by a belief that a certain thing, e.g., the resurrection, actually happened, combined with evidences from history) if faith is not to "hang in the air"? Trying to "know" should not be replaced with "the privilege of Christian proclamation" and its peculiar securities. Replacing rational knowledge with believing the proclamation was appropriate for an "exclusively revelational theology."

But this theology has reached a dead end, as it had to. For if we shut God out of the world and human experience, the only outcome must be the abandonment of the idea of God. This is the explanation for Robinson's *Honest to God* and the American "God is dead" movement. They are the inheritance of Barth and Bultmann. So, says Pannenberg, we must accept the task of verification as a mandate for theology. Only thus can theology escape its ghetto and enter the wide world of history.

Anyone who ignores the task of verification is doomed to walk an isolated — be it supernatural — way to revelation. He must first accept revelation in blind faith and only then move on to a second phase of faith in which understanding of the faith is sought *(Fides quaerit intellectum)*. But the schism remains intact, for the origin of faith is explained as a miracle "from above," and this means that what one believes is beyond dialogue, beyond communication, because it is beyond reason.

As we reflect on Pannenberg's analysis of the two phases, we should be aware that the problem he raises has been thought about before. I recall meeting with a committee at Vatican II where we discussed motivations for believing in connection with genuinely human insight into truth. The Roman Catholic thinker P. Rousselot, who wrote a book called *The Eyes of Faith (Les yeux de la foi*, 1910), came in for a lot of attention. Rousselot was concerned with the nature of believing within the total context of human existence; he, like Pannenberg, wanted to avoid separating faith into two phases. He saw the Roman Catholic system as an example: first one submits to the revelation handed him by the church and then one goes on to seek an understanding of his faith.

Obviously, we must take Pannenberg's rejection of the "two phases" seriously. And yet, it seems clear that his view of faith also divides faith experience into two periods. In his view, faith married to reason comes first; thereafter comes faith as trust. The evidence of history comes first. Faith (trust) comes second. He must be aware of this, for he says that, while there is a logical sequence, there need not be a psychological one. Trust always reaches out for a basis for itself. The act of trust and the act of searching for a ground for that trust cannot be isolated from each other — even though they can be distinguished from each other. "In the psychological enactment of faith, both can be taken up in the same act" *(op. cit.,* p. 33).

The remarkable thing in this synthesis is that Pannenberg started out by insisting that one must "know" historically, otherwise faith is really isolated from history. But then he goes on to say that the believer himself need not search out the basis for "knowing" the facts (as a ground for his trust), since that search is the business of theology. But this is where the problem lies. For, according to Pannenberg, it is the certainty that one's trust is well placed that is at stake. And this certainty is lacking as long as one does not have the historical evidence.

It was not his intention to underscore the connection between faith and the historical event, and to let it go at that. If this were all there was to it, his point about the difference between a logical and temporal distinction in the act of faith would be of no relevance. He may say, as he does, that the individual believer "can trust on the assumption that things are in order with respect to the ground of his trust" (*ibid.*, p. 33). But this does not help him deal with the *evidence* that Pannenberg considers so important. It is hard to see how Pannenberg can avoid a time distinction, by which a person becomes dependent on historical research even though not on the church.

The reformers were not strangers to Pannenberg's problem. They also thought about the nature of faith and they, too, used various words to get at it: words like *notitia, assensus,* and *fiducia.* Interestingly, they never thought it necessary to set these off into different time periods of Christian experience. Calvin used the word *cognitio,* but did not reduce faith to intellectual knowledge with it because he insisted that this *cognitio* was directed to "the benevolence of God toward us" and was more an affair of the heart than of the head. They were not offended either by words like *notitia* and *assensus.* Intuitively, they refused to isolate aspects of faith from one another. "How could it be *fiducia* without at the same time, and because it is *fiducia,* being *notitia* and *assensus* too?" (Barth, *CD* I/1, p. 269). The reformers never talked as if one first accepted and agreed to something and thereafter believed and trusted.

Undeniably, the reformers' rejection of the time distinction between phases of faith was of a piece with their understanding of the authority of the Word. Pannenberg, however, is bothered by the tendency to make the church the same sort of authority, and considers it practically impossible for people to work with authority in this way. For him, everything comes down to the truth question, and therefore to the question of whether the truth is to be verified. To direct men to the message, he says, is useless, because the question is whether that message is true. If we are not convinced of the truth, all we can do is simply *decide* to believe, and then the act of decision becomes the basis for the structure of faith. So, we are back with what Pannenberg fears most: reduction of faith to decision, to an act of intellectual suicide, to spirit-subjectivism — and to the rupture of contact between faith and the truth that meets us within history and persuades us of itself there. For this reason he wants to de-positivize faith.

Pannenberg is calling for a rerouting of theology along an avenue different from that on which it has been travelling for the last fifty years. He misses, in the last half-century, the theological courage it takes to do theology on Mars Hill. He does not want rationalism, not Barth's "all-powerful logic." But he does want respect for humanness and reasonableness instead of irrationalism and monologue.

We might wonder whether this apologetic would actually be effective in dialogue with modern atheism. The question one would face is to what extent his analysis of the human condition is convincing, and then whether it would in fact open the listener to the meaningfulness of the Christian religion and the perspectives of the Christian future. Even if old caricatures and misunderstandings are cleared away, if Christianity's genuine concern for the world in all its terrifying aspects were credible, and were not emasculated by escapism and quietism, even then the theological problems would still face those who took the dialogue and the convictions of the participants seriously.

The question about dialogue is whether the "question-asking nature" of man does lead to the "Reality that determines everything." Does the nature of man imply the "Reality" beyond? Is the implication clear and convincing? Indeed, would it stay on the agenda as the most important question? Berdyaev once said: "The problem of reconciling the existence of a powerful and good God with the evil and pain of the world — this is the single serious argument of atheism." Berdyaev puts his finger on what a great number of people have confessed. "I know that I am set within a simply hopeless situation. I cannot believe that the world we observe is the result of accident and yet I cannot consider that everything is the product of purpose" (Darwin, in 1860).

Questions like this go deeper than many that arise in modern anthropology, or that come up in the quest for a new empirical theology based on inductive reasoning — or, in other words, building from the ground of fact up to transcendence. The deeper question seems to plague Moltmann more than it does Pannenberg. It is not just the argument of atheism; it wells up in the bosom of the church. And while theodicy may be a futile undertaking, and while the problem of how to justify man (anthropodicy) seems more fitting than that of how to justify God, the deep problem still haunts us. We need not resort to an "I believe because it is absurd," as though our dilemma can turn absurdity into a virtue. Nor need we commit intellectual suicide. Nor need we resort to an authoritarianism that only suppresses problems rather than solves them. And certainly we should not anticipate a kind of theoretical explanation that will unexpectedly throw a revealing light on everything to clear up all that was problematic. This is surely not going to happen by means of a metaphysical theology, no matter what form it might take.

"The Reality that determines everything" is not a promising concept for solving all problems. More likely, the problem of evil and the question of theodicy will be the more pressing as one takes such a God concept seriously. Everything depends on the two words "determines" and "everything." For this reason alone the quest for reasonable faith will have to find another avenue. And whatever route we follow, we will have to keep the *content* of the gospel within the quest; if we abstract the quest for reasonableness from the content of faith we will always end up with bleak abstractions of a religious metaphysic that multiplies rather than solves questions.

One may hope that theology will indeed choose to take the route in which the content of faith is always part of the assumptions, and that it will plow through in spite of caricatures and misunderstandings. I am talking of an apologetic that does not isolate itself from the message it intends to make credible. I am talking about an apologetic that seeks its basic resources within the gospel itself (Colossians 4:6). Theology has no dispensation from the toughest questions. And if it makes its appeals to empirical evidence and the inductive methodology, if it tries to move from the bottom upward, its users are likely to be awakened from their dream and find themselves without perspective. For on waking up, they will find that the problems have not gone away. In short, they will experience what Pannenberg feared for the kerygmatic theologians.

I do not mean to suggest that the discussions about transcendence and immanence are not useful. Nor do I mean to say that anthropological analysis has no point. We see today an intense interest in these questions among both Protestants and Catholics, in what H. Bouillard called a "symbiosis between Christian faith and human experience." But everything is lost in all this if the question of faith is turned into an abstract existentialist question that is not really being asked by people in concrete human experience. The danger is real that the "symbiosis" could turn God into an abstraction, with no answer at all for actual questions confronting real believing people who are trying to understand the meaning of the questions in the light of the gospel. Unless we keep these questions at the fore of our concern, all our reflections about "reasonableness" will evaporate, no matter how subtle our analysis may be. Within the horizon of the actual and authentic questions it may be possible for the tradition of the church and its theology to shed critical light on life. For it will use a standard that will not demand blind obedience, but will ask us to try to understand the message of the gospel, the message that somehow keeps coming back to lead theology along exciting and surprising ways.

7

The Earthly Horizon

THE WORD "HORIZON" HAS CREPT INTO THE THEOLOGICAL JARGON of our time for very profound reasons. No one can help being impressed with the expansion of our horizons in outer space and inner consciousness, though we have yet to see whether the expansion will bring weal or woe in the end. As the horizons of reality have expanded, our certainty about the things we used to "know" has diminished. We are not as sure as we used to be. We have quadrupled our information and have become less sure of the truth.

We look back and see that what people wrote and said in earlier times was conditioned by their limitations. The time-limits of the past have to be reckoned with, too, in what the church said in the past, and even with what the Scriptures said. For the writers of the Bible, like all others, thought and wrote within the confines of their limited horizon. But there is another, very concrete matter that awareness of limited horizons raises. It is the outlook on the future, the relationship between our actual todays and our expected tomorrows, between our narrow horizons and the hope that leaps over them into the promised future.

The shocking catastrophic experiences of contemporary history give an urgent relevance to the question of the future. For theology this has meant that eschatology — the doctrine of the "last things" — has become something far more than an innocent little chapter that winds up a textbook. Current eschatological questions are not wholly out of touch with problems that the church has always wrestled with. There have always been people who were more interested in the future than in the present. People have always been fascinated with John's judgment that the world lies in evil (1 John 5:19) and that, in the last days, things are going to get much worse until the Antichrist (1 John 2:18) climaxes our evil history.

In this perspective there is at least no illusion or false optimism about the world. People who lived in anticipation of the Antichrist were not people who talked about Christianizing the world, or winning the world for Christ. Christians were summoned to withdraw from the present evil world, to remember that they had no abiding city here, and to keep their eyes fixed on the city of the future (Hebrews 13:14). Our horizon was seen in terms of what God would one day do, in his marvelous future, when he would make all things new. All sorts of personal and historical experiences played a role in shaping this attitude. But the one thing crucial to it was the expectation that our horizon would be overcome only at the end, when the Lord himself would lead us beyond it.

Another horizon-experience posed a direct antithesis to this one. God's future was seen not as a discouragement to our concern for this world, nor as a negation of all possibilities for this world. People who thought this way did not mean to underestimate evil. But they refused to capitulate to it. They refused to be quietistic in the face of it. Indeed, the presence of evil only impressed them with their responsibility for this world.

These two attitudes toward the world were given a new color by the crisis of modern times. For in our era the sense of lostness and forsakenness has become more intensified than ever. How, then, ought one to live now that it seems that ours is a time in which "offenses increase"? How ought one to live when program after program for world improvement fails? How ought we to live in a time when we have to be thankful merely for a balance of terror in the world which seems, for the present, to give some sense of security?

Is there any hope for genuine, humane life, even on short term, without a bit of chiliasm, without some sign that raises hope for a coming kingdom? (Cf. Barth: "Without at least a touch of chiliasm, there is no ethics.") C. F. von Weizsäcker, who was convinced he should impress his Göttingen students with the "sober facts with which atomic physics confronts us," asked this question: "How can we live in the atomic age?" His answer was that the strongest guarantee we had for world peace was the presence of hydrogen bombs and the possibility that they would make war unthinkable. There is something horrible in the thought that the existence of such destructive weapons is our best reason for hope. Could this really set hearts at ease? But the theological question is: What is the relevance in this of the Christian expectations for the future? How are we to bring Christian eschatology within the horizon of our daily lives?

Kuyper, back in the nineteenth century, was shocked at the enormous dangers of his own time. But this did not tempt him into an escapist apocalypticism; it led him instead to warn the church *against* world-flight. His warnings were so strong, in fact, that he was accused of secularizing Christianity. He was said to have "de-eschatologized" the faith. Oscar Cullmann, closer to our time, refused to call any lopsided expectation of the future that led people to world-denial *Christian* eschatology. Escape into the future is not eschatology, but eschaton fever.

The fever rises in apocalyptic times, times of catastrophe, crisis, wars and disasters. But emotions aroused by world troubles do not have to cause this fever. M. A. Beek, in a book about Jewish apocalyptic in the Old and New Testaments, remarked that people in those times experienced crisis in this way: they saw the flames coming from the volcanoes, and they listened for the horsemen of judgment, and they had ears peeled for the sound that would move the sun, moon, and stars from their courses, but then they would — in spite of it all — bend over their Book and give themselves in new energy to loving God and their neighbor. But most people have more trouble than the ancient Jews did coming to terms with the apocalyptic events. Even when Christians managed to get the future adjusted with the present in theory, their hearts did not always follow suit.

In the midst of estrangement and disillusionment, in the barrage of disasters, Christian theology has recently had to busy itself anew with the primary question. It is a question that goes beyond typical differences between optimists and pessimists. It zeroes in on the significance for the present of the salvation that has appeared and is confessed and preached by the church of Christ. Salvation has *appeared!* There is surely more here than a slight "touch of chiliasm," and more than an "incidental and fragmentary" infusion of Christian reality into the world.

Martin Buber had a conversation (back in 1933) with Karl Ludwig Schmidt and insisted to Schmidt that we were obviously living in an unredeemed world. We have goals, he said, but we have no means in history for achieving them; and this is true because the world has not yet been shaken open at the foundations. The Jewish philosopher echoed something of what Schalom

Ben-Chorin wrote: "The Jew knows in his heart that the world is not redeemed, and he refuses to opt for little enclaves of personal redemption in this unsaved world. The notion of a redeemed soul in the midst of an unredeemed world is essentially foreign to him."

Christian theology cannot but remember Jewish voices like these as it considers the salvation which has in fact come, perhaps in the form of a "realized eschatology," and which gives content to history even as it points to a kingdom still to come. This is not a matter of individual enclaves of personal salvation, but of a broad, worldly impact of salvation for the present and future. Albert Schweitzer discerned that *expectation* was the key to understanding New Testament eschatology, but that this expectation was never fulfilled. Cullmann tried to rescue this "consistent eschatology" by pointing to the decisive importance of the cross and resurrection of Jesus Christ for the present time, to the Victory that the salvation, once-for-all arrived, achieved — a Victory that guarantees the future. "The decisive battle of a war can be won in an early phase of the war even though the war goes on for a long time thereafter," writes Cullmann. But others saw this as an evasion; the terribly long postponement of the final victory calls that early victory into question (Fritz Buri). And one might ask whether, in view of the state of our world, the fitting time to remember is not a Victory Day, but those awful days of Europe's long stillness under the Nazi occupation.

Such questions as these haunted theology, especially as it confronted those dramatic phrases of the New Testament about everything being made new: the new creation in Christ (2 Corinthians 5:17); the new light that shines over the darkness (1 John 2:8); and the new situation created by the disarming of the powers (Colossians 2:15). The discontinuity between the present and future seems to be wiped away here. For we have not only the promise of a coming age, on the far side of our horizon, but the reality of a radical new power within our horizon. We hear of powers belonging to the future that have in fact broken into our world, the coming reality which we can already taste (Hebrews 6:5). We can taste "the kindness of the Lord" (1 Peter 2:3). "Taste"! — a word that suggests the "personal experience of salvation" (J. Behm, in G. Kittel and G. Friedrich, eds., *Theological Dictionary of the New Testament*, I, pp. 673f.).

The theology of our century is preoccupied with questions about *our* experience within *our* horizon. It is caught in the tension between the "having come" and the "not yet appeared." Theologians were nagged by this even before the advent of the Theology of Hope. How can we, in concrete instances, think about our world within the perspective of the "not yet"? What must we think about Buber's perception of the "unredeemed" state of the world, about demonization and disasters that hardly impress us as signs of a dethronement and disarming of the evil powers? These are the sorts of questions that haunt us about the state of affairs within our horizon, and force their way into every contemporary consideration of eschatology.

They are part of the single problem of our human prospects, our expectations, and our destiny. Early on in dialectical theology there was a strong protest against cultural optimism, in which people, Christians in particular, were counted on to build and spread the kingdom of God. Barth stoutly denied that the world's salvation lay in our hands, in our Christian action programs. Jesus Christ is the only way. And he is not "the keystone in the vault of human thought" and certainly not the crown of our activity. Rather, the kingdom comes straight from above, as a miracle, a gift, a new birth, as a resurrection from the dead, as an event that far exceeds our horizons. The church, therefore, can only await it in utter thankfulness and humility.

The same horizon question was on the agenda during and after the ecumenical conference at Stockholm in 1925. There a tension developed between so-called Anglo-Saxon and German Christendom. For one, the realizing of the kingdom of God *within* this world was paramount. For the other, the acts of God trespassed our horizons, intruding from a transcendent arena. One German theologian startled the conference with the statement: "Christianizing the world is impossible," and another attacked the "profane worldliness of some Americans." Those who were influenced by Rauschenbusch's "social gospel" were the special targets. For the "social gospel" saw the kingdom coming through the penetration of its power into concrete society. But its advocates heard the German critique as unproductive defeatism, a defeatism that abandoned the world within our horizon to corruption and demonization, with no hope other than that of some far-off future.

Americans themselves were acquainted with those who viewed the task of the church to be only that of calling people out of the Babel of this world. American dispensationalists were sure that the thousand-year reign of Christ would invade the world one day wholly independent of our human development and not as a product of human, not even Christian, programs of action. In contrast, others wanted to put their hands to the plow and, in the power of the gospel, go to work at renewal and transformation. They would have been sympathetic with a response Dorothee Sölle gave when Günter Gaus asked her if she believed that man was changeable: "I think that is an atheistic question. Anyone who doubts that man can be changed does not really believe in God."

After the Stockholm conference, the tensions persisted. The two sides were characterized as *evolutionistic* and *eschatological*. Later we talked in terms of *horizontalism* and *verticalism*. But the issue was the same. The former — the evolutionistic or horizontalistic — appealed to the parable of the yeast. The latter — the eschatological or verticalistic — appealed to the promise that *God* would make all things new. And the question was whether the kingdom was primarily a mandate or a promise. Almost a quarter-century later, the discussion was still at full steam.

Reinhold Niebuhr wrote a piece in 1948 that once again referred to the contrast between Anglo-Saxon and continental theology in their approaches to the kingdom of God. Karl Barth had given his famous address to the first assembly of the World Council of Churches in Amsterdam. He spoke of the world's disorder and God's plan of salvation. In one of his side remarks, Barth said he had been dismayed to discover in the preparatory papers so little awareness of the fundamental significance of that which had happened, once for all, in the cross and resurrection of Jesus Christ. He branded as nonsense the notion that we now lived in a post-Christian era. How could this be possible now that Jesus Christ is risen and is coming again? To consider this — the event of Jesus Christ — is now and always will be the prime task of Christian theology. We have, said Barth, no mandate to build a new tower of Babel, nor to light candles in a world into which *the Light* of the world has shown. He warned against "Christian Marshall Plans." He cautioned against programs that the church might devise to rescue the world. At the end of his speech he recalled Isaiah's word: "Take counsel together, but it will come to nought; speak a word, but it will not stand, for God is with us."

Niebuhr entered this situation with a critique against Barth's one-sidedness. He granted the validity of Barth's indictment of a "Christian Marshall Plan." But he thought that Barth underestimated the prophetic task of the church. He suspected "crisis theology" of reintroducing quietism into the church, and he feared that it proclaimed victory without struggle. Barth made things too easy; he encouraged flight from struggle and cultural obscurantism. Though Niebuhr had become a socialist during his pastoral period in Detroit, his objections against Barth were not motivated by Rauschenbusch's social gospel nor by an "evolutionistic" eschatology. In the social gospel, Niebuhr discerned too much American optimism, as though growth and goodness were all but inevitable; the social gospel, he had seen, was unaware of the depths of evil within the impersonal social structures. His experience in Detroit with the Ford Motor Company had impressed him with the immorality of institutional life. So his judgment of Barth was not born of optimism for life within our horizon.

Personal conversion and sanctification is not able to overcome the immorality of society. We cannot count on personal conversions to renew the structures of life. Niebuhr had criticisms of Billy Graham on this score. He did not want to abandon the world; he wanted to subject it to the power and judgment of the gospel. And this is what he found lacking in Barth's "defeatism." In his Gifford lectures (*The Nature and Destiny of Man*, 1935) he called dialectical theology to account for its failure to give any guidance as to what should be done in concrete situations. He referred to people like Barth as Protestant skeptics. And he was confirmed in his opinion after Barth's speech to the World Council.

Niebuhr's name is not mentioned in any of the volumes of Barth's *Church Dogmatics*. But we do not have to guess Barth's response to his criticism. For Barth, the significance of God's salvation for this world was not really at issue. He called for the sort of activity in the world that would get at what was most essential in the gospel: freedom and righteousness, fellowship and responsibility. Barth had no quietistic impulse. This was manifest in the struggle against the Nazi regime, in the Barmen declaration and in other decisive matters relating to it. His was not a quietism as opposed to concrete obedience. But he did want a christological analysis of authentic obedience.

We cannot grasp Barth's critical stance unless we keep in view the distorted brand of obedience that was being urged by the church. It was a time when Goebbels' propaganda sheet could publish a sermon preached by Bishop Dibelius in Potsdam. It was a time when 600 preachers joined a group of National Socialists in thanks to God, the Lord of history, for giving to Germany a leader and savior named Hitler. It was a time when national unity was called for in obedience to God's command. We ought not indict Dibelius on this score; he himself joined Niemöller in prison in 1937. But the fact that Nazi propaganda could use his sermonizing for its own ends contains a summons to make sure of what we are doing when we call for obedience in concrete situations. So, when Barth raises deep and disturbing questions about Christian action, he is not flirting with defeatism or quietism.

Barth's friend Günther Dehn wrestled with the same question when he was branded by 2000 students at Leipzig and Jena as a traitor against German honor. He had protested vigorously against Nazi tendencies, but was told to translate his Christian piety into action. Action, however, meant action *for* the National Socialists. Barth saw what was at stake in Dehn's situation. He knew that Dehn was definitely not undermining concrete obedience in favor of waiting for the eschaton. It was Barth who, in 1939, faced up to the French Protestants and asked why they had kept silence during those days — as though the church no longer had a prophetic office to fulfil. And to this question, Barth added the observation that if the Christian church had not gotten so used to silence, the catastrophe in Germany might not have happened.

The Niebuhr-Barth tension was a symptom of the sort of problem that the church faces now as well as then. It is the problem of our Christian concern for the world as we live it within our horizon — but, above all, of the grounds and motives for our concern.

The impression has often been given that Christian faith is really intolerant of a concentrated concern for *this* world. Others may be preoccupied with the concerns of the world, but Christians have a perspective of higher things. Kuyper, in his day, saw this tendency; in fact, he said that "believers have carried on throughout our whole century in a dualism over against the world and have been all too one-sidedly spiritual. . . . They have dared not grasp any higher than to rescue spiritual life within their private circles" (*Gemeene Gratie*, III, p. 10). Kuyper's protest has been echoed through the years. Not everyone who picked it up went as far as Kuyper in claiming every inch of territory on earth "pro-Rege" — for the King. But many were just as emphatic as he was in their rejection of Christian indifference for life within our horizon.

But the summons to keep faith with life within our horizon evoked a counterreaction. Now, the danger was secularization. And Barth, to some people's surprise, was criticized on this account. Zahrnt, for instance, saw even in Barth's vision of the world, which was reflected in his own life-style (his love of Mozart, for instance), a new form of being Christian; our earthly environment offered the possibility for being God's co-laborers. Humanizing of existence, building the city of man — these are things we are concerned about when we turn the theology of sin and grace into a theology of God's kingdom and substitute for the soteriological Christ a vision of Christ's Lordship over the world. Some saw Christian concern for the world as a humanizing of God's kingdom and an offense against Paul's injunction to seek those things that are above the earth (Colossians 3:2). The service of God was replaced by the service of man in the seductive summons to be faithful to the earth.

Those who suspected the call to earthly service could only be the more disturbed by the dialogues that were organized between Christians and Marxists. Earlier, most Christians assumed that the antithesis between Christianity and Marxism excluded any possibility of dialogue. Everything seemed to have been said on both sides. So when the dialogues began many interpreted them only as signs of a willingness to relativize the antithesis between atheism and Christianity, and, in view of Marxist dogma, this could only mean capitulation of the Christian faith to Marxist ideology. Besides, many saw dialogue as a fad that offered no real hope for genuine communication.

Certainly the dangers in dialogue are not imaginary. Dialogue can be a maneuver by which one side hopes to demonstrate its power. If a dialogue is meant to be more than a chance to deliver a message, or make a witness, more than a chance to speak *to* rather than *with* the partners, it can be a serious affair. This is what Pope Paul meant when he said: "The Church must be in dialogue with the world in which she lives."

Dialogue can sometimes seem unreal. Milan Machovec recalls a conference at Marienbad (in East Germany) in 1967 during which the theologians confessed that Christianity often preaches death too much and life too little, transcendence too much and immanence too little, spirituality too much and social concern too little. The Marxists responded: "Not so fast, brothers, *we* are the ones who have fallen short, *we* are the ones who have neglected the ethical, the existential, the real." And "it is we who have accented the transcendent." Machovec describes this role-reversal as comic (cf. M. Machovec, *Gottfrage und moderner Atheismus*, 1972, p. 69). But he does not mean to ridicule dialogue; what he wants is *serious* dialogue, not a dialogue of phoney tolerance. He recalls an experience with a certain printer. He had written an article in which he said that if there was to be dialogue he wanted an opponent who really would try to convert him. But the printer read this as a typing error ("Machovec is not *that* stupid"). So the sentence was printed as: "I want an opponent who will *not* try to convert me." Machovec concludes: "We do not want half-baked believers in dialogue; we want to confront real Christians." Here we have more than openness and friendliness in communication. Not a faddish conversation, but an authentic encounter — this is the way to fruitful dialogue. V. Gardavsky, in this vein, commented on Rahner's notion of anonymous Christianity by saying that a communist would not accept "the honorary title 'anonymous Christian.' "

One motive behind the dialogues is the common awareness that we all share a threatened world. But this is not the only motive. Marxists became interested in dialogue as they sensed that Christians were in fact rejecting a spirituality that ignored the the world and were rejecting the notion of a future that lured men away from concern for the present. Teilhard de Chardin played a part in this; his view of evolution flew in the face of a doctrine of original sin that led to complacency and conservatism. But there were others, Pope John XXIII, for example. Marxists listened to such men. And they noted signals of a concern for the world in which faith in the hereafter did not exclude struggle for the earth. They discerned a new kind of Christian concern that was different from the Marxist image of traditional Christendom. Now the hope for the future, far from discouraging concern for the world, became the stimulus and basis for it. So it was mutual care for this world that led to dialogue. That eschatological hope could be the basis for worldly concern flatly opposed any tendency to empty present life of genuine significance. Fretting about a balance between a more or less worldly accent, or between this-worldly or other-worldly visions, was stopped. But the new focus on earthly life did raise questions. It was a phenomenon that captured theology quite suddenly. Rahner asked: "How do we account for this sudden revival of horizontalism?" He suggested, as one explanation, the difficulty people have had in experiencing God in a world that is increasingly explained by natural causes — a world where God no longer breaks in to do his special work. This does not impress Rahner as an argument for atheism, however. Indeed, as he puts it, we should be especially hospitable in days like these, for we may be entertaining angels unaware (Hebrews 13:2). And, we may even meet Christ in the form of hungry, naked, and imprisoned men (Matthew 25).

Nonetheless, our *experience* of God within the world has become more questionable; it is harder to relate experience of God with the other experiences of reality. The proportions of misery, poverty, injustice, and inhumanity have grown terribly great. And they are brought close to us now; we are forced to see them in living color. We are refused the luxury of retreat into a private world of religion and piety. In *The Winds of War*, by Herman Wouk, we hear a young woman crying in the rubble of Warsaw: "Can't we help? Can't we do something?" The world has broken open, and its poverty, hunger, war, injustice, and discrimination shout to us that flight from reality is closed off. We are forced to see that there is no escape either in a pious refuge of today or a promised land of tomorrow. We all must ask: "Can't we do something?"

The state of affairs we live in must give Christians pause before they judge other Christians for being too wrapped up in the concerns of the world. We ought not see in it merely a horizontalist shrinkage of the Christian horizon. We are in touch here with a question of crucial significance for understanding the gospel. Does the Christian faith call us away from the world or does it push us into it? Only as we come to grips with this question can we speak a helpful word in the current discussions about the unfortunate dilemma — horizontalism or verticalism?

When we create false dilemmas like this we lose our vision for the many dimensions of reality, and in our narrowed scope we cause needless reactions to arise, even to the point of dividing the church and sowing distrust of the brethren. That this should happen is amazing. In the context of Christian faith almost no one contends for a total indifference to our world. The gospel testimony is too strong to allow complete unconcern. The image of him who was ever ready to stop, to see and care for the blind, the deaf, the sinner and publican, the poor and the sick, the sheep without a shepherd, to stop and be moved to compassion — the image of such a concerned One is too sharp to excuse indifference. Is it thinkable that the disciples of this Lord would be unwilling to follow him in his seeing, his caring, his acting? And yet . . . to recognize our Lord's concern does not resolve the tension.

We cannot give a full account of the biblical appeals for concentration on this world. They come from any number of facets within the Scripture's message. The gospel sends us en route through the world, and asks us, as the angels asked the disciples: "Why do you stand looking into heaven?" (Acts 1:11). The disciples went back to Jerusalem where the storm would sweep over their heads, and we must go to our own Jerusalems. An immense activity is called for as life in our world is seen as it is. But all Christian activity is beset with temptations. The foremost, perhaps, is the temptation of *self-reliance*. It is the seductive tendency to act without setting human action under and within the acts of God. Kuyper was often reminded that Zechariah's word might indict his activity: "not by might, nor by power, but by my Spirit, says the Lord of hosts" (Zechariah 4:6). He tried to respond exegetically: the words, he said, were not a defense of quietism, but had to do with the tone and temper and background of human action. The apostles' disclaimer of miracles done through their own "power or piety" (Acts 3:12), Moses' promise that the Lord would fight for the people while they had "only to be still" (Exodus 14:4), the psalmist's word about the God "who *alone* does wondrous things" (Psalm 72:18) are all necessary. But they have meaning only within the activity to which we are summoned. Human activity is never minimized. And it cannot be reduced in priority to a "secondary" issue, as though it is of less importance to whatever is given top priority.

We observe a growing resistance to making human action a "secondary" matter. This does not mean that one wants to reverse the order and make it top priority. It means that a scale of priorities is contrary to the gospel. Theologians have thought again about all those biblical passages that focus on man as he lives in the world into which salvation came, passages that overcome the dilemma that forces a choice between the vertical and the horizontal. The interlocking connection between justification and sanctification — as seen by James as well as by Paul — has never wholly escaped the church's awareness. But the inescapability of the connection has taken on a new sharpness as theology confronts the gospel's clear rejection of dualism. Theology has recognized that the gospel makes the choice between human action and divine initiative impossible.

When John writes about one who sees his brother in need and yet closes his heart, he does not indict the man of closed heart for reneging on a *secondary* duty. Rather, he asks: "How does God's love abide in him?" (1 John 3:17). This is the radical unity between the love of God and concern for man. The love mandate is not a legalistic appendage; it lies at the heart of God's own innermost being. To see another in need and to refuse action has catastrophic effects for one's abiding in God's love. There is a kind of "seeing" that was illustrated by the priest and the Levite who saw a man in need and passed him by. There is a kind of "seeing" illustrated by the Samaritan who saw the same man and redirected his life in response.

We are not dealing with a synthesis between religion and moralism. The parable of the Samaritan reveals a mystery. It is the mystery of the broad planes to which our vision is opened. It is the mystery of the divine concern for life within our human horizon. So every sign that men are awakened to this mystery is reason for rejoicing. A man on his way to the altar with a gift in his hands for God was stopped, held back, and sent to make things right with his brother before he came back to offer his gift to God (Matthew 5:24). This, too, could be concluded with: "Go thou and do likewise."

Dorothee Sölle has observed that the isolation of the individual from his fellow man is always coupled with devotion to an unworldly God. And she suspects the traditional doctrine of forgiving grace just for this reason. But when we hear this, we need to recall David's prayer of confession for sin against men; he confesses that, in its deepest dimension, his sin against man was against God alone (Psalm 51). This is his plea for grace. But

even then we cannot simply reject Sölle's sense for the unbreak-
able connection of man with man; we cannot reject her unwillingness to set man's duty to man on a subordinate shelf. Bonhoeffer's
word is relevant here: he whose heart does not cry out for the
Jews is not qualified to sing the Gregorian chant. When the heart
is divided, turned away from man and only to God, the harp
and the hymn (even of David) become a curse. How can there
be any confusion about the bi-focal concentration to which we
are called? Surely the twofold Great Command does not cause
confusion; there is no primary and secondary ranking here. The
second command is not-appended as an afterthought. If this were
so, the second would not be "like unto" the first. And Paul would
not have summed up all the commands of God under the second
table and then declared that he who fails in love to his neighbor
has failed to obey the law (Romans 13:8-10).

The Old Testament has come to loom large in theological
focus on life within our horizon. And this is most understandable,
for here the prophets witness to the radical demands our neighbors
make on us, demands that arise from our covenant with Yahweh.
There is no problem here of a shift from focus on God to concern for man. And there is surely no flat moralism. But the mandate for humanity stands in the light of the message of salvation
and the knowledge of the Lord. The prophets never felt the
dilemma between vertical and horizontal religion that has cost
the church so much energy and time. The prophets were not
troubled by the question of where to lay the accent. They simply
probed through to the living of every day with the knowledge of
the innermost desire of Yahweh. They called for worldly concern
without relativizing the transcendent message; they appealed to
justice without a thought that justice competed with God's
promise. They did not talk in terms of "first this and only
secondarily that." They called for a walk with God and with
man together.

Modern theological literature, not surprisingly, is filled with
reminders from Amos and Isaiah. We hear Amos proclaiming
God's word: "Seek me and live" (Amos 5:4). But in this context
we also hear his protest against corruption, callous oppression,
and rejection of justice — all made in the name of him who had
made Pleiades and Orion: "Therefore, because you trample upon
the poor and take from exactions of wheat . . ." (5:9-11). Amos
breaks up Israel's feasts, tough and radical prophet that he is.

But he is not calling an end to the history of divine salvation; he is pointing the new way that can skirt the edges of the threatened judgment.

Within this horizon of injustice, where Yahweh's attention is riveted, one cannot merely long for the day of the Lord. For the common life has been broken apart by the heavy hand of man. God hates their sacred festivals, the noise of their songs and the melody of their harps (Amos 5:21-23). So it goes with the entire Old Testament. It focusses constantly on life within our horizon; the cries of the poor, the appeals of the needy are all set within the searching light of God. This is why they must be the concern of Israel (Exodus 23:1-9). It is ridiculous to suppose that the Old Testament is guilty of being too heavily accented and one-sidedly concerned with the horizontal dimension of life, as though love for God might somehow get shortchanged by it. The service of the God of Israel and total concern for life within our horizon are inseparable.

The prophetic message, with its concentration on God and man, is seen in its strong rejection of any religiosity that takes the form of unfruitful piety (cf. Isaiah 58:14). Harvey Cox was right in seeing here the very essence of Old Testament worship. The prophets did not dance between competing accents, nor did they wrestle with dilemmas. They could rage when people tended their own houses and left God's house in desolation (Haggai 1:9,10). The Psalms certainly do not present a cult wherein concern for brother competed with concern for God. The house of Yahweh is not an arena for competition between God's praise and man's need. The Lord God of Israel is he who sets prisoners free, gives sight to the blind, lifts the downtrodden, rescues the stranger, and supports the orphan and the widow (Psalm 146). This is Israel's God. His people can truly give all their attention to him without being lured away from their neighbors. For it is in this hour of this God that the Hallelujah resounds to the God who is not far away, but very close at hand, so close that the entire horizon may and must know of it. This is the breathtaking vision of Isaiah: "They shall not hurt or destroy in all my holy mountain; for the earth shall be full of the knowledge of the Lord as the waters cover the sea" (Isaiah 11:9).

No wonder, then, that the "least of these" brothers of our Lord come into focus throughout the church's history. James Baldwin was in step with the Old Testament when, on a Sunday afternoon at Uppsala, he spoke about the race problem in terms of the cup of cold water. With this cup of water our Lord tied the affairs of our horizon to the fact that Christ's glorification at God's right hand was one with Christ's real presence on earth.

Visser 't Hooft, at the same World Council Assembly in Uppsala, spoke about the "mandate of the ecumenical movement" with respect to the horizontal and vertical dimensions of the gospel. He pointed to the cross of Jesus Christ as the decisive event in human history which keeps us from eliminating either dimension in our mandate. On another occasion, Visser 't Hooft was preceded by Francis Jeanson, who addressed the students with the comment that Christendom appeared to an outsider as "simple morality." To this Visser 't Hooft responded: "Have we become such moralists that they who hear us do not even have the chance to see that the center of Christian existence is the cross of Christ?" At Uppsala he warned — with no sense of tension with what he had said before — against all engagement with the vertical that entailed a flight from the world and against all involvement with the horizontal that gave second place to love for God.

The relationship between love for God and love for neighbor appears in almost all theological discussions of our time. In most cases, the discussions center on the dilemma that the relationship appears to create for our love. Karl Barth was foremost among those who attacked the exclusive concentration on neighbor-love that typified the disciples of Kant and Ritschl. In this line, love for God was represented as a "religious romanticism." Barth contested the notion that we have no place for a spontaneous love for God, as though the Holy Spirit inspired us only to days of labor with an "abolition of a true and direct love for God" (CD IV/2, p. 795). He recalled the anointing scene in Bethany (Mark 14) and how some were offended at the wasting of a valuable substance while the poor had need. Here, said Barth, an "ethico-religious Puritanism protests against a very doubtful pietistic undertaking" (ibid., p. 797). We must not let such hypocritical protests distort the fact that the lonely woman's act of costly devotion is *not* a reason for unconcern for the poor. In the presence of Jesus (cf. Mark 14:7), the poor cannot be shoved aside as something less important, a second-rate concern.

Barth's radical resistance to one-sided piety is bound up with his insight into our knowledge of God. Knowing God issues in an authentic doxology which goes beyond all human dilemmas. (Interestingly, Moltmann, of all people, reminds us that Barth is the only theologian of the European Protestant tradition who has dared to speak of the beauty of God, in contrast to the one-sided "Western" accent on the almightiness of God; cf. Barth, *CD* II/1, pp. 734, 739; J. Moltmann, *Theology of Play*, E.T. 1972, p. 38.) In this sphere we need not think too cautiously; nor need we pretend to be too wise. And we need not create a "quiet zone," as though that would do our neighbor any good. Christian people can (like the priest and Levite) isolate themselves within a piety directed to God that leaves the neighbor out in the cold. Or they can try to create a new world and forget about love for God (cf. Luke 11:42). But neither ought we, as a third option, accept the notion that love for God *is* love for neighbor, understandable though it would be to do so.

When Barth speaks of the "unique form of the love for God" he is not going back into an isolated piety. Nor is he saying that only the first part of the Great Commandment is really important. For Barth the special "form" of love for God is the "source of the stream" that flows to the neighbor.

Not without reason Barth warns against exchanging one cult for the other — abandoning the worship of God for service of neighbor. For he sees the danger of another reaction. With an appeal to the gospel, pietists, mystics, and romantics will run from a distorted, corrupt, and inhumane world to ask again only for the "Source," looking again to the "alabaster jar of ointment of pure nard" (Mark 14:3). They may again look to this religious cult as being far more important than the "poor" whom we in any case have among us always. The truth lies in neither. In the "special form of the love for God" a new life is visible, not a life of isolation, but a life of involvement in the deep divine philanthropy that has once for all appeared in history. In the environment of this mystery, no one can go far wrong. Neither side will be neglected, not God, not the neighbor. And no reactionary spirit gives us any right to divide the great mystery into fragments, and to let our full obedience become a tension between primary and secondary accents.

One aspect of the horizontal-versus-vertical discussions is the protest against "splitting" reality into two levels, the this-worldly and the other-worldly. There is steady opposition to a view of God's transcendence that places him outside the world in a way

that requires us to seek and to worship him detached from the
world. It is a view that suggests the real world is the higher world,
beyond ours. Thus we are led to flee from or reject the world in
which we actually find our home.

The word "supernaturalism" is sometimes used to typify this
"splitting" of the worlds. "Supernaturalism" unfortunately carries many senses, but in Robinson's *Honest to God* (1963) it was
given a fairly specific meaning. For Robinson supernaturalism
was a spatial image – the "God up there" – suggesting a distant
being, a super-being, whose existence could be demonstrated (or
disproven, as the case may be). Robinson suggested that one
could rightly ask whether this God-concept is nothing more than
a projection of our own spirit. It was this God-concept he had in
mind when he spoke of the "end of theism." Tillich agreed: "the
protest of atheism against such a highest person is correct."
Robinson was declaring bankrupt the "splitting" of reality that
posited another world which made this one unimportant and
lured us away from concern for the acute questions of life within
our horizon.

It is clear, however, that flight away from reality within our
horizon really has nothing to do with what transcends it. We can
speak about transcendence in a way that drives us into our world
as well as away from it. Paul, for instance, has a reality behind
this world in view precisely when he talks of our struggle on
earth (2 Corinthians 10:5; Ephesians 6:12). Here, in fact, lies
the touchstone for the question of whether a flight from the world
or involvement in the world is demanded.

I recall Kuyper using the metaphor of a curtain to sharpen
our concern for this world: "If once the curtain were pulled
back, and the spiritual world behind it came to view, it would
expose to our spiritual vision a struggle so intense, so convulsive,
sweeping everything within its range, that the fiercest battle ever
fought on earth would seem, by comparison, a mere game. Not
here, but up there – that is where the real conflict is waged.
Our earthly struggle drones in its backlash." Kuyper is not splitting
up reality with the phrase "not here, but up there." He was certainly sensitive to a tension in this. He recalled how he once had
been tempted "to slide off into Baader's theosophic stream, entranced by its hypnotic spell and tempted by its ethical force."
But the vagueness of it all could not interest him for long; its

attraction paled as Kuyper was brought back to the biblical reality of the "background" behind our horizon.

Only a superficial thinking will connect world-flight with faith in the reality of a spiritual background to this world. It may be that sheer spiritual inertia holds our vision within the boundaries of our earthly horizon, robbing us of the sense of transcendence. It happened with the disciples who came back to the Lord with excited talk of what had happened to them. But the Lord told them what *he* had seen in the background: "I saw Satan falling from heaven" (Luke 10:18). And so their earthly victory was given a meaning deeper than they had known (Luke 10:20). Stephen, too, saw what no one else could see; and what he saw in the background had fundamental point for what was happening on earth (Acts 7:56). The final book of the Bible is full of apocalyptic language that carries insight and warning, comfort and perspective for life within our horizon. It uses language that makes Kuyper's own colorful battle-metaphors sound timid. The point is this: the transcendent, the background to earth, is what gives events on earth their profound importance.

To anticipate the future stimulates concern for this world. But it does raise problems about the *relationship* between the eschaton and the time of the present. Johannes Weiss and Albert Schweitzer saw the eschatological perspective as being central to the New Testament message, but saw it as void of any mandate for action in our time. But dialectical theology saw it otherwise; the dialectical theologians read eschatology as being vitally relevant. Barth's remark has often been repeated: "If Christianity be not altogether eschatology, there remains in it no relationship whatever with Christ" (*Romans*, 1963 ed., p. 314).

Early on in dialectical theology, the transcendent was said to illuminate the whole of human existence; but history itself, on its way toward the future, was not really talked about much. At that time, Ranke's word characterized the relationship between eschatology and history: "Every epoch is God's epoch." Althaus separated eschatology from all notions of "the end of history"; eschatology had nothing to do with an end to time. In this he was akin to Windelband, who telescoped the telos, the goal and end of things, into the experience of the present. So history, en route toward the future, got short shrift. But Althaus, like Barth, later came to recognize a greater importance in ongoing history. In his *Die letzten Dinge* of 1933 he stoutly insisted that eschatology had everything to do with the horizonal line of history. Here he was reacting to Bultmann's "eschatology of the moment" in which the future is completely absorbed into the moment of personal decision here and now.

Barth showed signs of some afterthought in the volume of his *Church Dogmatics* that came out in 1940. Here he admitted that he had earlier failed to take adequate account of the actual coming of God's kingdom in his concentration on the "far-sidedness" of the kingdom (*CD* II/1, p. 635). He acknowledged that he had missed the real point of Romans 13:11 ("Salvation is nearer to us now than when we first believed") in a one-sidedly "supra-temporal understanding of God" (*ibid.*). Time, he now emphasized, is not empty; it participates in the presence of God, and this gives ethics a new importance. We must not, he said, let eschatology lapse into a mere religious experience of decision. If we do, we deny the real meaning of history.

At this point, Barth is parting ways with Bultmann's under-standing of eschatology. In 1926, Bultmann wrote an article (in *Zwischen den Zeiten*) about the eschatology of John's Gospel. Here he contrasted the existential, vertical relationship which is present in the events of the here and now with what he called the dramatic eschatology that has to do with events at the end of time. The process of history as it moves toward the end-time is almost wholly ignored in Bultmann's view. And he has stuck consistently to this eschatology of the present moment. He con-cluded his book on eschatology with a discussion about the mean-ing of history. His view is crystallized in this remark: ". . . Do not look around yourself into universal history; you must look into your own personal history. Always in your present lies the mean-ing of history, and you cannot see it as a spectator, but only in your responsible decisions. In every moment slumbers the possi-bility of being the eschatological moment. You must awaken it" (*The Presence of Eternity. History and Eschatology*, E.T. 1957, p. 155). Faith, then, is really a vantage point outside of history because, as Herbert Butterfield also agrees, every moment is an eschaton.

Dorothee Sölle launched her sharpest criticism against Bult-mann's penchant for taking faith out of the realm of history and for reducing existence to an individual experience. For, as she said, with this the question of history's meaning simply fades away, and with it the hope of the Christian. (Ernst Bloch attacked

Bultmann on this same count.) As a result, life is "de-politicized" and history is left to its barren fate. Sölle pleads instead for a concrete vision for all of human history. She agrees with Metz's statement: "In order to get at human existence we must avoid being totally existential." The meaning of real life in this world and its history must be our central concern, Sölle insists. And, ironically, she says that the move from the existential to the political is really to follow through consistently from Bultmann's own view. What she means is that human existence has a wider spread than individual existence in the moment of the here and now. What is at stake is life in the world as we move toward the future. If we are to be truly earnest about concrete life in our world, we must avoid flight into transcendence or into the far future. But we must equally avoid flight into the individual existential situation. Flight of any sort is ruled out.

There is clearly a sturdy tradition within the church that supports Sölle's admonition about the importance of history and the significance of what happens every tension-filled and responsibility-laden day within our horizon.

Once, this sense for the significance of earthly life was affected by a kind of eternalizing of the real events: the crucially important decisions were made in eternity. The decisions, then, were made "before" time with the effect that earthly history was not the arena where crucial decisions were made. Idealistic christology — the Christ of the Christ-idea or the Christ-symbol — saw the *work* of Christ as basically irrelevant, at most an illustration of what was eternally valid. The eternal emptied history of its significance, and this undermined the importance of what actually happened in Christ's ministry on earth.

This formed the background to Cocceius' conviction that *actual* forgiveness could not occur until the event of the cross actually took place in history to remove the barrier of guilt. Cocceius' viewpoint worked its way into nineteenth-century theology via the theology of the history of salvation. And it is strong in such views as that of Oscar Cullmann in his polemic against Bultmann (cf. Cullmann, *Salvation in History*, E.T. 1967). It is seen as well in the Dutch scholars Herman Ridderbos and Hendrikus Berkhof.

The renewed awareness of history led naturally to the question of history's future, and to the question of how human decisions are incorporated into *the* once-for-all decision that was made in the cross and resurrection of Jesus Christ. Concern about earthly events, not in the abstract but in their brim-filled reality, was charged with urgency by the needs, threats, corruption, and dehumanizing of life around us. Thus it led to a new thematizing of theology — expressly, the Theology of Hope. When Moltmann's book with that title was first published and a great deal of discussion was aroused by it, some wondered how anything new could be involved in it. After all, hope is a self-evident biblical theme and had been part of theology all along. But the theology of hope, nonetheless, sent disturbing new waves into theology because it focussed so concretely on the *process* of history; it was eschatological without being futuristic.

Though we are mentioning Moltmann's book in the context of Sölle's critique of Bultmann, we do not mean to put Moltmann and Sölle in the same bracket. Sölle sees in Moltmann too much of a "mythology of apocalyptic promise" for her liking. But there is some common ground. They both stress the importance of history and the inadequacy of an individualistic, existentialistic experience with no real bond with the moving stream of our full and real life together in history. For Moltmann, history is given its central meaning through a grounded expectation. Is human longing merely a postulate, a utopian desire, or is there a "basis for expectation"? Moltmann believes there is a basis for hope. Hope has its foundation in the cross and resurrection of Christ. Christ has broken life open for the future: "Christianity stands or falls with the reality of the raising of Jesus from the dead by God" (*Theology of Hope*, E.T. 1967, p. 165).

Precisely here lie profound and far-reaching consequences for our concern about the world and its history. For the risen Christ is the Lord. Christian eschatology implies, as Moltmann says, a "responsibility of hope in our worldly plans and actions of today." Eschatology is above all "the medium of Christian faith, the keynote by which everything else is harmonized, the ray of light heralding the expected new day in which everything now is waiting to be fulfilled." Being on the way, reaching out and waiting for the new — this gets a growing importance and urgency in a direct coupling with all those facets of the New Testament in which the city of God and the new earth are promised by the God of hope (Romans 15:13). Again and again, Moltmann confronts existentialist theology with the criticism that it has no eye for the broad ranges of history, that it sees life on the precipice of eternity only in one's individual encounter.

Genuine hope, he contends, implies that the hopeful stretch themselves out, in tension and longing, for what is still to come; and this manifests itself in protest and rebellion against all the structures of this world that impede the fulfilment of hope, and against any tendency to rest in the status quo of our time. What is called for in this theology is not a vague appeal to the future, not a tranquilizing utopian vision, but an eschatological urge to action.

The future-oriented theology of hope is allied with a new reflection on the essence of human nature — man's *ec*-centric posture, his openness, his readiness for new possibilities. In this connection we meet the name of the Marxist philosopher Ernst Bloch. Bloch had been deeply impressed with the dynamic of the Hebrew-messianic expectation of the future. This future orientation did not imply, for him, a theistic faith or the reality of God. Indeed, theism actually threatened hope because it set history's future in God rather than in the hands of men. A perspective on God as Creator and Redeemer discredits what men do; the divine apocalypse signifies a leap into the future in which human productivity and creativity have no role. Bloch sees this discrediting of human agency in Augustine and, later, in a more radical way, in Barth, especially in Barth's commentary on Romans. God's No to man and the world only touches the edge of the human sphere and then in the form of a declaration of war against all human activity.

Bloch's criticism is no trivial criticism of religion; he means it to be a positive contribution to human life. Hope must be liberated from the shackles of theism and be set loose as a stimulus to *relevant* expectation of the kingdom. (Cf. Bloch, *Atheism in Christianity*, E.T. 1972.) Thus, "only an atheist can be a good Christian," he writes, because an atheist knows there is "no God up there" who releases men from their responsibility. This is a criticism that echoes those of Feuerbach and Marx.

The difference between Bloch and Moltmann is very clear. But Moltmann, the Christian, accepts Bloch's critique as a challenge to stress the dynamic of the future-directedness of life. This appears in his conviction that the eschaton is more than a mere unveiling of what has really already happened in redemption.

Discussions about eschatology have frequently focused on this notion of "unveiling." Is "unveiling" the right category under which to think about the eschaton? Is the end an *apo*-kalyps, a lifting of the curtain behind which our reality is now hidden? Moltmann sees a danger in thinking about the apocalypse in these terms. In fact, the eschaton "does not illuminate a future which is always somehow already inherent in reality" (*Theology of Hope*, p. 85). It is more like a creation out of nothing, a resurrection from the dead.

But the notion has, nonetheless, taken a large place in eschatology during the last while. We meet the "unveiling" motif in W. Kreck (*Die Zukunft des Gekommenen*, 1961) and in H. Berkhof, who talks about the future as an "extrapolation of what has already appeared in Christ and the Spirit" — and of "the experiences that we have with God in our own world and time" (Berkhof, *De Christelijk Geloof*, 1973, p. 545). We find the same motif in Karl Rahner. Eschatology, he writes, is in the final word christology. Anything in eschatology that cannot be read as a christological expression is mere "fortune-telling and apocalypticism" (*Theological Investigations*, IV, E.T. 1966, pp. 323ff.).

Pannenberg, too, is interested in the "unveiling" motif. When he talks of the "real revelation events" of the future, he immediately adds: "The end events bring nothing decisively new, nothing that was not already present in the resurrection of Jesus," and what was complete in him does not have to be completed (*Basic Questions in Theology*, II, p. 44). And, finally, Barth has a strong word about "unveiling." For him the end-time will indeed be a disclosure and not of a second, different reality. "On the contrary, it is already the one reality which here and now still encounters us in concealment, but there and then will make itself known, and will be knowable and known without concealment" (*CD* IV/3/2, p. 489).

Moltmann does not want to deny the fact that an unveiling will occur. And of course this would be unwarranted from the point of view of the New Testament; for the New Testament is emphatic about the significance of all that happens here and now even while it points, often in urgent warning, to the future (cf. 2 Corinthians 5:10; Galatians 6:8). But, says Moltmann, "The revelation of Christ cannot then merely consist in what has already happened in hidden ways being unveiled for us to see . . ." (*Theology of Hope*, p. 228). He becomes more emphatic when he says that "the expression 'unveiling' for revelation must be dropped, and in its stead revelation must be conceived as an event that takes place in promise and fulfilment" *(ibid.)*.

Moltmann's view runs parallel with Bloch's thoughts. For Bloch, too, denies the "unveiling" motif as he meets it in the "it is finished" of Christian faith. The Christian notion that "it is finished" means that the future can be only a disclosure of what is already present (*Atheismus*, p. 190, E.T. *Atheism in Christianity*, 1972, p. 195). Of course, Bloch sees this as a "theistic" weakness. For Moltmann the "unveiling" motif implies that everything important happened in the past, and that the church now must only continually remember this past and in its light look forward to the coming disclosure of what is really present now, even though hidden. It means there is nothing basically new that lies ahead in the future. God's revelation in the future will not, then, be the "beginning of a new and different future," but only the "disclosure and true interpretation of the ongoing reality." Revelation does not give us a trumpet call to hope; it only puts us "under the spell of remembrance." This, says Moltmann, is not a vision of a new possibility, not the promise of a new thing created out of nothing, and, for that reason, not a meaningful summons to struggle and protest in our time.

Moltmann has been criticized for the heavy accent he places on the newness of the future, and especially for the implication he sees in it for what must be done by us in the present time. Has he not minimized the importance of what has happened "once-for-all"? And does he not suggest that the realization of the eschaton lies in our hands, within our horizon? And, instead of a "realized eschatology," does he suggest an eschatology that must yet be realized? Moltmann responds to such suggestions with a touch of irony. The decisive significance of the newness of the future, and the dynamic for the present implicit within it, does not entail a future without a foundation laid in the past. The cross and resurrection were God's incursions into the world which evoke our tension-filled expectations for the future. In fact, after his *Theology of Hope*, Moltmann never gave signs of lapsing into some form of optimistic evolutionism. His book *The Crucified God* came out in 1972 (E.T. 1974), and in it he shoves aside evolutionism and futurism. He has been asked whether, in moving from *Hope* to the *Crucified God*, he turned off the "Bloch music" and listened again to an "eschatology of the cross," stopped singing "the Hallelujah chorus of Easter and began the penitence hymns of Good Friday." But Moltmann insists that he has not changed his thinking; the theology of hope was an eschatology of the cross from the beginning. It was a theology of the risen Crucified One.

Remembrance need not spellbind us, but it is undeniably a remembrance of the death of Christ. This remembrance makes hope realistic. The cross means that the hope created by the resurrection is concretely tied to "its mobilizing vision." Here — with hope founded in the cross — Moltmann feels a keen kinship with J. B. Metz, whose "political theology" also accents the "remembrance" of the cross. Precisely because of what the church remembers, it excludes the possibility of quietism. For the cross and resurrection open up the future to men and set them on the way toward the future in an active anticipation. Life and the world now come into the light of their real meaning. Life is now no longer "a mere waiting room in which one sits around until the door is opened to God's office." Rather, we are now summoned to *do* what is promised for tomorrow. But for that reason there can be no Prometheus-like struggle; for the powers that are at work now are the conquering powers of the coming age (Hebrews 6).

Christianity must mobilize the powers of the future. It must mobilize them so that we can bring something of the future into the personal, social, and political realities of the present time. The future has a liberating power that must now be engaged.

The notion that the liberating power of the future contains a call for political action has occasioned some criticism. We could even say that it has inspired some mistrust, a fear that it could lead to humanizing and horizontalizing of faith. H. E. Tödt, for instance, recalled that, according to the New Testament, man "does not have the potential, not even with faith, to bring in the kingdom of God" (cf. Tödt in W.-D. Marsch, ed., *Diskussion über die "Theologie der Hoffnung" von Jürgen Moltmann,* 1967). Tödt sees a chiliastic component in Moltmann's talk of liberation, a tendency to overestimate man's ability to realize in history what is promised for the future. This reminds us of earlier eschatological discussions in which Barth put the question to the religious socialist movement: "Can we then erect forms of the kingdom of God?" There is, in the fear of horizontalism, a suspicion of the ugly head of pride, and an inflated estimate of Christian power in our movement toward the eschaton.

The discussion of the Christian's labors in connection with the eschaton gets more complicated whenever quietism is disavowed at the same time as horizontalism is signalled as a threat. We feel the tension in A. van Ruler as much as anywhere. He vehemently sets himself against horizontalism, but does so in connection with his own ideals of a theocracy. Theocracy, he believes, reveals the "right correlation" between eschaton and history. A genuine concern for humanity is mandated by the eschaton. For the Lord God is most interested in the social life of men; he offers the social ideal (Van Ruler, *Theologische Werk*, 1961, VI, p. 45). Therefore the church, with its message, is the mediator between the gospel and the world. It has "enormous pretensions" to be sure; but the church does not annul the worldliness of the world. Rather it summons the world to its highest potential. Van Ruler uses the boldest expressions he can find to spell out the worldly concerns of the Christian community. He talks about "synergism" and speaks of the Reformation as being "radically and totally mariological." He objected to the title of H. Berkhof's book, *Christ, the Meaning of History;* it is *man,* he said, who is the meaning of history (*ibid.*, pp. 67ff.). Van Ruler was fascinated with the "deification" of man as a pneumatological category; and this "deification" entails a kind of synergism in which men become fellow judges of the world, a radical worldliness, and even "self-redemption" (*ibid.*, I, 1969, pp. 230f.). Van Ruler lived into the Reformation denial of the meritorious worth of human works; but this did not permit him to minimize the importance of human activity. Indeed, he accented its importance to the full. And this is all bound up with his vision of theocracy. Eschatology is *per se* secular; what Communism envisions as history's route to the eschaton of world revolution is child's play compared with the Christian vision. Faith has limitless hope for the world.

This passionate call to world-concern brings Van Ruler into the spirit of Moltmann, and of J. Verkuyl (cf. Verkuyl, *The Message of Liberation in Our Time,* E.T. 1973). There is no finicky arrangement of accents, no making sure that we give just the right accent to eschatology and the precisely correct accent to the world of the present. For Van Ruler the eschaton is not merely the *appearance* of what has already been redeemed; it is the unheard-of new thing, the consummation of the whole historical process in which all the life of this earth is taken along. This is the "most decisive perspective offered by Reformed theology." And man himself is, in a certain sense, the purpose of it all: the structure of love is "not theocentric, but anthropocentric" (*op. cit.*, II, 1971, p. 143). This was Van Ruler's thinking as of 1969: the church has everything to do with the world and all that happens in it. "Concern for the world belongs to the essence of the church. And that concern is gospel-mandated. For the gospel is the gospel of the kingdom" (*ibid.*, p. 102).

But it was the same Van Ruler who at the same time attacked horizontalism — sometimes gently, sometimes in wrath. His distaste for horizontalizing the gospel in no way reflects a turning away from his premise: he is not opposed to the vitality, the concern, or the synergism that characterizes horizontalism. He is not opposed to its worldliness, certainly not to Christian participation in the world. What he is against is the *substitution* of human work for the work of God. Dorothee Sölle is one of his targets. He rejects the "exclusive concern" for the political and social, and he vigorously opposes any Christian call to transform the world that is "wholly and exclusively directed to this life and this world," which is to confuse historical with redemptive movement.

His polemic against horizontalism is not a subtle way of retracting his own world-oriented theology. Van Ruler is against isolating world-concern from the gospel of salvation. He does not want to go back to the notion of salvation as a primary concern and worldly needs as a secondary concern. He does not want to balance off neatly the spiritual and heavenly against a less-important worldly. But he surely is opposed to a reduction of the spiritual to the earthly.

Understandably, Moltmann has responded to such critiques, explaining that he never intended a triumphalistic conquest of the world; and evolutionism and pride were not in his intentions. God's kingdom has not been put in man's hands; the world does not move naturally into God's kingdom. God's kingdom is entirely his own. Moltmann makes a distinction between the future and the advent; it is one thing for history to move toward its destiny, but it is another for the kingdom to come in the parousia. The Christian waits for the advent. There is an anticipation of the future only in the sense of waiting for something new that is proclaimed by the New Testament. Here we are not in the category of a self-evident movement "out of the inner tendencies of the present time." But there is a proclamation that "comes into the present time." And with this, there is ground for creative and militant hope within our history.

Movement into the future does not happen by way of the inner dynamics of history; we cannot build for the future unless the future itself is given. For this reason, Moltmann agrees that the future we hope for is not "identical with the results of our activity; all our activity is ambiguous just as we historical creatures are always ambiguous." But since the future is coming from God, our activity can never be in vain. None of this, however, can justify a defeatist or quietist attitude toward life. We may disclaim hubris and reject evolutionism, but this does not mute the appeal for obedient action. Nor does it discourage hope for concrete new events within our horizon, short of the eschaton. In this vein, we can understand Moltmann's lament at the loss of creative élan that comes with readiness to give up on the world, a faith without hope. He wants to rise above the dilemma: either an eschaton that only unveils the meaning of the past or a titanic struggle in a Marxist sense. We might mention J. M. Lochman at this point. Lochman, who found a home in Basel after leaving Czechoslovakia in 1968, also contends that grace may never be an excuse for quietism. We may rightly be offended by the Marxist Prometheus complex (Prometheus, says Lochman, is Marxism's greatest saint), but this should not tempt us into an unbiblical reaction, standing unemployed along the way in the style of the disciples (Matthew 20:7), waiting for what the Lord alone will do in his future.

In spite of the differences with respect to the future as a mere unveiling, Moltmann is not all that far from Barth. Moltmann recognizes that Barth is too complex to be typed as a theologian who sees no newly creative event in the eschaton. Barth, he knows, teaches more than a sheer noetic event, a future that is new only to the observer. Barth is not immunized against a genuine promise for the new future by the "It is finished" motif. When Barth spoke against what he called "the pan-eschatological dream" he did not mean to minimize the importance of the future; what he did intend was to emphasize that "the One hoped-for" sets the church beneath his present Lordship. Barth too, no less than Moltmann, warned against escapism, against a "flight of thought into heaven." Here, too, there is a possibility of hubris, of overestimation of our own work. The world around us, as it stands before our eyes, says Barth, shouts to us that we have no reason for hubris. The life under sin, typified by death, marked clearly on every battlefield, in every prison and every asylum, sends the message: This life is not yet the redeemed existence. Nonetheless, to be alert to the little lights ignited along the way as signs of the coming kingdom is not a forbidden option. For in this life, expectation and service are bound together as a way of proclaiming the great light: "To hope is to work, and only thus is it true hope" (CD IV/3, pp. 937ff.).

Both Barth and Moltmann radically reject Bloch's critique of theism as a God concept that excludes human activity. The picture is totally different. Without trust in God protests against injustice and the struggle for justice are crippled. There is no place for anthropocentrism, not in the century of Auschwitz and Hiroshima. And there is every reason to be critical of a kingdom hope that promises a future without God. There is every reason, too, for rejecting a waiting-room quietism that, as tribute to divine majesty, squeezes human action out of the scene for fear of God's jealousy. Barth puts it this way: The construct, "God is everything, man is nothing," as a description of grace "is not merely a 'shocking simplification' but complete nonsense" (CD IV/1, p. 627).

Dilemmas always are a source of polarization. We quickly go over to simplistic either-or's (e.g., individual piety or human concern) in which the fulness of truth is torn apart. And in the atmosphere of false polarities, we often stop listening to each other and lose our ability to understand each other's words. With this, irritation and pique poison the theological discussion.

But it is striking and, at the same time, reassuring that the clear intent of the gospel comes through even in the midst of theological polarization, especially when all the parties intend to be faithful to the gospel.

The old tensions between concern for personal salvation and concern for the world provide occasion for searching out the implications of the gospel. The same is true of the contrast between so-called political theology and mysticism. It is sometimes feared that even a theology with so splendid a label as "theology of hope" loses sight of the individual and his salvation, and turns hope into a new form of human activism. Helmut Thielicke, in this connection, criticizes "political theology" on the grounds of its christology, not on the grounds of its concern for the affairs of this world. In this christology, Thielicke thinks, Jesus is viewed as a *model* of human activity in such a way that the issue of his divinity evaporates. He sees this as a natural upshot of a christology that has concern only with man and his world. Jesus becomes a substitute for an absent God. Transcendence is lost, in this view, and man tends to transgress his limits in order to replace the lost God. Naturally, in the mind of "political theologians" Thielicke's fears are misplaced. For, they say, what they want is not to replace the gospel, but to trace its bearing on worldly affairs. This leads us to say that the problem for Christian theology lies in the *manner* in which the work of man is integrated into the work of God.

The discussion goes on, however, to ask about the *concrete* bearing of the gospel on life. With this, we encounter very deep differences. The question of how the gospel bears on politics is an old one, and it is far more than an interesting theoretical problem. Rather, it is one that touches on man's life in his concrete world. And we are dealing with real people, not just imaginary cases. Pannenberg rightly warned against the "stupor" of enthusiasm for distant revolutionary heroes in far-off places while ordinary work needing to be done here and now is ignored.

In the midst of many discussions about the theology of revolution and nonviolence, transformation and concrete changes, we encounter many options. (Cf. L. Smedes, "The Ethics of Violence as a Last Resort" in H. Kuitert, ed., *Septuagesimo Anno*, 1973.) But the possibility of various options leaves life in tension. Uncertainty can lead to an ill-considered use of the gospel to support specific causes or it can, on the other hand, lead to a new indifference to the gospel. Even the accent on hope does not pave a way out of this impasse. And if it does not show that the gospel's speech about liberating power has concrete meaning, it could end in fruitlessness. But the promising factor is that the very problems encountered in the discussion compel us to recognize the clear thrust of the gospel.

It is important, in this connection, to note the equally timely discussions about the *consummation*, particularly in reference to whether it is an immanent or a transcendent event. Rahner has put the question in these terms, somewhat parallel with Moltmann's distinction between what can be anticipated *in* history and what must be expected as an intervention *into* history (*futurum* and *adventus*). The decisive question is whether we can anticipate the kingdom of God within this world in a realistic sense. We hardly ever meet an absolute denial of the possibility of the kingdom of God within history. Vatican II itself spoke of a this-worldly anticipation: "Thus the end of the age has already come to us, and the renewal of the world is irrevocably begun and can be anticipated in a real way within our time." But this anticipation is present, for Vatican II, in the *church*. For the church is that which is "given a real, be it incomplete holiness." So Vatican II did not mean that we experienced a foretaste of the consummation within the alienated and corrupt life of humanity. Nor did it mean to identify the presence of the consummation with the groanings of creation for liberation from our bondage to this perishable life.

But the council did speak in other settings about our anticipation of the future in life outside the holy church. In the *Constitution on the Church,* we read that the laymen of the church are empowered to bring the gospel into daily life, into both the family and society. The people are children of promise, and they ought not cluster their hopes around their private and inner lives, but rather live them out "through a continuing transformation of life, through struggle against the worldly powers of darkness and the evil spirits, including those within the structures of earthly life." Rahner discerns in such statements a revolutionary posture and a strike against the tendency of the church to sanctify conservatism and all that suggests religion as the "opiate of the people." It is regrettable, says Rahner, that "the will to conserve has become for us the cardinal virtue of life" (Rahner, *Theological Investigations*, X, E.T. 1971, pp. 242ff.). He sees in Catholicism a special sympathy for the structure of Christian hope. In the Protestant doctrine of justification the important element is the forensic relationship in which the sinner is lifted out of his sinful status as a person, but without a real presence of grace in life. The Catholic view allows for a more immanent consummation of Christian experience. God's absolute self-giving, which is the transcendent side, is immanent within the creature. And therefore the consummation is both transcendent and immanent; both are aspects of the one consummation. Seeking that which is above does not reduce but rather magnifies our duty to build a more humane world. This is the kind of thinking that Rahner finds encouraging in the council. Rahner insists that no matter how "probingly and carefully" we do our human work, whatever progress takes place in an improved structuring of human society is of "highest importance" for the kingdom of God.

Rahner summarizes the question by asking whether the new earth "from above" descends into a "neutral" territory of an unredeemed and untransformed world or whether it is "built by men" *(ibid.)*. This is a question that haunts the relationship between Marxism and Christianity. It pervades the issue of whether Christians are really prepared to take this present world seriously. Is the world merely the raw stuff for the exercise of our personal Christian virtues or is it the arena for realizing actual goals within the world? For Rahner a persistent difference exists between history and consummation (both in the personal and social sense). There remains within the social humanization of life a place for "radical conversion." But there is no radical discontinuity between them. Much rather, the present life is "radically significant" — history itself moves toward the future of God and this fact dissolves the dilemma between history and the kingdom of God.

Rahner reveals a fascinating similarity to Kuyper in all of this. It was Kuyper who talked about the eternal hope as a "hidden germ of life, the basic significance of things" within the world. And he called Christians to the task of bringing into reality some of the glory and honor of the New Jerusalem. He spoke of the "connection between this life and the life to come" (Kuyper, *Gemeene Gratie*, I, pp. 458ff.). This was not a horizontalizing of the gospel. Kuyper certainly did not suppose that the kingdom would come through an evolutionist dynamic within the world that would break through finally as the kingdom of Glory. But he did see that the hope of the kingdom to come gave an eternal value to this earthly life and to our human work.

The *continuity* between the present and the future also intrigued Bavinck. "Everything that is authentic, noble, just, pure, lovable, and of sound repute in creation . . . will be brought together in the future city of God, but renewed, recreated, and raised to its highest glory. The material is already present in this earth" (Bavinck, *Gereformeerde Dogmatiek*, IV, p. 702). Bavinck and Kuyper were fighting an other-worldly spirituality, and were especially concerned with the problem of the *cosmos* and its significance in relation to eternal life. The present discussions are oriented more to the relationship between the movement of *history* and the transcendent origin of the time to come. The discussions therefore tend to focus on the temporal horizon; the question has to do with our responsibility for this present time where justice does not dwell and our hope for the new earth of the future wherein justice will dwell (2 Peter 3:13). That is, current discussions do not touch on Kuyper's "life-germ" of eternity within the world or Bavinck's earthly "material" from which the future kingdom will be fashioned, but rather on the hurly-burly of human life as it moves on its way toward the future of God. Here we confront the question of man on his way in the service of the future kingdom, a service to this tragedy- and injustice-infected world as we anticipate the world to come.

The passionate protest we have seen in our time against defeatism and quietism, against an irrelevant consciousness of transcendence and against a hope for the future that is cut loose from affairs of our world, is not a secularized estrangement from the gospel. That it is interpreted as a secularized gospel must be charged to the carelessness with which the protest is often made. Sometimes the appeal for this-worldly responsibility is sounded without the kind of qualifications that Moltmann, for instance, applies. So, very understandable reactions are evoked, reactions that also fail to honor the connections between the gospel and human responsibility for the world.

Naturally enough, the theological discussions find their way into congregations. There the impression is created that theologians are offering an inner-worldly salvation that lies in our own hands. And with this the suspicion is evoked that the real Christian expectation of God's future, when God himself will make all things new and provide a new Jerusalem that comes from heaven (Revelation 21), is being undermined. To counter this suspicion, we are reminded of the biblical themes about human calling and responsibility. We are reminded of the victory theme of the New Testament — the disarming of the powers (Colossians 2:14) and the new creation that has already come. But this is countered with the reminder that the New Testament also speaks of a "not yet" which renders all triumphalism inappropriate. We are reminded too of our daily experience which stifles optimism about our own future; the disarmed powers still have amazing power.

Discussions within the Reformed Churches of the Netherlands are typical of the tensions Christians feel with respect to the this-worldly and the other-worldly aspects of faith, and to the relation between man's earthly work and the redemptive acts of the transcendent God. At a synod assembly in 1971/72, the question took this form, among others: What does the Bible mean when it says that the new Jerusalem will "descend from heaven"? Here the transcendent-versus-immanent theme is crystallized: Can we legitimately speak of a realization of the kingdom within our earthly history? On the sidelines a discussion was opened between assembly delegates and members of the theological faculty of the Free University. From this discussion emerged a consensus, set in a series of themes.

1. The meaning of history is defined by God's redemptive acts for the redemption and renewal of our world. Man, with his human responsibility, is implicated in his acts. This is why the church calls all men to faith and conversion.

2. The fulfilment of salvation-history lies beyond the present horizon of our existence. Therefore, Christian discipleship has the character of a pilgrimage.

3. The revelation of God's salvation does not take place outside the context of our earthly knowledge and experience, but it is also true that God's acts are not confined to our field of knowing and working.

4. In our world, life is heavily burdened with evil. This puts faith in tension and struggle. But God tells us that he will one day triumph powerfully over the forces of darkness. . . . Thus, without fatalistically accepting the evil of the world, we are encouraged to persevere in the struggle to appropriate his salvation.

5. We encounter outside the church manifestations of humanity that often put Christians to shame. We believe that these fragmentary snippets of human goodness are somehow related to the saving work of God. This does not undo the fact that only the gospel of God's grace in Jesus Christ is the revealed way for the whole world to be saved.

The assembly received this statement and used it to express a general consensus on two points, as stated by the synod:

a) The fulfilment of salvation-history lies beyond our present earthly existence and will occur in the day of Christ.

b) The church has the mandate, with the gospel of God's grace in Jesus Christ that was entrusted to it, to call all men to faith and conversion in which a conscious, personal faith-relationship with Christ is discovered.

Certainly a brief churchly declaration like this does not answer all the explicit and implicit questions. But space is created by it for further reflection on the concrete significance of the lordship of Christ for the struggles of this earthly life. It leaves us open for the terribly serious business of life in our world. Life is too serious to permit flight from it. And when men like Bonhoeffer speak of the "deep this-worldliness of Christianity" they do not mean to de-eschatologize the gospel. To become "this-worldly" is not to empty the future of its radical character of "beyond this world." What it does do is close the door to flight into the "beyond." It tells us that such a flight is a caricature, not a profile of Christian hope. The summons to "this-worldly" living is a response, as Rahner puts it, to "God's redeeming love for the world in all its dimensions" (*op. cit.*, III, E.T. 1967, p. 48).

Our ongoing struggle can give us a longing for a consensus that the source and power of our human action lies within the love that God has for this world. It is his enormous philanthropy (Titus 3:4) that blazes the way into the future that he prepares. With this the deepest intention of our human action can be tested. And as we are confronted again and again with the message of his love, we can be liberated from caricatures of the gospel that could otherwise release Christians from responsibility for justice and mercy. On the route of faith and action, along with hope, we see that the gospel we believe is far removed from the picture of a future without bearing on the present, a heavenly hope without concern for the neighbor and his world. We can break through caricatures, and when we do the light will always shine through all our fabricated dilemmas and appear as the light of *men* to the glory of our Father who is in heaven (Matthew 5:16).

8

Concern for the Faith

NO ONE WHO HAS LIVED CLOSE TO THE CHURCH DURING THE LAST several years will be surprised at the title of this final chapter. Perhaps he will recognize in it something of his own doubts about theological trends. There are symptoms of concern everywhere, and they touch on deep and central issues. Some of the problems have sneaked up on people, catching them unprepared; many of today's problems seem foreign to all their experiences with the faith. Some people feel betrayed, threatened with a loss of something profoundly important. For Protestants, it is tied to a fear that the complete trustworthiness of Scripture is somehow being subverted. For Catholics, it is related to a loss of respect for the authority of the church as the last word for questions of faith. In both places, people have a feeling that theologians are taking a critical attitude toward the church's past, that they are breaking continuity with the church of all ages and its universal and undoubted Christian faith.

We seem to have set out on a path without knowing where it will lead us. This suspicion is not limited to any one communion; it is present in almost every denomination. Every problem that one church encounters has its parallel in other churches. A familiar example of the sorts of questions that have plagued evangelical churches is the set of questions that cluster around the creation and fall of man. Some people are sure that newer interpretations spell a clear threat to the faith and are reason for concern and alarm. Others, after early hesitation, have become convinced that, as long as we continue to confess God as Creator and the reality of human rebellion and guilt, along with the utter need for God's grace, we can fit the newer interpretations within the church's faith.

We have labelled the unrest as concern for the faith. This concern is for more than the dogma of scriptural authority or, as in Rome, for the dogma of papal authority. It reaches out from these basic matters into a large complex of beliefs that seem to have become unglued as a result of watered down authority. And some of these issues touch the heart of the church.

One does not have to be boxed into dead orthodoxy to share this concern. It is true that dogma can become petrified, and faith can be hardened into a legalistic network of beliefs. But it is also true that the mystery of Jesus Christ is part of the church's dogma. Dogma is a living reality within the house of God; here it sounds as the love song of the congregation. Concern for dogma is concern for faith. The task of theology is to help preserve the doxology of dogma. This is why unrest about dogma, concern for the faith that was once-for-all delivered, is the more unsettling when theology seems out of tune with the faith of the church. Reassuring people about the good intentions of theologians does not set them at rest; they know it is a matter of truth and not simply of good intent.

We cannot trace out all the components of concern for the faith within the churches. What we will do is point out some areas of unrest and concern within theology itself. Uncertainty is always the companion of those who search out new ways. And theology has embarked on many new directions. There is tension in theology as new ways of interpreting the old dogmas conflict with traditional ways. We will look at some of the conflicts that have caused concern for the faith.

One area of tension that has been with us for several years, and remains one of the most difficult, is the effort to reinterpret dogma.

Everyone understands that the faith needs to be interpreted. But is there something more afoot than an interpretation of the faith? We have always known that the faith has to be understood in the light of its origin, its content, and its implications. But many suspect that current reinterpretations involve something more dubious than this. That their suspicions need not be well founded is seen in that reinterpretations of the faith have always taken place whenever we try to confess the faith within the critical moments of our own time. The message of the gospel is understood in new generations. Even this causes a certain amount of tension. For the question always arises as to whether the new form has preserved the old message intact or whether the content itself has undergone transformation, in part or as a whole.

What the faithful want to know is whether reinterpretations of the faith preserve continuity with the faith of the fathers. Those concerned to keep the faith alive in new forms, meanwhile, try to assure others of their convictions that the continuity is intact. Reinterpreting the faith of the church is, in fact, an effort to preserve the deepest intentions of the church when it formulated its dogmas, and to revive that original faith in new expressions.

Of course, ours is not the first century of reinterpretation of dogma. The nineteenth century was busy with it, even more critically than ours. And when theologians were critical of Chalcedon and the Apostles' Creed, they also claimed to be doing nothing more than piercing to the true intent of the faith, recapturing the essence of the Christian faith. Both Protestant and Catholic modernism claimed to be only reforming the antiquated concepts in order to preserve the essence. It is the memory of this kind of reinterpretation that causes concern today. For it is a reminder that reinterpretation can be an honorable label for a less than honorable affair.

Some suggest that reinterpretation is more dangerous than outright criticism of the faith. The former can soothe the church into supposing that it is still in touch with the true faith while in fact a profound shift has taken place under its nose; a break with the faith has occurred under the camouflage of reinterpretation. Thus, the issue is always: Are we dealing with the creation of a new meaning or only with a new way of pointing to the old meaning?

The tensions exist in the church because the work of reinterpretation has not gone on in some ivory tower. It touches the lives of people for whom the church and its faith are the heart of life. And it is carried on by theologians whose heart is just as close to the center of the church. Sometimes, this very fact causes intense problems, especially if their reflections bring them to conclusions which they deeply believe are in line with the traditional faith. (To recall some names of the older days, we might mention Berenger of Tours with his reformation of transubstantiation, Gottschalk with his doctrine of predestination, and Galileo with his view of the relation between Scripture and science.) There have been others who, out of integrity, declined the option of continuing within the church under the guise of retaining the essence, though not the form, of the old faith. A famous example is Allard Pierson of the nineteenth century. He finally concluded that he could no longer believe in the doctrine of vicarious redemption; so he wrote to the congregation he had pastored for eight years, accounted for his convictions, and resigned his office. He saw no way of translating his opinions within the framework of the church's faith, and had no desire to urge the church to expand its parameters of toleration. Pierson was sometimes called the *enfant terrible* of modernism; he was one of the few who decided on their own that there was no place within the church for their convictions. Most modernists were convinced that it was their convictions the church ought to preach, that only thus could the faith be liberated from its orthodox confinement.

The Pierson affair illustrates how the problem of reinterpretation of the faith can strike deep into the vitals of the church. There is often more afoot than a new, somewhat refined manner of expression. And there is more than a simple development of dogma, a kind of organic growth, an unfolding of the truth from the implicit to the explicit. If this is all there were at hand everyone would recognize reinterpretation as an enrichment of faith. The question, for many, is whether we are dealing not with a new manner of expression but with a new faith, a faith with ties somewhere other than that which was "once-for-all delivered" to the church *for all times* (Jude 3; 1 Timothy 6:20).

Reinterpretation of the faith usually assumes a fundamental distinction: the distinction between form and content, between the formulations of dogma and the truth that is expressed in those formulations. The question is whether the church can work with this distinction. It has been a burden for the Roman Catholic Church, whose doctrine of papal infallibility might, on first thought, provide minimal room for reinterpretation. Nor does it seem flexible enough for making dogma more understandable to new generations. After all, truth formulated *infallibly* ought to be relevant for all times. The more striking, then, is the fact that reinterpretation of dogma has been going on intensely within Roman Catholic theological circles in a deep awareness of the historically conditioned character of the church's speech. Since H. Boulliard made a distinction between the affirmation (truth) and the representation of truth (its form) some thirty years ago, the process has gone on apace. Resistance to it came almost immediately. Some saw it as a relativizing of truth, and were sure it would undermine the certainty of faith. They were convinced that the Holy Spirit was involved not only in affirmation, but in giving truth its verbal form. But even after the first official protest was sounded in 1950 (in the encyclical *Humani Generis*), the problem was not washed away. The same complex of problems was evident in 1965 when the encyclical *Mysterium Fidei* used the same arguments against reinterpretations of the doctrine of transubstantiation that had been used fifteen years earlier.

The question of the criterion for judging between form and content was bound to come up in this connection. The church, it was said, expressed its intentions in these particular words, and not other words, so therefore the form cannot be touched without touching the content expressed in it. As a matter of fact, the distinction between form and content was used only after we became conscious of the difference between the wider horizons of our knowledge and the narrower limit of earlier generations. In any case, it was not a simple task "to make a clear distinction between what was essential and unchangeable in the faith and the church and what is only the external form or time-bound expression and therefore can be changed with no loss of content" (Cardinal Alfrink).

Hence, an uneasiness haunts all talk about the time-bound character of older formulations, about antiquated concepts and "the garments" of thought (Schillebeeckx) worn in previous times. Profound questions cling to the project of reinterpreting the faith, questions having to do both with the church's continuity with its own confession and with personal faith experience. Personal faith gets involved with all sorts of questions — the doctrine of the eucharist, christology, eschatology (especially in relation to modern crises). For instance, one's personal hope seems affected when theologians appear to de-liberalize the biblical teachings about eschatology. What the latter comes down to is the question of whether the things the church always taught about the future have lost their original *literal* sense. And so, again, the question is raised whether there is not much more loose in the church than a simple distinction between form and content.

The urge to reinterpret dogma is occasioned in part by the rise of problems that earlier generations were wholly innocent of and to which they could therefore hardly have given an answer. This is involved in the way the Council of Trent treated the dogma of original sin and the way this dogma has been reinterpreted in the light of later discoveries about man and his origins. Was there some way of distinguishing Trent's unchange-able "affirmation" from its changeable "representation"? Well, the problems remained, and with them a general sense of the legiti-macy of reinterpretation. The challenge was that of finding a *hermeneutic* for reinterpreting the affirmations of the church.

Questions like these came, not from those whose commit-ment to the church was notably weak, but from committed Catho-lics who wanted precisely to maintain their witness to unchange-able truth through the changing times. When John XXIII opened the Second Vatican Council, he said something that relates to the whole question of reinterpretation. "This certain and un-changeable doctrine, to which we must be faithful, ought to be studied and expounded with methods appropriate for our time. For we must distinguish between the inheritance of faith itself, or, if one prefers, of the truths contained in our holy doctrine, and the manner in which these truths were formulated, naturally in the same sense and with the same meaning." At the opening evening, a group of German bishops gathered and discussed the Pope's statement with enormous enthusiasm; Hans Küng, who spoke for the bishops, seized on it with particular zest. The Pope's words were hardly "revolutionary," of course. He set clear limits and made sure that the "ever the same" of the church sounded clearly through all he said. But he made the distinction between content and form respectable, and even spoke of its necessity. This was certainly notable.

Putting the task of reinterpretation on the agenda no doubt showed the influence of Cardinal Bea. But it also showed the influence of others, like Karl Rahner, for instance, who never tired of speaking about the difference between the "method" and the "content" of the church's speech. Men like these were not criticizing the affirmations of the past. They meant to cover an important aspect of the infallible dogma.

Further discussions, however, brought theologians face to face with the very question of infallibility; surely, it was held by some, we cannot have a revision of *infallible* utterances; "the in-fallible utterances of the church's teaching office" are "off limits" for Catholic theologians (M. Löhrer). We may talk of interpre-tations, but not of revisions or corrections. But others contended that *all* the formulations are *always* temporal, inadequate, and limited. This is the way Karl Rahner, first, and then Hans Küng talked. As they talked of the limited character of their church's utterances Catholic theologians also began thinking about Catholicism's relationship to other churches. If one's own statements are time-bound, and in a certain sense limited, we become aware that others may really be committed to the same truth which both of us express only in part. Hence, without wiping out the differences, we may be able to have converging interpretations of the one truth. Thus spoke men like Küng.

Dogma-historical studies of the councils like Chalcedon and Trent added fuel to the fire. The time-conditioned aspect of churchly statements became very evident. But at the same time, the difference between *correction* and *interpretation* became fuzzier. What are we dealing with? Are we touching only on "technical concepts" and "scholastic niceties"? If so, then we need not worry about corrections. Or, is our sensitivity to the horizon problem leading us into actual criticism of statements of faith? If so, then the disquiet among the churches cannot be shoved aside as more stubborn conservatism.

The problematics involved in the interpretation of dogma climaxed in a very important debate about the infallibility of the Pope and his statements of dogma. For years this most sensitive matter was never discussed. But now it has surfaced in the name of the church's responsibility as it faces the future in a new age. The question was often discussed as to which statements, among all that the previous popes had made, were infallible. But *that* the Pope spoke infallibly was never doubted in public. All this changed when Hans Küng set papal infallibility itself on the agenda in his book *Infallible?* first issued in 1970 (E.T. 1971). This book was the forerunner of an extended discussion in which the contention that had been made with respect to other dogmas, namely that the truth always comes to us in the stream of history and is expressed in fallible, inadequate forms, now was applied to papal statements. Paul's word about our partial knowledge (1 Corinthians 13:12) became a sort of proof-text. "All churchly formulations of the faith are fragmentary," and concepts appear in them that certainly "do not participate" in infallibility. Such notions as these were out in the open, notions that called for delicate distinctions, and were certain, as Rahner said, to create uncertainty about the very content of the churchly teachings.

The question of whether we are dealing with criticism or only interpretation now became obviously relevant. In fact this question arose in response to earlier books by Küng, such as

Structures of the Church, 1962 (E.T. 1964), and *The Church,* 1967 (E.T. 1967). But now the issue was sharper and more critical. The First Vatican Council (1870) spoke about the church's need, for its own well-being, of the enclave of infallibility. The enclave was created by the Holy Spirit in the form of irrevocable, infallible teachings which are lifted above all discussion and criticism.

But Küng called for a hard look at the actual history of papal statements in which error was, as a matter of fact, mixed with truth. He wanted complete honesty and integrity. (He wrote a book called *Truthfulness: The Future of the Church,* 1968.) Has the time not come, he asked, for a "genuine demythologizing and de-ideologizing of the church's teaching authority?" The *church* is, Küng insisted, indefectible. But this does not require, as a *conditio sine qua non,* that its *teachings* are infallible nor that the church's path is marked by irrevocable statements. We should rather think in terms of being guided and sustained by the Spirit as he leads us through the valleys of possible error. "The church is sustained in the truth in spite of the possibilities of error." For this reason, it puts its trust in the promise of the Holy Spirit who was given to *lead* the church into all truth. Küng talked in the same vein as Bavinck did and as the Belgic Confession does: the church is preserved by God as it walks amid enemies (Article XXVII).

Küng was greeted by a sharp attack from none other than Karl Rahner, who, along with others, published a criticism of Küng's book, *Infallible?* Rahner publicly asked the sensitive question: "Is Küng still Catholic?" And he answered by saying that Küng should be treated as a "liberal Protestant" for whom neither the Scriptures nor the councils were binding. Küng was clearly hurt by Rahner's frontal assault; after all, in his thought about the historical conditionedness — and relativity — of dogma, he had identified closely with Rahner himself. It was hardly understandable for Küng, then, that Rahner turned on him.

For many, it had been Rahner himself who disturbed the church by his rather free and uninhibited use of the distinction between content and form of churchly definitions. His own distinctions seemed to carry crucial consequences in their wake, as his views of creation and evolution and of the plural origin of man seemed to demonstrate. The Council of Trent, after all, had all but excluded the possibility of a plurality of human origins;

and the church in 1950 emphatically spoke against the poly-
genesis of man on the grounds that only monogenesis could be
harmonized with Trent's doctrine of original sin and its exegesis
of Paul's statement that all have sinned in Adam.

Rahner waded straight through traditional interpretations,
and raised many questions in Catholic minds. In 1971 — in the
midst of the infallibility debate with Küng — Rahner found himself accused by Cardinal Höffner. And Küng appeared on German
radio to ask ironically: "Is Rahner still Catholic?" His answer
was that it would be utter absurdity to doubt it.

Without going into the background of Rahner's criticism
of Küng, we might recall his remark to J. B. Metz back in 1968 —
prior to his dispute with Küng. He said that, while for twenty
years he had gained the reputation of a progressive theologian, he
now found himself having to defend the truly central and traditional positions of the church. He believed, he said, that he had
not changed, but that others had. He saw himself standing within
the church, defending it against radical opposition. And the foes,
as he saw them, were touching issues on which the church stood
or fell. He did not have Küng in view at the time. He had his
eye on what he called un-Christian views against which a clear
No needed to be said — probably he had radical forms of secularization in view. But we cannot help wondering whether, later,
Rahner did not suspect that Küng fit the label of desacralizer.
Only in some such way can we account for the intensity of Rahner's response to Küng's views. In any case, the unrest created
by the Küng-Rahner debate is an example of concern for the faith.

We sense the growing concern in Jean Daniélou. During the
Second Vatican Council he was (along with Henri de Lubac)
one of the most visible representatives of the "new theology."
There he spoke earnestly about the historical limitations of the
church and about the cultural garments in which the faith is
clothed. He appealed to the church to untie itself from Aristo-
telian philosophy and seek contact with modern modes of thought.
In 1968, however, Daniélou said that he was concerned about
the apparent loss of the objective, definitive, and absolute
language that has come about because men now doubt the ability
of human reason to have objective knowledge of the truth.

Getting clear focus on the backgrounds and motives behind
the tensions is very difficult. But we can see quite clearly that
the problem of interpretation is at the center all along the line.

The question is one of limits: where does reinterpretation of the past slide over into critique of and break with the past? At the present stage of discussion, the question is being asked whether Küng is reacting against a straw man, whether he has interpreted the real intentions of Vatican I correctly. It is asked, for instance, whether Vatican I ever meant to assert that it was impossible for the church to err. Might it not be that the council never intended an *absolute* unchangeability of dogmatic formulas, but only to say that the Pope's magisterial *judgment*, which was, in any case, inexpendable in situations of conflict, was the last and final word? (Cf. A. Houtepen, *Onfeilbaarheid en hermeneutiek*, 1973, pp. 342, 349.)

We may ask whether the problems that Küng has raised would be any different if Vatican I had intended only to say that the Pope's final word of judgment was beyond appeal. It seems to me that Küng's questions would be essentially the same. They are aimed, not at whether "infallible statements" are possible or justified, but rather at the problem implicit in all that the church, in its historicalness, says. Thus, he is saying that *nothing* is beyond appeal. Even the Pope's judicial pronouncements would be in question. For Küng, what is at stake is whether Christ the Lord is the one final judge.

Protestant churches are occupied with the same problem. Confessional Protestant bodies, in particular, have felt the tension between current theological reflection and the confessions of the church from earlier centuries. The question of how to make contact with modern thought is the main cause of the tension. For the Gereformeerde Kerken (Reformed Churches) of the Netherlands, the tension surfaced dramatically back in 1926 around the name of J. G. Geelkerken and the actions of the Synod of Assen. The struggle that began then has continued without interruption until the present moment. It concentrated on the interpretation of Scripture, though, as now, it took the churchly form of the question of one's commitment to the confessions of the church. At the Synod of Assen, the question focussed on the "utterly obvious" literal intention of the biblical account of the creation and fall of man. (I have given a rather full account of the dispute in my book, *Holy Scripture*, E.T. 1975, and will not enter into detail here.) It is enough to point out that the question of whether the Bible speaks "literally" or "symbolically" — the question raised at Assen — has been considerably broadened since then. New questions have arisen that have to do with the further development of science and with the hermeneutics of the Old and New Testament, especially with respect to Genesis 3 and Romans 5. These questions run on parallel tracks with the problems the Catholic church faced in the confrontation between the church's teachings about creation and the theory of evolution. The difference between them is that, forty years afterward, the Gereformeerde Kerken officially abandoned the decisions made at the Synod of Assen. For Roman Catholicism, given its doctrine of the church, a decision to annul a prior churchly definition is unthinkable. But for the Reformed churches, with their doctrine of the church and its dogma as a form of human confession, it was not unthinkable, in spite of the tensions that such an action creates, tensions that are inevitable because of a desire to maintain continuity with the church's confessions along with a calling to cope with the development of human understanding in an honest manner.

The Synod of Assen had declared that a "literal" interpretation of the "speaking serpent" was required by the confessions of the church. When this decision was retracted the common conviction was that the retraction in no way estranged the present church from its confessions about the creation and the fall of man. The consensus was that the unity of *faith* was not broken. The synod stated in a mood of doxology that it discerned "with joy that all the members of the synod were committed to the confession that God created man good unto a fellowship of love with him, but that man in arrogant disobedience rejected and rejects this fellowship, that all of mankind is estranged from him, has fallen into the bondage of sin, and can be rescued only through God's gracious intervention." It would be an exaggeration to say that everyone in the church shared this joy, but it is true that the conviction prevailed that, in the midst of remaining differences of opinion, there was no radical break with the past, and that shifts in interpretation are not the same as rejection of the authority of Holy Scripture. This helps explain why the discussions since then have not been submerged, and why the older issues keep rising in the background of newer problems. We can only be glad when concern for older questions stays alive. They are related to many aspects of Christian faith and confession, and it can hardly be claimed that they have been clarified to everyone's satisfaction.

I have the sense that many, including theologians, feel themselves caught in a web of uncertainties, what with questions posed from the corners of modern biblical studies, consciousness of the relativity of human thought, the problems of modern science, and the broad question of the limits of our horizon. Even more important is that differences arise as to what, after all, is *central* to Christian faith. When Catholics discussed the hierarchy of truths, the question of which were central to faith always hovered nearby. And the same question haunts the Protestant world. But it is precisely here, when people sense that the center may be affected, that it is obvious that all seeking of the truth involves unrest and concern.

We will now proceed to review some important theological discussions that have been most directly involved with the reinterpretation of unquestionably central issues of the faith. We have in mind the quest for a responsive interpretation of the church's confession of Jesus Christ. This quest is interlocked at many points with our interpretations of the church's past confessions to which both Catholics and Protestants are committed. The definition of the natures and person of Christ at Chalcedon is a clear instance.

We should not be surprised that, in connection with the christological questions raised in recent times, the confession of the trinity also gets involved. We cannot deal with the faith as though we could divide it up neatly into compartments *(loci)* of doctrine. We are dealing always with basic questions, whether earlier or later ones, that affect the preaching of the whole gospel. I will not pretend to do more than provide some orientation within certain phases of the quest that strike me as particularly important. In doing this I cannot help sensing that, whatever unrest and concern such quests provoke, our interest in them is sustained by an expectation that the bond between seeking and finding ("Seek and you shall find") will not fail us. Without this hope, theology loses its primary stimulus.

The confession of Christ's genuine humanity has become a focal point for modern christological discussion. Modern christology is dead set against any sort of docetism, any tendency that shaves anything away from the Lord's humanity. It is as though theologians want once and for all to undo the damage that ancient docetism did to the church's appreciation for the manhood of Jesus Christ. Naturally, the emphasis on Christ's humanity can give the impression that theologians want to reduce Christ to humanity. We had the same concern when theologians "rediscovered" the humanity of the Scriptures, a concern that they were reducing the Holy Scripture to a human book.

It is not forgotten here in the Netherlands that it was Jan Hendrik Scholten — the father of Dutch modernism — who devoted his inaugural address at the University of Franeker (in 1841) to the dangers of docetism. Could it, then, be likewise true that current stress on Christ's humanity and the dangers of docetism arises from a basically modernistic trend? Could the attack on docetism really stem from a thinking that has no sympathy for the great mystery of the Word becoming flesh and no concern to keep alive the church's confessions of him "in whom the fulness of God dwelt bodily" (Colossians 2:9)?

Such suspicions are unnecessary if only for the reason that the church itself has expressly confessed the true humanity of its Lord. This is not only true of Chalcedon, but of the Reformed confessions as well. Does not the Belgic Confession put it as sharply as any? "Our salvation and resurrection," it says, "depend on the reality of his body" (Article XIX).

Modern stress on the true humanity of Christ is not validated only by the church's confession. It is proper just because the humanness of Jesus has frequently been minimized in the church; the faithful have often concentrated wholly on the other side of Chalcedon's statement, the true *divinity* of Christ. Docetism has always crept into the church with subtlety, not so as to lead to an outright denial of the Lord's humanity, but to minimize it. Moltmann remarks that "a mild docetism runs through the christology of the ancient church" (*The Crucified God*, E.T. 1974, p. 89). Bavinck thought he discerned some docetism in both Roman Catholic and Lutheran churches — in distinction from the Reformed, which he thought kept the balance intact between confessions of Christ's divinity and humanity (*Gereformeerde Dogmatiek*, III, p. 298).

But why does theology consider docetism a threat in our time? And why is Roman Catholic theology suspect above others? Whether Catholic theology is still tied to docetic tendencies of the earlier days (as Bavinck saw it) is not really to the point. What is to the point is that exegesis of the New Testament is giving intense address to the biblical witness which sets Christ's humanity so vividly before us. It is turning again to the confession that he *emptied* himself and became a servant of man as a man (Philippians 2:8).

Understandably, then, sayings of Jesus like that in which he disclaims knowledge "of that day or that hour" (Mark 13:32) have become newly relevant to the discussion. Theologians have long had trouble with such explicit self-limits of Jesus; their problems with it led many to rephrase Jesus' words as meaning that he could not *divulge* the day or hour. Modern theologians (Rahner, Schillebeeckx, A. Vögtle, H. Riedlinger, to name a few) have pointed to these words as decisive against docetism; if Jesus anywhere prohibits a docetic view of himself it is here. Jesus' limited knowledge was cited in the days of Roman Catholic modernism by A. Loisy in his plea for unprejudiced exegesis. And while Loisy's view was criticized by men like Maurice Blondel as a humanizing of Christ, the words themselves have kept coming back on the agenda. Jesus' admission of limited knowledge played a large role in the papal condemnation of modernism; it seemed to undermine the Catholic conviction that Jesus enjoyed the "blessed vision" from the beginning of his life. And Catholics held that this vision gave Jesus power to know the past, the present, and the future perfectly.

This tradition had other problems with the biblical portrait of Jesus — his dread in Gethsemane, and his *learning* of obedience (Hebrews 5:8). So, in our time, a more unprejudiced approach to the New Testament picture of Jesus has emerged. Catholic theologians began to reckon with the background to traditional exegesis, and recognized there a tendency to approach the New Testament from a dogmatic viewpoint extracted from Chalcedon, particularly from its confessions of Jesus as "truly God." The accent on Jesus' humanity was seized by men like Deodat de Basly as opening the possibility for a psychological study of Jesus. His ideas were answered in an encyclical, in 1951 *(Sempiternus Christus Rex)*. Here the possibility of a psychology of Jesus was endorsed, but with one qualification: it could not assume that the humanity of Jesus was an independent subject. This would be in conflict with Chalcedon. And shortly thereafter the uninterrupted "blessed vision" enjoyed by Jesus was given fresh affirmation in the encyclical, *Haurietas aquas.* We must not think of Jesus as "truly man" without keeping the "truly God" in view: "how can anyone who confesses that the Word became flesh suggest that there is anything that the Wisdom of God does not know?" Jesus' admission that he "did not know" is interpreted in a way that does not allow for genuine ignorance: the Mark statement is interpreted in the light of texts from John's Gospel. Thus we find that Gregory I, who in the fifth century began the interpretation of "not knowing" as a "not making known," casts his shadow over the official Catholic exegesis of our time. It is not hard to understand why resistance to it keeps growing as theologians seek to do fuller justice to Jesus' humanity. They are convinced that respect for that humanity must be pursued the full route, with no turning back.

The New Testament profile of Jesus comes to the forefront in the current stress on his true humanity. We find frequent references to his human dread and to his experience of God-forsakenness at Calvary, for instance. Rahner strongly criticized what he called "piecemeal psychology," and meant by it a tendency to ignore the fact of Christ's bitterly real pilgrimage as a man. To make too much of the "blessed vision" easily leads to a heretical denial of Christ's passion. The gospel gives us no tolerance here; it confronts us with Jesus' "consciousness of questions, of doubts, with the experience of learning and being surprised, and with the inner conclusions of one who had gone into deadly God-forsakenness." These are voices that echo the Reformation; Calvin had no problem acknowledging Jesus' limits (cf. *Institutes*, III/XVI/12) and Luther denied that Jesus had complete wisdom from the moment of his birth.

Tensions are still apparent, however, as we see in Rahner's view that Christ, his limits notwithstanding, had a "foundational insight" into things, an insight that is not the same as an infinite encyclopedic store of information. He remarks that Christ, in his human development, consistently drew on what he knew "im Grunde" (fundamentally) (Rahner, *Exegese und Dogmatik*, 1962). But this only seems to raise the same questions that Rahner himself had asked.

Tensions are evident in many areas of Catholic christology, especially in so far as it sticks close to the Council of Chalcedon. For at Chalcedon the *vere Deus* was stressed as strongly as the *vere homo,* and, more importantly, both natures were united in one divine person. The big question of *how* these two natures are related keeps protruding into the discussions, especially where docetism is sedulously avoided. It has been claimed that docetism cannot be rejected in all seriousness as long as we maintain the two-natures doctrine, for in it the human nature is always overshadowed and given second place to the divine. If this is true, it is surely out of tune with the New Testament. The New Testament never gives the impression that when Jesus speaks only "one part of his person is speaking" or that "what he is saying might not be entirely true to the whole of his person" (J. McIntyre, *The Shape of Christology*, 1966, p. 85). "It was left to later apologetic to invent subtleties" *(ibid.)*. The two-natures doctrine, in spite of its function in warding off docetism, seems to betray an inner antinomy. This was seen in the definitions of the two natures found in the letter that Pope Leo wrote to Flavianus just before Chalcedon. Leo speaks of acts that are obviously divine acts and others that are clearly human. One must ask whether such distinctions do not inevitably draw a shadow over the human Jesus. And is not the history of this dogma a proof that the two-natures doctrine just does not give us a chance to dispel the shadow?

Not surprisingly, a Greek term from sixth-century christology still haunts christological discussions in our century. I refer to *anhypostasis*, a term first coined by Leontius of Byzantium. It is translated as the "impersonality" of Jesus' human nature. What may now look like a subtle and strange theologoumenon was a focus of sharp dispute in the Middle Ages. (Cf. H. A. Oberman, *The Harvest of Medieval Theology*, 1963, pp. 251ff.) Anyone tempted to smile indulgently at theologians' games should remember that it was the *church's* confession that gave rise to the questions. For Chalcedon poses the question of whether the unity of Christ's person can be understood in any other way than by saying that Christ's humanity was an *impersonal* humanity. It may sound strange to say, in view of the modern perception of what it is to be human, that he who was like us in all things should not have had human personality. But if he had two natures, how could he be an integral, unified person except by having only one person, and that the divine person?

Long before the term *anhypostasis* became a critical object of discussion in modern Catholicism, D. H. Th. Vollenhoven had sparked a debate in the Gereformeerde Kerken by branding it as monophysite. It tended, said Vollenhoven, to negate the genuine humanity of Jesus, a negation that the Reformed Confessions did not tolerate. He was in turn accused of Nestorianism by V. Hepp, the dogmatician of the Free University. Nestorianism, the name given to the notion that there really were two persons in Jesus, was equally intolerable. (Cf. my extensive discussion of this debate in *The Person of Christ*, E.T. 1953, chapter 12.) Vollenhoven's view was a common-sense observation that an impersonal human nature was not a complete human nature. I recall that, at the time, I wrote that we should be more precise as to what we meant by "person"; but Hepp insisted that we were dealing not with definitions but with a matter of profound consequence for the church. His complaints were the same as those levelled against de Basly by Roman Catholics; in questioning the two-natures doctrine, it was said, de Basly was introducing Nestorianism through the back door.

The question keeps coming back as to whether the notion of impersonal humanity is not entailed in Chalcedon's two-natures doctrine, even though the term "impersonality" never gained status within the church's dogma. If so, it raises the further question of whether Chalcedon itself does justice to the humanity of our Lord. If Jesus was not a human person, does it not follow that Jesus of Nazareth was really no more than an instrument played by the divine Logos? (This is a point raised by Oberman, *op. cit.*, p. 253.)

We must also note that the term *anhypostasis* has earned considerable praise. Those who admire it do, of course, take pains to cleanse it of docetism. Barth, for one, wrote a letter to Thurneysen, in which he said that the doctrine of *anhypostasis* could well be replaced in its "candle-holder." We must, said Barth, take a good look into the old dogmatics and find out what "impersonality" is all about; it was hardly a "terrible doctrine." Others defended "impersonality" while at the same time rejecting Nestorianism. Their point was always that the humanness of Jesus was united to the person of the Son of God and cannot be abstracted from him.

This interpretation has much in common with a distinction that H. M. Relton made between *anhypostasis* and *enhypostasis* (*A Study in Christology*, 1929). But the push against anhypostasis only became stronger as it seemed more obviously to suggest that Jesus was not, after all, *fully* human. For even *en*hypostasis, as an effort to say that Jesus' humanity was rooted in the personality of the Word, left him without human personality. Donald Baillie (*God Was in Christ*, 1951) was appreciative that *an*hypostasis was a tool to combat Nestorianism. Nonetheless he saw *an*hypostasis as a poor indicator of Jesus' identity. H. Berkhof sees a "neomonophysitism" lurking in *anhypostasis*, making Jesus' humanity a costume for his real divine self (*De Christelijk Geloof*, 1973, p. 303). But Berkhof thinks this was against the intent of Chalcedon. And so, once again, we meet the problem of interpretation. What did Chalcedon — one of the most crucial conciliar declarations in the history of the church — really mean to confess about him who is the heart and source of faith?

Its bad treatment at the hands of the nineteenth-century critics brought out strong defenders of Chalcedon. The defense focussed on the need to interpret Chalcedon in terms of its intent within the specific historical situation. One aspect of the situation was the double threat coming from Nestorius on one side and Eutyches on the other. Chalcedon intended to maintain the biblical faith in the face of threats from these two opposite directions. Barth insists that Chalcedon was not a captive of a particular ontology, and was not interested in a metaphysics of nature (*human* nature, for instance) that had nothing to do with Jesus' saving impact. Barth pointed to the "positive meaning of the formula." He was sure that modern theology had broken with the church's ancient confession and substituted a totally different vision out of an honor it felt for the very "being of God in revelation" and for "the realism of the biblical relevation: the Word is made flesh."

Brunner thought very differently. He saw Chalcedon as introducing mythology into christology, or at least teaching metaphysical redemption. Bultmann's response to the doctrinal basis of the World Council of Churches was in the same mold. "Jesus Christ as God and Savior," he said, "smacks of a metaphysical notion that has little in common with the New Testament witness to Christ as the Messiah, the Son of David, and the Son of God who was obedient to the Father." The New Testament is not interested in Christ's nature, Bultmann argued, but in his saving effect. So, again, we see resistance to ontology and a preference for a functional christology.

Oscar Cullmann, Bultmann's untiring opponent, does agree that the New Testament, unlike "later Greek speculations about substance and natures," is interested in the history of salvation. "Therefore, in the light of the New Testament witness, all mere speculation about his natures is an absurdity. Functional Christology is the only kind which exists" (*Christology of the New Testament*, E.T. 1959, p. 326). The New Testament does not "give information about how we are to conceive the being of God beyond the history of revelation . . ." (*ibid.*, p. 327).

On first impression, we might suppose that Cullmann is as opposed to Chalcedon as Bultmann is. But this is not the case. He was criticized by Father Bavaud, who objected to the notion of a functional christology, and by P. Gaechter, who thought a functional christology was a form of modalism. But Cullmann answered that he was one with Chalcedon. The New Testament, indeed, bears witness to the God of Abraham, Isaac, and Jacob, not to Christ's *being* God independent of his revelatory and saving significance. But this is not to say that the New Testament is in conflict with ontology and certainly does not rule out a preexistent Christ. When we ask the New Testament who Jesus is, we do not get a word about his divine nature; we hear about his work. But, Cullmann says, Chalcedon is a later *reflection* about the natures of Christ. It is a reflection Cullmann considers an "absolute necessity," but it is *not* exegesis of the New Testament. The exegete limits himself to functional christology, and resists identifying later christologies, like that of Chalcedon, with the New Testament christology. Chalcedon, however, "corresponds to what the Christology of the N.T. presupposes" ("The Reply of Prof. Cullmann to Roman Catholic Critics," *Scottish Journal of Theology*, 1962, pp. 36ff.).

An unresolved problem still remains. The church meant to found its confession of Christ on the New Testament. It did not mean to separate dogma from the New Testament in the sharp manner that Cullmann does in his answer to the charge of heresy. The problem of ontological versus functional christology still challenges us. The contrast has a modern sound; it may be a symptom of a general distaste for abstractions and a modern penchant for what is functional, operational, and existential. More to the point, however, is the way Chalcedon describes the joining of the human and divine natures in one person. Pannenberg speaks of Jesus, as he appears in Chalcedon, as "bearing and uniting two opposed substances in himself. All the insoluble problems of the doctrine of two natures result from this conception" (*Jesus — God and Man*, E.T. 1968, p. 284). Hans Küng, in a similar vein, says that classic christology is oriented to Greek metaphysics and gives an ontological interpretation of the incarnation and divine Sonship (*Menschwerdung Gottes*, 1970, pp. 661ff.).

In dealing with the problem of the unity of Christ, we tend to talk as though there were two separate components that had somehow to be joined. This is especially true if we abstract the problem — even though only in thought — from the saving action of Christ. No one would suggest that the theologians of the two-natures doctrine saw the saving significance of Christ's work as anything but a living reality. Still, as they dealt with the theological problem of the union, the historical work of Christ and his historical revelation were set aside. This is evident in the later monothelite controversy — the controversy about whether there was one or two wills in the Savior. Did the decision made at Constantinople (680) — that there were two wills — correspond with the Christ-profile of the New Testament? The New Testament, after all, speaks of Christ's will and the Father's will (as seen in Gethsemane), but never of two distinct wills operating in Jesus. The point is that in such discussions the single living person of the biblical Jesus, in all his revelatory activity, seems to be somewhere in the background.

It is striking that most theologians set limits to their criticism of Chalcedon. Pannenberg, for instance, has no objection to the *vere Deus et vere homo;* it is, he acknowledged, "an inexpendable expression of Christian theology." The criticism is focussed wholly on the two-natures doctrine, on the two-sidedness that seems to disrupt the personal unity of Christ. Thus, the question is posed as to whether we might better stick with the way in which the earthly, human Jesus appears on the scene in the pages of the New Testament.

In current christology, we often meet a distinction between a christology "from above" and a christology "from below." The christology "from above" stands for classical christology which moves from the divine Son, the second person of the trinity, who assumes human nature when he descends from heaven to earth. This christology is sometimes also called incarnation christology or even descendence christology. The Son descends from above, from his exalted preexistent status in heaven. This is the christology, says Pannenberg, of the ancient church; but he says it is also the christology of Barth and Brunner and others. From the newer exegetical studies, however, comes a christology "from below." It is formed out of the givens of the New Testament, the history of Jesus; here the experience and discovery of the mystery of God in the flesh is prior to dogmatic reflection. Rahner and Cullmann call this approach that of the history of salvation. It is more inductive than deductive, more exegetical than dogmatic. Rahner thinks this method makes for a better missionary and pedagogical approach, since it makes christology existentially more credible. From below: this means that the earthly Jesus, in his life and death here below, looms before our view. We follow him in his earthly pilgrimage, and come, as we follow, to the amazing discovery of the mystery of his real identity. His life is not set within the framework of his deity and his preexistence; it is read off the pages of the Gospels, and is understood as it comes to us from them.

We must ask whether the distinction between christologies "from above" and "from below" is a real option. At least we encounter unusual complications in regard to the question. Pannenberg, for instance, criticizes christology "from above" because it beclouds the real manhood of Jesus by its deductive preoccupation with the Godhead of the Son. But he hesitates a bit in the midst of his analysis. Though he opts for a christology "from below," he also grants a relative legitimacy to a christology "from above." The old christology is not sheer error; there is truth in it. But *our* way has to be the way of a christology "from below"; only in this way can we ask about his deity without submerging his true humanity.

Rahner is less dogmatic. The "descendence christology," as he calls it, is present in the New Testament — in John's prologue, for instance, and in the christological hymns. But this "descendence christology" was set within a specific framework, the category of the trinity. It begins with the Logos and his preexistence rather than with an experience with the crucified and risen Lord. "God has become man": christology "from above" can interpret this only on the basis of the "axiom" of ancient christology, not on the basis of an experience with the biblical Jesus. So he admits the legitimacy of the ancient christology. The church, from its earliest days, *had* to deal with christology in the manner that came to expression in the Council of Chalcedon.

But the christology "from above" contains the danger that the connection between soteriology and christology is submerged into the problem of how two natures can be united in a single person. It creates the impression, what with all the concern about two natures, that in Jesus Christ we are dealing with an ontological problem in its own right, cut off from the work of saving history. We seem to be coping with a metaphysics of Jesus rather than with the saving ministry of Jesus. The confession "Jesus is God" does not guarantee orthodoxy; it can easily be construed in a heretical monophysite denial of Jesus' manhood. The initial and accurate Christian intuition is to reject this heresy as a caricature. But intuitions are not theologically adequate. So christology's task is not to repeat the ancient formulas, but to dig out their true meaning so that misunderstanding can be avoided. And this, it is said, can be done today only by way of a christology "from below."

Otto Weber is preoccupied with the same set of problems. The christology "from above" that dominated the earlier centuries ended up in objectionable metaphysical intrigues (cf. Weber, *Grundlagen der Dogmatik*, II, 1962, p. 23). It forgot that God can be known only through what happens "below" the heavens. Yet, Weber refuses to opt for a christology "from below" as the alternative to a christology constructed from the movement of the Son from heaven to earth. He fears that a christology "from below" may slice away the truth of the reality "from above." And he asks whether the current interest in a christology "from below" is prompted by oneness of mind with the New Testament or by the modern quest for the historical Jesus.

Weber recalls that Luther appealed to the humanity of Jesus countless times as he wrestled against the "theology of glory." But Luther never set himself aloof from the old church dogma. Naturally, Luther's allegiance to classic christology depends on his interpretation of Chalcedon. And Luther's understanding of the ancient counsels has been the source of a lot of scholarly debate. W. Joest, in his study of Luther's christology, has said that Luther never bothered his head about the metaphysical problem of the unity and distinction of the two natures. His approach to the ancient definitions was uncritical, though he held on to them (W. Joest, *Ontologie der Person bei Luther*, 1967). Joest's judgment is very understandable, especially as we note how Luther on occasion warned about speculation concerning the two natures. "Christ is not called Christ because he had two natures," Luther wrote. "What has that fact to do with me? He bears this glorious and comforting name because of his work and his office; what he did provides him with the title." Luther here is responding to the way "the Sophists have put Christ through their mills" (A. Harnack, *History of Dogma*, VII, p. 2).

That Luther held with the ancient formula is due not to a metaphysical concern, but to a desire for continuity in the church's faith.

The continuity must indeed be preserved. We must keep continuity even as we criticize abstractions in the older christology. Even in remarks like Melanchthon's famous word about knowing Christ, we recognize a desire to stay within the historical faith. To know Christ, Melanchthon said, was to know his saving acts; to know him is not the same thing as to have a correct view of his natures and the method of his incarnation. Yet, Melanchthon did not scuttle the ancient christology; he merely side-stepped its dangers.

There is a place for marvelling at the mystery of the union between the divine and human natures, even for that mystery by itself, apart from the work of Christ. And to marvel at the "from above" in and with the appearance of Jesus whom we meet "from below" gives an opportunity of reinterpreting the creed without breaking with it. This means that we do not deal with a "descendence-christology" that is set apart from the history of Jesus to become a metaphysical problem in its own right, a problem of how two different substances could be united.

The church's path, like that of the disciples, is the pathway of ongoing discovery — right through all the misunderstandings and misjudgments made along the way. It is this discovery-experience that the New Testament relates from page to page. All the vital decisions of the church's preaching are made in connection with its discovery of Jesus "from below." For in the church's preaching the saving significance of God's wonderful acts in Christ are set before the listening congregation. We are talking about the discoveries of Christ's glory (John 1:14), that he is the Holy One of God (John 6:69), that he is the word of life, experienced by seeing and tasting it (1 John 1:1). We are talking about experiences like those of Nathanael who, overcoming his skepticism, finally had to "come and see" and so to find (John 1:47, 50), and of Thomas who, after his bitter disappointment and doubts, discovered reason for a doxology (John 20:28).

These discoveries were not made by speculating about an abstract notion of preexistence and a coming "from above." Nor are they made by sacrificing the intellect at the two-natures doctrine, as if one had first to get this doctrine straight and only then enter into an experience with the Father.

A HALF CENTURY OF THEOLOGY

In these matters, the church has a lively fear of speculation. Speculation works in this way: it uses the "from above" truth to construct an objective doctrine of Christ that is then loaned out for further deductions, in which Christ's work of salvation is set in the background, if not neglected altogether. Pannenberg is off the mark when he typifies the christology "from above" as a doctrine by which the believer sets himself "at God's standpoint." The intention was quite different, as Rahner, Weber, and Moltmann recognize. Moltmann is right in saying that we are not taking necessarily a divine standpoint if we try to "follow the way of the Son of God in the world" (*The Crucified God*, p. 89). There is only an *apparent* conflict between the christology "from above" and "from below," and if we assume it is a real conflict we will be forced into the dilemma that Bultmann posed: "Does Jesus help me because he is the Son of God or is he the Son of God because he helps me?"

We might illustrate the problem posed by the "from above" or "from below" antithesis by noting John's prologue, which has frequently been cited as a case of christology "from above." The prologue, it is claimed, begins with the *a priori* category of a preexistent Logos and only then speaks about the Word who became flesh (John 1:14). Ridderbos counters this suggestion by saying that John's real point is not the revelation of the Lord who, at a given point, appears in the form of the person of Christ. The gist of the prologue is that here the Logos is interpreted from the vantage point of all that had already happened in Jesus Christ before the eyes and ears of the writer. The gospel is a witness of what people had seen, heard, and touched. There is no *a priori* christology here at all. The view of the eternal Word is a view "from below," from the vantage point of human vision, human search, and human discovery in the history of Jesus. Barth sees the situation similarly; the exegesis of the fourth-century confessions, he believes, was "basically on the right track" and managed to speak of the eternal Word without falling into metaphysics.

The matter of a christological framework or scheme comes up in many recent studies of classic christology, especially that of Chalcedon. The question is whether the schematization into which classic christology fits the revelation of Christ harmonizes with the portrait of the New Testament. Sometimes, while acknowledging that Chalcedon was not trying to dispense a metaphysics, theologians stress the danger of where Chalcedon can lead.

Korff, for instance, warns about drawing conclusions like *anhypos-tasis*, duotheletism, and even the famous extra-Calvinisticum from the definition given by Chalcedon. This is a legitimate concern that we do not abstract the question of Christ's person from his work and thus get bogged down in the problem of the unity of his distinct natures. Even those who respect the motive within the post-Chalcedon developments will admit to the dangers.

Keeping our eye open for abstractions, we can then locate the connections between the church's confession and the living, concrete portrait of Jesus found in the Gospels. And then we can preach the living Lord in the church. This does not mean that fair criticism of the ancient confession is out of order. But right at a time when so much attention is given to a reinterpretation of dogma, it is helpful to recognize that the form given to christology at Chalcedon was not tied to metaphysics, at least not in the sense that the church was trying to teach an official metaphysics in its confessions. The accusation that the church was really trying to put over a certain metaphysics is not really a sincere effort to purify the church's tradition and to preserve our continuity with it. Some theologians of our time want a christology that is no longer ontological, no longer turns the living reality into the "thingness of a two-natures ontology," but rather is a "functional, personalist christology." But we must ask whether the juxtaposing of these two categories — "thingness" and "personalist" — are really helpful (cf. H. Ott, *Die Antwort des Glaubens*, 1972, p. 257). It certainly gives a simplistic picture of what happened at Chalcedon. It assumes that Chalcedon pretended to provide a complete and exhaustive summary of the biblical teaching about Jesus Christ. And it forgets, quite unhistorically, that Chalcedon did not intend that its formula be abstracted from the total profile of Jesus Christ that was known and confessed at that time.

The specific formula cannot be plucked loose from the whole confession of the church at a given period. What Rahner says about the "self-transcendence of every formula" is relevant here; for the formula points to a specific *feature* of dogma that happened to be in the crucible at a given moment. This is why it is misleading to speak of Chalcedon as the high point or climax of the confession of Christ. Korff puts it this way, and he was understandably impressed with the threats to christology that were rife at the time. But it is wrong to suggest that Chalcedon is the final stopping place for christological understanding, as though it perfected every thought and said everything that could be said. If we assume that Chalcedon is the end of christological discussion we are likely to isolate the confession and lose sight of its place within the fulness of New Testament revelation. Set apart from its place within the total confession, Chalcedon can very easily be interpreted as a cold and negative statement (as Harnack did), as a metaphysics, or a speculation on the question of how two different natures could be united in Christ. In short, it can be taken by itself and twisted into an independent formula that has lost touch with the living Savior.

We can overestimate Chalcedon by seeing its "negative definition" as a final focus for the mystery of how Jesus could be God and man in one person (F.W.A. Korff, Christologie, I, 1940, p. 197). The mystery of Christ is then the theoretical problem of how two very different natures could be united. And Chalcedon's formula is seen as putting the mystery in sharper focus, limiting it, finalizing it, and thus setting limits to further progress in understanding. Over against this notion, we should see further progress in christology, not as transgression of the limits set by Chalcedon, but as growth into the full possibilities of preaching Christ.

Chalcedon has entered little into the preaching of the church. This is understandable in view of the polemical orientation of its creation. More, the Chalcedon confession is hardly known within the churches. If anything from Chalcedon has gotten through to the churches it is the phrase "true God and true man." The disputed sections, about Christ being known "in two natures, unmixed and unchanged, undivided and unseparated" and yet "brought together in one person and one essence," are hardly known. The confession "true God and true man" is encountered in preaching, not as a dualistic metaphysical notion, but as an echo of Thomas' discovery: "My Lord and my God." The tradition of faith experienced the time-bound language of Chalcedon as an abstract ontology far less than has theology. The reason for this is that Christ is preached from the Gospels; and therefore whatever the church set in difficult formulas cannot be the final word or highest word, because it is not the language of preaching.

I suspect that the "difficult" language is made more difficult by treating Chalcedon unhistorically. That is, it is judged without taking into view its real intent. If we keep its intention in mind we can understand how the preaching of Christ avoids dualism

without any sense of breaking with Chalcedon. Preaching is in
touch with the revelation of the mystery — not the mystery of
how we can solve the problem of a metaphysical union, nor the
mystery of whether Christ had two wills or one, but the mystery
of godliness that is seen "from below" and is seen so deeply that
it takes the wind out of all human speculation.

In times when the church is concerned about the faith, restless about the church's dogma, and confused about what is
really going on among theologians, talk about Chalcedon could
give the impression of another alienation from the church's
confession. It is worth remembering then that any fixed definition
can fossilize, especially if the definitions are no longer understood. Indeed, we should remember that no definition is adequate. Calvin was keenly conscious of this; he refused to fight
about words. He recalled the differing use of language by the
different councils, especially the semantic problems Greeks and
Latins had with each other, and agreed with Augustine's comment that the church's words are pressed out of the poverty of
human speech (*Institutes*, I/XIII/5). Augustine's reserve was,
for Calvin, a hint that we should not too quickly put a label on
people who do not swear by the same words that we use. He
had the word *anhypostasis* in mind. Calvin was willing to bury
any set of words as long as the faith is alive. He was not lapsing
into semantic defeatism; he was only recognizing that the distinction between heresy and orthodoxy is not tested by conformity with certain words. Orthodoxy is maintained only in
conformity with the truth that the church had in mind when it
tried to state the truth in its inadequate formulas. If we grasp
this, our perspective on the church's confession of the mystery
of him "in whom the fulness of Godhead dwelt bodily" will be
safe. And it will not be preserved as a theoretical problem, which
theology has the task of solving, but as a message given to the
congregation that lives by this mystery and the grace that it
reveals (Colossians 2:9, 11-15).

Modern christology has wanted to avoid dualism, especially
any dualism that conflicts with Chalcedon's own statement about
the "one and the same Christ." Schillebeeckx, for instance, does
not like expressions such as: "Besides being man, Jesus is also
God." The word "besides" is misleading, he thinks, because the
divinity must be seen *in* the humanity of Jesus, not alongside of it.
The mystery of Christ's person must not be sought somewhere

"behind" or "under" the man Jesus, but precisely *in* him. Christ himself said: "He who has seen me has seen the Father." He would not be the revelation of God for us if God appeared alongside of him, as though his divinity had to be revealed in a "divine nature" alongside his own human nature. "The man Jesus is himself the presence of God, and anyone who sets his divinity 'beside' Jesus opposes the whole of Christian tradition."

Rahner works with similar thoughts. He recalls the notion of Duns Scotus, that the primary motive for the incarnation was not the bearing of human guilt, and that therefore we can think of the incarnation apart from the fall of man. This view, Rahner submits, was never condemned by the church, so we may see the large context for the incarnation as the total process of creative evolution without fear of being judged heretical (*Theological Investigations*, V, E.T. 1966, pp. 184f.). In an interview with Eberhard Simons (cf. Simons, *Zur Lage der Theologie. Probleme nach dem Konzil*, 1962), he pleaded for a new christology that would take anthropology into account. He wants to bring christology out of its isolation and set it in the context of a universal revelation that is coexistent with human history. But he does not want to sacrifice the uniqueness of the *contingent* revelation in Christ; he only wants to recognize its place within a universal revelation. There are shades of Teilhard de Chardin here; we are dealing again with the relation between Christ and creation, Christ as the first and the last, in whom *all things* are reconciled (Colossians 1:20).

Clearly, Chalcedon is not merely an interesting, if complex, chapter in the history of interpretation. It stays within the focus of theological discussion because we need to keep working at the best way to understand the mystery of Christ. At Chalcedon the mystery was formulated in the "true God–true man" language in the midst of a polemic struggle that concentrated on the nature of the union between the two. Later, the task of the council was abstracted from its place within a large setting, abstracted too from the context of preaching and the life of the congregation. Hence, it hardly came to the attention of people within the churches. The problems that arose in relation to Chalcedon were so profound and often so broad that some people preferred to avoid the whole challenge of reinterpretation. And they sometimes did this out of their concern for the unchangeable truth which seemed to be threatened by reinterpretation of the ancient formula. Trying to reinterpret the church's confession from the viewpoint of new images of man, whether in phenomenology or existentialism, looked like a rejection of the confession.

There is unrest about the church's dogma, concern for the church's faith, in this reaction to reinterpretation. The tensions sometimes muffle the doxology of the church, the doxology that ought to unite us and bring to light the deepest meaning of the dogmas. We cannot take refuge in a mere repetition of the formulas as a way of setting the concerns at rest. What Augustine said about human words is to the point here: we do not speak as though we can say what ought to be said, we speak only "because we cannot be silent." His comment does not give warrant to relativism, but it does remind us that the reality always transcends our words and thoughts and is never fixed within the grasp of human formulations. This is why we are urged to go on toward greater understanding of all the dimensions of God's love in Jesus Christ (Ephesians 3:18-21).

The preaching of the church, in every new age, challenges us to give our answer, in our time, to the question that echoes from the neighborhood of Caesarea Philippi (Matthew 16). Preaching cannot be a repetition of the dogma of the church, not the dogma of two natures, nor any other in which the church focussed on a single aspect of the faith in order to point to the wider dimensions. Dogma, even that of Chalcedon, cannot encapsulate the tradition of the history of Jesus Christ. If we thought it could, we would miss genuine orthodoxy, the orthodoxy that is expressed in the doxology or, if not, is not worthy of the name orthodoxy.

When Bavinck wrote that theology, at least for the time being, can do no better than to maintain the two-natures doctrine (*Gereformeerde Dogmatiek*, III, p. 288), he was suggesting that the coagulation of the church's speech in historical formulations has no real meaning unless it is taken up into a living confession that later believers can carry with them into a still deeper understanding of it. The perspective of Thomas' confession — "My Lord and my God" — must prevail through all our thinking and all our reinterpretations. Indeed, all reinterpretation should be tested by whether it can participate in *this* confession.

Certain words Jesus spoke have played a large role in recent christological discussions, words that have always been important in preaching. We have in mind such words as these. reported by John: "He who has seen me has seen the Father" (John 14:9).

Philip's request, "Show us the Father," received a question in reply: "Have you been with me so long and not known me?" Philip's wish to get to the depth and height of Jesus' identity is misplaced in view of the fact that he had lived close to Jesus for many months. And Jesus' answer, therefore, has unique significance. To see Jesus *is* to see the Father.

We have seen Jesus' truly surprising words interpreted in amazing ways. They are used by Bishop Robinson in *Honest to God* (1963) and by Paul van Buren in his *The Secular Meaning of Christianity* (1963), for instance, as indicators that *all* of christology should be defined in terms of the man Jesus. Van Buren understands Jesus to be telling Philip that he should not look but confine his concern to Jesus. He wants to read Chalcedon in this light too: if the Word has actually become flesh, we can understand the Great Commandment simply as meaning that we should love our neighbor after the model of Jesus in his freedom. Hence, Chalcedon *really* means that Jesus is the model of freedom and love.

It is utterly clear that van Buren missed the point, not only of these particular words, but of the entire Gospel of John. Van Buren was not merely rejecting dualism. Nor was he merely setting aside questions that ignore the man Jesus and probe into regions totally unknown to us. Van Buren's notion of transcendence is congenial only to a wholly secularized Christianity, which in turn simply ignores the real problems that the ancient church wrestled with. It is not hard to understand why people who thought in this vein found themselves attracted to Arius, against whom the ancient church had to defend the deity of Christ, even though, when the chips were down, they moved back from him (cf. N. Pittenger, *Christology Reconsidered,* 1970, p. 8; Pittenger in responding to M. Wiles, "In Defense of Arius," *Journal of Theological Studies,* 1962).

It is in such discussions as these that we feel how tortuous the process of reinterpretation can be. It is full of tensions. And we also see how the prejudices of one's own time control reinterpretation of the past. But not even such extreme forms as Robinson and van Buren should tempt us in reaction to reject the effort. To do so would be to commit an historical error; we simply cannot avoid the fact that the ancient formulations were time-bound. But, more seriously, we would miss the connection between the confessions and contemporary preaching. It is the church's preaching that is really at stake. It was for the sake of the clarity of the salvation message that the church wanted, with its confessions, to focus attention on the voiceless lamb who opened the door to the possibility that men, like the Eunuch from Ethiopia, could meet him in preaching and go on their way rejoicing (Acts 8:35,39).

We have noted the danger of isolating the questions that orbited around the person of Jesus Christ. To isolate the question of his natures, for instance, from the total biblical picture could lead to the assumption that Christ's natures, and especially the possibility of uniting his two natures in one person, were self-evident and not a mystery. But isolation of this question was not possible for any length of time, in any case, for the overpowering portrait of the Gospels came back to prevent an abstract definition of the "union" from being the only truth about Jesus. The gospel picture kept calling us back to the concrete life of Jesus within the confession of the unity of his person.

The history of theology, nonetheless, presents us with various questions which seem to flow quite naturally from Chalcedon and which therefore compel us to deal with them. One of the most compelling questions lies in the thought that, while we indeed should pay attention to the concrete life of Jesus, we must do so within the perspective of his deity. From this has come the question of God's *impassibility*. It seemed to be implied in Chalcedon that the "true God" who was united with "true man" could not suffer. It was a view of God that avoided anthropomorphic traits. This brought back past echoes of older controversies about so-called theopaschitism (the suffering God); it has to do with the terribly profound question of how the "true God" was involved in the sufferings of the man Jesus. I discussed Barth's views about the passion of God in my book, *The Triumph of Grace in the Theology of Karl Barth* (E.T. 1956); and when we spoke together about my book, on a visit to Basel in 1954, Barth immediately urged that we talk about "the question of theopaschitism." From this conversation, and also from what he later wrote about my book in the *Church Dogmatics*, I became quite convinced that Barth was hardly one of those who had only a christology "from above." I think Pannenberg is wrong in interpreting Barth's christology as defined "from the standpoint of God." Right at the point of the suffering of our Lord, Barth most clearly does his thinking about the mystery of the atonement from the givens of the New Testament witness and not from any *a priori* notion of the inability of God to suffer. The theology of the cross and God's participation in the passion of Christ — in whom God was present reconciling the world to himself (2 Corinthians 5:19) — dominates Barth's thoughts. Barth saw no way to divide up the work between the "true God" and the "true man," leaving God out of the experience of passion. Rather, it is in Jesus Christ that the "final depth of the being of God" is recognized (*CD* II/1, p. 588).

By seeing God himself involved in Christ's passion, though in an unfathomable way, Barth stoutly rejected any "conflict" in God, a notion that he thought bordered on blasphemy. Now that God is revealed here, as he truly is, without any horrible confrontation of "God against God," there can be no "conflict nor any self-contradiction" (*CD* IV/1, p. 186). Here we can answer the question of whether God capitulated to the powers of evil and somehow abdicated from his Godness. The answer is that God, far from abdicating, maintained and revealed his deity in the most living way precisely in the passion of this man as his only son. Therefore, what was involved was not just an important historical event, but the very redemption of the world with God. Hence, Barth's sharp position against the kenosis doctrine of the nineteenth century (the notion that God set aside his divine attributes in order to be incarnate): God revealed his divine attributes precisely in this way and is, indeed, God just in this way.

The church has always had an intuitive grasp of how impermissible and impossible it is to isolate and divide the life of Christ. We see it in Ignatius, in Augustine, in Luther, Calvin, and Barth, as well as in many English-speaking theologians. It was Luther especially who wanted to say that in Christ God was actually present, and that Jesus was not simply the instrument of God, nor the proclaimer, and certainly not a mere illustration of how God works; Luther spoke of the "crucified God." Anselm would never have spoken this way. Asked whether the doctrine of the two natures did not make God somewhat peripheral to the sufferings of Christ, Anselm said that questions like this were born of misunderstanding, for the divine nature cannot suffer. Still, we confess Jesus Christ as one person in two natures. "So when we say that God experienced limits or weakness, we understand that to refer, not to the dignity of his (divine) nature, but to the weakness of his human nature." Boso, who asked the question, was not satisfied. For, after all, Christ was God's beloved Son and God had led him into this passion. Anselm's answer stood pat, and we still have the impression that it is just a little too clear to be wholly credible.

Something about this clear and neat solution keeps raising doubts. I think that Bavinck was wrestling with this very notion when he remarked that the Scripture often speaks of Christ's divine nature as the subject of humiliation. Further, he remarked that the church fathers often expressed themselves in this vein. This was one of those comments Bavinck made now and then, touching on difficult matters without working them out further. But it serves to underscore his awareness that some things cannot be given simple solutions, no matter how logical they appear. We can speak *too* clearly about some things, and in our wish to be clear miss the depths and heights of the matter. We may keep Paul's word in mind: "But we impart a secret and hidden wisdom of God. . . . None of the rulers of this age understood this; for if they had, they would not have crucified the Lord of glory" (1 Corinthians 2:7,8).

Not surprisingly, Romans 8:32 always comes into consideration in discussions about God's involvement in the sufferings of Jesus. God's being *for* us is set in the context of God's *action*. "He who did not spare his own Son but gave him up for us all, will he not also give us all things with him?" God's involvement is indicated in a unique way. (It was he himself who spared not his own Son. We should keep John 3:16 in mind here, as well as the parable of the unrighteous tenants in Matthew 21:33ff., and the word about the only beloved Son in Mark 12:6.) Paul's point — perhaps made in recollection of Abraham's sacrifice of Isaac — is this: if God did all this, the other gifts to us become simple in comparison, embraced as they all are in the sacrifice of him than whom, in Calvin's words, nothing "was more precious or excellent." Nothing could demonstrate God's love more clearly, said Calvin, than this unhesitating involvement right to the uttermost limit.

Here we confront a divine sacrifice, a divine giving-over which, as H. N. Ridderbos puts it, is not "an impersonal decree, behind which God is hidden as the Great Unknown," but rather God is seen as the "one who offers, who gives himself." God does not give some*thing*, skimpingly, but "sacrifices his own beloved Son into human forsakenness." For Paul, nothing could be deeper, more revealing, and more real — and therefore it is filled with awesome perspectives.

The divine "giving over" — how often have we not tried to set this crucial dimension of God's act into some sort of exegetical or dogmatic formula? "Giving over" comes up in contrasting contexts in the Bible. Paul speaks of it in a judgmental sense in Romans 1:24-28. Judas gave Jesus over to his enemies. It is, as Barth noted, not a mere semantic accident, this "giving over." But the interesting thing is that divine and human actions are coupled in it, and in this way the "for us" dimension becomes apparent in this action of God.

In an earlier work, I mentioned Stauffer's notion of "the law of reversal" in the relationship between the acts of man and the acts of God (cf. E. Stauffer, New Testament Theology, E.T. 1955, p. 207, and my The Providence of God, E.T. 1952, p. 100). The "law of reversal" is a mystery that comes to view in the life and death of Jesus as nowhere else. The word "law" is, obviously, not a fortunate choice, but Stauffer means to indicate God's teleological action which is effective straight through human sin. There is no way to make a clear separation in our thought between the human and divine acts. The New Testament can speak emphatically about human involvement in the course of Jesus' suffering. "You denied the Holy One." "You killed the author of life." "You crucified" Jesus (Acts 3:14,15; 2:36). And, in the great contrast: God raised him from the dead (Acts 3:15). But Paul can speak of God's act in "giving over" Jesus to the cross. Paul is not unaware of the history of Jesus' pathway to the cross; what Paul wants to say is that it was "for us." This act of mercy is intertwined with the human darkness, and on the way to the shocking unveiling of human guilt the light is shed on the mercy of God (Acts 3:36).

In 1971, H. Wiersinga wrote a doctoral dissertation on the doctrine of atonement (De verzoening in de theologische discussie) which provoked a heated controversy. The discussion focussed on the relationship between the human events surrounding the life and death of Christ and the saving mercy of God in redemption. Wiersinga stressed the human action that brought about Christ's death, as well as the human response to his death. There could, of course, be little controversy about this; the New Testament is plain enough about human guilt in connection with Christ. We may forget or minimize human involvement by concentrating on the divine action at the cross. But, following the New Testament, Christ's passion cannot be segregated from human implication. To do that would be just as absurd as to ascribe some creative value to the sorrow in reaction to Christ's death that was said to have overcome the generations of the earth. Questions arose with respect to God's act and Christ's own self-offering, and centered on the substitutionary atonement. Romans 8:32 became a key passage: "He who did not spare his own Son but gave him up for us all. . . ." Wiersinga wrote: "God gave up his own Son; Jesus gave himself up to death; and he was the victim of other men." Put all these together and you have a complex problem of understanding. Wiersinga wrote that there were "more dimensions to the relationship between Jesus' suffering and our reconciliation" than one-sided dogmatic theories would sometimes suggest. And he was particularly concerned about aspects of our doctrine of "substitutionary atonement" that becloud the realities of reconciliation.

The doctrine of substitutionary atonement has seen hefty debate quite often. Dorothee Sölle and Helmut Gollwitzer had a spirited argument about it in the sixties (cf. D. Sölle, *Christ the Representative*, E.T. 1967, and H. Gollwitzer, *Von der Stellvertretung Gottes*, 1967). Sölle contended that substitutionary atonement is a caricature of what the Bible means by substitution. Why Sölle reacts as strongly as she does is not hard to figure out. She is sharpest when she opposes Karl Barth for stressing that Christ's salvation lies in its having happened "*for us*" but "*without us*" (Sölle, *op. cit.*, pp. 88ff.; cf. Barth, *CD* IV/1, p. 249). There is indeed a decisive point of view involved.

Sölle sees a real danger in this, the danger of objectifying Christ's substitution, turning it into a fact that is independent of our response, an event that has its full significance in and by itself. She especially opposes the notion that Christ stands in our place, rejected in place of us sinners, as Barth put it. She sees in this a kind of disqualification of human responsibility; man is represented here, she thinks, as a creature without will, without a genuine relationship to Christ, and therefore shorn of responsibility. This is the part of Sölle's analysis that Gollwitzer rightly branded as a caricature.

When Barth says that Christ's suffering is "God's act for us" he does not mean that Christ is a kind of ersatz offering. He is concerned with the crucial dimension that Paul indicates in the

justification of the ungodly (Romans 4:5) and in Christ's dying
for us while we were yet sinners and enemies (5:8,10). There is
no vacuum of relationship between us and Christ in this. But it
does have to do with the revelation of radical grace. The "without us" does not mean that human beings are set out of God's
sight; it only opens the door to grace, to *sola gratia*. Gollwitzer
compares Sölle's protest to the old Socinian objection to substitutionary atonement on the ground that it appeared to negate
human worth; but, says Gollwitzer, they thought this only because they stumbled over their own interpretation of an exclusive atonement as a causal-mechanistic event that was played
off wholly irrespective of us.

Wiersinga does not take Sölle's route. He explicitly affirms
the radicality of Paul's "when we were yet sinners . . . Christ died
for us." The problematics of the atonement lie, for him, in a
fear that the "for us" dimension becomes isolated and objectified,
and thus becomes an atonement without real effect on people.
The explains why the problem of an *effective* atonement has
played such a large role in the discussion. This is odd, it would
seem, since effective atonement is a tautology; we cannot cir-
cumscribe the atonement in the simple categories of objective
or subjective.

Sölle thinks of substitution as an objective thing, completed in a way that makes human renewal and reconciliation
superfluous. But when we hear this we can recall that Paul, in the
context of God's atoning act in which he "made Christ to be sin
for us," immediately calls man to be reconciled in the name of
Christ. Paul did not see this call as a threat to the justification
of the godless, nor an overshadowing of his proclamation of
salvation "by grace alone." He did not think the summons to be
reconciled was a synergism that had to be brought in as an
afterthought. But he did not take man out of the picture either.
Salvation was completed, and yet the reality of the cross was
taken up into the *ministry* of reconciliation (2 Corinthians 5:18).

Earlier discussion focussed on the *direction* of the atonement:
was it directed toward God or toward man? Was God turned
about by the achievement of Christ or was the renewed and
reconciled man turned about? Gradually this antithesis was seen
as unreal. But it still appears, at least implicitly, in consideration
of the dimensions of the passion in which our guilt was borne and
carried by the Lord. This is why, in my judgment, we should be

sensitive to the dangers that Sölle fears, and respond to them, not by rejecting the doctrine of substitution, but by distinguishing it from any juridical game and from all calculation in which the juridical beclouds the gracious action of God. There is only one way to go, and that is the way of understanding how precisely in the substitution of Christ all human alibis are eliminated. In view of the cross — with its utter darkness — and in view of Romans 8:32, there is no possibility for thinking of substitutionary atonement as if it were a mechanical ersatz that does not really touch us. If this misconception is closed off, not only in dogmatics but in the actual life of the congregation, then faith can point to the substitution, total and radical as it is, and see the new creature in Christ embraced within the radicality of this rejection of the Son of Man.

The discussion centering around Wiersinga's views is carried on fully "from beneath," in the context of the mystery and strangeness of the cross. Wiersinga wants to let the mystery be a mystery — that of human guilt and the room God gives to human rebellion. We could also think of the mystery of how God allowed his Anointed to go into this way of forsakenness and rejection. This strikes me as a hint of the depths of Romans 8:32, not as a theoretical problem, but in respect to Paul's amazement at the Christ "given over" for us. In this environment, human alibi is forbidden. Walking in the footsteps of the Lord is not an addendum, but is embraced by him whose healing comes through being crucified and dead to sin and alive to righteousness (1 Peter 2:24).

Anyone who fails to respect this bond between us and the vicarious atonement has lost the ability to grasp the reality of reconciliation. The New Testament speaks about the possibility of "crucifying the Son of God afresh" (Hebrews 6:8). If we are unsettled by this word — or by Pascal's remark about the agony of Christ lasting till the end of the world — we probably need to reconsider the terrible possibility of crucifying Christ "afresh." What seems to be suggested here is a "possibility and reality" — in a constant vice-versa relationship (Hebrews 6:4-6) — in which grace and reconciliation are an "objective" point of departure with an uncertain result. The possibility may or may not be realized. The "possibility" of rendering the cross of no effect after the heavenly gift, after the good Word of God and the advent of the powers of the coming age, is the possibility that has become an impossibility. It is the possibility that guilt might not be undone that has become an impossibility to one who knows the Christ who covers his own forgiven guilt.

We might well be shocked at the relationship between justification and sanctification after this. It is not as automatic as we might think. The shocking reality is hinted at in Gollwitzer's words: "He sets his affairs in fearsome ways into the hands of men, his disciples and his church." Here alibis become lame, and excuses are out of order. We may present excuses on the premise that human action is only secondary when it comes to reconciliation. But they will not hold water. And the only way to pull the rug from under human alibi is to keep hold of both a genuinely substitutionary action of Christ and the necessity of the new creature in Christ.

I have had occasion to mention that Barth frequently speaks of the "passion of God" but never of the "death of God" (*The Triumph of Grace in the Theology of Karl Barth*, p. 307). And I said that this seemed to me a kind of holding back from the consequences of his own thought. Barth remarked in a conversation with me (in 1954) that he was not that interested in following this thought through to its possible consequences. He was concerned with the actual involvement of God in the sacrifice of his own Son; Christ was not merely an earthly instrument of a totally other God. God himself is present, not in weakness that permits men to suffer without hope and perspective, but in the sovereignty of his love. He was giving himself! This is why 2 Timothy 2:13 has such point here: "He cannot deny himself" (2 Timothy 2:13). The older theology gave the right answer, Barth insisted, to the questions of whether and how far God the Almighty can lie, deny himself, sin, or die. Barth said we should not speak of God as though we were playing games with general concepts about "ability." The notion that "God can do everything" can turn God's power into powerlessness. Barth writes about what God cannot do as a form of God's "abundance and perfection." In response to my questions, Barth wrote that we were in agreement about God's involvement in the sufferings of Christ, and that "christological thinking must always be a matter of the perfection, apprehension, understanding, and estimation of the person who according to the writers of Holy Scripture discloses himself as the crucified and risen Son of God and Son of Man" (*CD* IV/3, p. 175).

This is where crucial decisions are made in our theological considerations. And they must not be made according to what we know beforehand to be likely or possible, nor on the basis of a theory of God's impassibility — or, for that matter, his ability to suffer — nor on the basis of a logical deduction from the doctrine of Christ's two natures. The decisions must follow from our sensitive awareness of God's own involvement along the way that he sacrificed his own Son. Here he is himself: "God gives . . . himself, but he does not give himself away. He does not give up being God in becoming a creature, in becoming man" (*CD* IV/1, p. 185).

Modern theology has set itself against the notion of divine apathy. This is true, not only with respect to God's involvement in the passion of Christ, but with his compassion, his empathy, his feelings for human suffering. In England, the thought of divine compassion surfaced markedly after the First World War; here there was talk of "the suffering God" as theologians wrote about his concern and compassion. (Cf. L. J. Kuyper, "The Suffering and the Repentance of God" in *The Scottish Journal of Theology*, 1969; and K. J. Woolcombe, "The Pain of God" in *The Scottish Journal of Theology*, 1967.) We meet it also in K. Kitamori's contention that Western theology gave the doctrine of God a bad orientation with its philosophical notions of divine unchangeableness (Kitamori, *Theology of the Pain of God*, 1966). He ascribes this to the fact that Western views of life and death are dominated by life and happiness. Lacking a feeling for the tragic in life it is easy to gloss over the suffering compassion of God. He suspects that this has influenced our understanding of God in important ways: "To overlook this decisive matter means a misfortune for the church in the entire world."

The Bible, of course, is full of incidents in which the compassion of God is revealed. In the Old Testament, God is involved in human life, his affections are stirred, his emotions aroused. We need only recall the pain felt by the Spirit (Isaiah 63:10) and the affliction he felt in people's affliction (Isaiah 63:9). The New Testament speaks of the inner mercies of God (Luke 1:78) as the light of Christmas, which shines through all the miseries of humankind. This is the light prefigured in the story of Jonah. Jonah was quite willing to let a godless city die, but God looks on that city with its 120,000 children with compassion. It is the inner life of God, which is open to us in all its depths. "I am

God and not a man" (Hosea 11:9), and this means, not that God has no inner life of compassion, but precisely that he does. And on this basis, we too are summoned to follow him in the surprising pathways of compassion (Luke 6:36) and to new life-styles that we put on as a new garment (Colossians 3:12). Divine compassion is the model for human emotional response to life (Romans 12:1).

The biblical witness to God's inner movement has had steadily more influence on theological thought, taking over from speculative notions of an unmoved essence. There are connections between the questions of the suffering God in the passion of Christ and concern about divine involvement in all human suffering. Both are reactions against the notion of divine apathy. But this has meant that the question of theodicy has crept into the picture. We may have given up on justifying the ways of God; we may have come to see that it is man who needs justifying. But the question has persisted: how can we conceive of God's relationship to human misery?

Barth contended that ordinary efforts at theodicy paled in view of the cross of Christ. He said this, however, in the conviction that what is involved is not a theoretical answer to the enigma of evil as such, but an answer of faith. For Moltmann, too, the question of theodicy is not merely a terrifying question for theoretical thought. But the way in which it is answered receives a special form. The title of his recent book, *The Crucified God*, makes it clear that he approaches theodicy and the problem of suffering within the context of the suffering of Christ. Moltmann, in speaking of the cross, is concerned with the union of God with the suffering, the oppressed, and the lost among all men — hence, not just with the older problem of the union of God with the suffering human nature of Christ. So, for Moltmann, the cross is the answer to the general theodicy question.

He does not let the general theodicy question pale. And here he parts with Barth. He takes the question, which for atheism is answered by God's nonexistence ("The only excuse for God is that he does not exist" — Stendhal), and finds the answer in God's existence as the God whose being is revealed in the God-forsakenness of Christ. God's being is expressed in earthly suffering, not in an "uninvolved heavenly holiness." The atheistic protest is rendered mute by the theology of the cross. For the God of the crucifixion manifests himself to suffering people through his own suffering. He displays himself in forsakenness. Not even the resurrection dissolves the reality of forsakenness; it underscores it and triumphs over it by opening the door of life to the future.

Moltmann is talking about a deeper concept than divine compassion. He is working with a consistent, thoroughgoing crucifixion theology. He coined the word *patri-compassionism*, as a twist on the old patripassianism. Compared to the old form of patripassianism Moltmann's probing goes much further. "He humbles himself and takes on himself the eternal death of the godless and the forsaken, so that all the godless and forsaken can experience communion with him" (*The Crucified God*, p. 276). And here the older efforts at theodicy are ruled out, for now it is clear *how* man is taken "into the life and suffering, the death and resurrection of God" (*ibid.*, p. 277). Thus, a "post-Auschwitz theology" is possible after all. For the abstract questions of theodicy fall away in the shadow of the event of the cross. The cross is "the beginning of the trinitarian history of God," a history in which God is so completely absorbed that the fourth word from the cross could aptly read: "Why have you abandoned yourself?"

Moltmann asks Barth whether the cross really does touch the very being of God and, if so, whether we do not need a revolution in our concept of God. It is true that Moltmann's thoughts about the conflict *within* God are not reflected in Barth. For Barth, who is no less turned off by the notion of divine apathy, draws a limit that he refuses to cross. Moltmann, on the other hand, goes beyond Barth's limit and sees the cross as the key to God's participation in the suffering within the whole world. It is the resurrection that tells us that the solidarity of God with suffering in the cross is not an isolated instance, not a powerless solidarity. Barth drew back from drawing this conclusion, and refused to universalize the event of Good Friday. And he refused to admit to a conflict within God, a God-against-God event, even though he resisted the portrait of an apathetic God who merely watched Christ suffer.

Almost everyone who has worked at a theology of the cross has groped his way very warily. But Moltmann goes beyond the boundaries into the thesis of the suffering God and the conflict within the God who was forsaken. To refuse to go this whole route with Moltmann must not mean a retreat to the apathetic God. Von Balthasar, on reviewing the whole problem, concluded that every human formulation is found wanting. One gets the impression that Moltmann, in driving through to the bitter end of thought about the suffering God, has not had von Balthasar's reserve.

The questions we are discussing here have played a part in no one's thought more existentially than in Bonhoeffer's. He put intense stress on the "powerlessness" of God in the theology of the cross. God is with us in weakness, Bonhoeffer liked to say. He confessed that he became speechless at the way God's redeeming and liberating acts touch on our lives, for it was a way, not of the God on high, but of the God in the depths, the pain, the hurt, and the humiliation.

And so, ideas that at first hearing sounded paradoxical and foreign compared to traditional views of "God the Father Almighty" have found their way into common theological currency. God's weakness — this is the way of thinking about God in our time. There have been justifiable cautions uttered, too, cautions lest we play dialectical games with the concepts of power and weakness. Gollwitzer speaks to this point when he remarks that the ordinary believer experiences what feels like the weakness of God, but what he wants to hear is the power of God; and his concern is bitterly serious, for he wants God's power and not his weakness to be the last and conclusive word (cf. Gollwitzer, *Von der Stellvertretung Gottes*, p. 123). He warns against "accenting the weakness of God, for this has the look of fantasy, a romantic game of paradoxes." Is it possible that Bonhoeffer too was bitterly serious about the power of God and that it was for this reason that his whole life and thought were dominated by what he *experienced* as the weakness of God?

We think again about Barth, who was as centered as anyone on the theology of the cross and wanted as much as anyone to let the cross dominate his theology, and who, in thinking of human weakness, could write: "But God is not weakness, neither in part nor in whole, but real Power" (*Dogmatics in Outline*, E.T. 1949, p. 47). The apostle Paul refuses to be caught in a dialectic of power and weakness; for the powers of evil have been disarmed at the cross by the power of God, even though his power looks like weakness in man's eyes (Colossians 2:15). At the same time, Paul brings thoughts together that astound us on first hearing: the foolishness and weakness of God. Paul is not throwing out words for shock effect, or dealing with theological subtleties for the sophisticated reader. He speaks out of a sense of wonder at the reality of the cross, a reality that offends human logic and counters all natural expectations of divine power. This is the foolishness and weakness that fascinated Luther; to him the unique and amazing thing about God's actions is that they showed his weakness to be strength and his foolishness to be wiser than human wisdom. Calvin thought that the word "foolishness" was a concession, a kind of irony in the face of human arrogance. There is truth in these approaches to the language of "weakness," but we must let Paul's words point the way to the light that comes into darkness. For in the face of this weakness, the high priests and scribes were compelled in spite of themselves to make a witness: "He saved others, he cannot save himself" (Matthew 27:42).

Taking the word "weakness" seriously, as contemporary theologians do, inevitably raises questions. Van Ruler, for instance, says he is not impressed with sharp-witted theologians who locate God's power in the weakness of the crucified. But he finds a truth in it, nonetheless. For God can indeed go that far: "He can let himself, in his Son, move into powerless forsakenness," into a "divine impotence on the cross." Van Ruler's qualification is that the cross is not *mere* weakness, but is the power of salvation. And so Van Ruler is not far from Barth and Bonhoeffer. "The divine rule is fashioned in the style of suffering. Even the omnipotence of God takes the route of love's work of transformation. His power is at once saving power and weakness" (A. van Ruler, *Ik Geloof*, 1969, p. 124).

Thus it is that we encounter various expressions, all of them inadequate, and all of which need qualification to ward off misunderstanding. Interpretations, for this reason, are never dead-end. Each one is open to new insights. Trying to avoid empty notions of transcendence and facile notions of supernaturalism, we counter with insights that come as a shock to many. But they come as a shock because they express what the heart already experiences of the emptiness of many older concepts that no longer are in touch with reality (cf. H. M. Kuitert, *The Necessity of Faith*, E.T. 1975). In the environs of Jesus Christ, we are conscious of both transcendence and closeness. It is a transcendence, however, that is not an empty transcendence. And it is a closeness that reveals that God's answer transcends even our highest concepts. If we keep this transcendence in view, we will not be easily shocked by the protests against misconstrued "theism" and empty "supernaturalism."

Considering the changes in christology during recent years, we will not be surprised that the doctrine of the trinity has also met with fresh approaches. The question here, as in christology, is whether the old formulas can still be understood. If the ancient definitions are no longer understood, they have become mere objects of belief that are agreed to without sensing any significance in them for life. The church's language in setting forth the trinity is as full of difficulties as was its language for the person of Jesus Christ. It spoke of the one God in three persons and three persons in one God. The formula had to be defended and explained as the church confronted the radical monotheism of both Judaism and Islam, on one hand, and tritheism on the other. Always, the incomprehensibility of God was confessed along with the trinitarian definition. But one could not resort to God's incomprehensibility in explaining the words we use. For instance, how God could be one when he was also three persons was a natural question.

In speaking of God the church has always talked of him as *a* person; it could hardly speak any other way as long as it addressed God in prayer. But at the same time, in dogmatics, the term "person" was reserved for the *three* persons. The semantic problem has always been acutely felt. Some have spoken of it as an insoluble problem. We can hardly talk of three persons without offering some explanation. For when modern people think of persons they think of individual, discrete beings. So dogmatics sometimes speaks of three distinct *subjects* — rather than of persons — that exist in personal relationship with each other.

Warding off tritheism, however, does not assure us that our confession will be clear. The church always took it for granted that it would not be understood as teaching that there were three Gods. Indeed, explicit tritheism was never more than a marginal threat to the church, so it felt no great urgency to be clear on that point. But it tended to forget the kind of impression that its words made on people outside the church — within it too for that matter. They sounded strange and paradoxical, and gave the impression of a doctrine that one simply had to accept as coming "from above" and handed down in the church's own odd language. But the Belgic Confession interestingly explains that we know the persons of the trinity "as well from the testimonies of Holy Writ as from their operations, and chiefly by those we feel in ourselves" (Article IX). This is a remarkable statement; we know this doctrine by what we feel of the work of the trinity *in ourselves*. But do people "know" the difficult terminology in this way? The words are not all that simple and unambiguous. And this is why problems arise which can only be answered in terminology that is an *understandable* witness to what one believes. Theology has made nuances and distinctions that have never been taken up in the church's preaching. Who today, within the congregation, grasps the meaning of *filioque*, over which East and West split asunder in 1054? And who can explain the difference between the ontological and the economical trinity?

The difference between the ontological and economical trinity is the difference between the inner being of God and the trinity as revealed in historical acts. The distinction has not gone down well in our day, mostly because it represents more talk about what God is in himself, cut off from his revelation. Gollwitzer has emphatically labelled all talk about "God in and by himself" as speculation. E. Jüngel responds to this by saying that God's being lies in becoming (cf. *Gottes Sein ist im Werden*, 1965, pp. 112f.). God, he says, wants to be to human faith what he actually *is*. The tension between him and Gollwitzer seems apparent. But it appears that Gollwitzer is concerned with how God is disclosed in his revelation, and has to come to terms with questions that have always been implicit in the doctrine of the trinity. His meaning is pretty much expressed in Otto Weber's contention "that God discloses himself to us as he is in himself through a threefold revelation and . . . he is that which he discloses himself to be" (O. Weber, *Grundlagen der Dogmatik*, I, 1955, p. 410). So there is no pushing back a God *behind* revelation. Rather we note a recognition of the genuineness of a revelation which excludes speculation just because "God who is reveals himself as who he is" (*ibid.*, p. 399).

The distinction between the ontological and economical trinity was used by the church in its effort to combat modalism. Modalism is the teaching that God is revealed in his actions in the *mode* of the three persons; hence, God is trinitarian only in his progressive stages of revelation. Modalism's attraction lay in its clear opposition to tritheism. It laid a strong stress on the unity of God (God as *Mon*arch) and in doing so underscored the biblical witness to his oneness (cf. Deuteronomy 6:4; Mark 12:49;

1 Corinthians 8:4; James 2:11, etc.). It read the New Testament language about Father, Son, and Holy Spirit, then, as expressions of how the one God *appeared* to the world in his saving work — the Father in creation, the Son in redemption, and the Spirit in sanctification. Its biblical overtones explain why modalism has always been "virulent" (L. Scheffczyk, in J. Feiner and M. Löhrer, eds., *Mysterium Salutis*, II, 1967, p. 166). Barth remarked that modern theology is a reversion back to modalism in fear of tritheism.

Our problem with modalism obviously cannot be its appeal to revelation. The Heidelberg Catechism itself answers the question of why we name God as Father, Son, and Holy Spirit, by saying that this is how he revealed himself in his Word (Lord's Day VIII). The problem is that modalism sees the trinity as *only* modes of revelation. And we must ask, as Barth did, what the word "only" means.

We meet the same question in functional christology, which is a parallel with the functional notion of the trinity. (Cf. I. Hermann, *Kyrios und Pneuma, Studien zur Christologie der Paulinischen Hauptbriefe,* 1961.) Schillebeeckx says that functional christology is modalistic in the same way that classic modalism is. When H. Berkhof published his book on the Holy Spirit, he raised the question in some readers' minds whether he was not modalistic. Berkhof suggested that the formulation of "one essence and three persons" compounds rather than resolves the problem of the trinity. He perceived a large gap between the modern sense of "person" (person as a self-conscious individual) and the older theological concept of person. Moderns almost have to see "three persons" as a three-God notion. The result is that the expression "three persons of the trinity" is a source of confusion rather than a formula of unity. So Berkhof proposes: "The triune God is not made up of three persons: he is himself a person who meets us in the Son and in the Holy Spirit." He prefers to say that the words Father, Son, and Holy Spirit have to do with God's actions as he came to us in saving history. This is not modalism, he insists, because modalism is a denial of the reality of God's being in revelation; it posits a contrast between revelation and reality. According to modalism, God only *appears* to be Father, Son, and Holy Spirit; the revelations are really costumes or masks. In contrast to modalism, Berkhof insists that

"We may believe that he is as he comes to us in his revelation" (Berkhof, *The Doctrine of the Holy Spirit*, E.T. 1966, pp. 109ff.). In his later work, *De Christelijk Geloof* (1973), Berkhof develops his thoughts more fully, but the basic polemic is the same. He is still against the idea of an abstract God-in-himself, and posits the revelational trinity over against speculative views, thus dissolving the distinction between a revelational and ontological trinity. He still stays clear of the modalistic notion that the three modes of revelation are "only" modes; indeed, he stresses even more that revelation is of the essence. "The triune events reveal the essence of God and steer us to that essence."

It may be that this concentration on the revelational trinity reflects precisely what the doctrine of the trinity intended. To say this is not to gloss over problems by putting the best possible color on the ancient formula. It is to try to do justice to the necessary task of getting at the real intention of ancient dogmas as we try to reinterpret them. No matter how foreign to us the terminology may seem, the intention of the doctrine is clear enough. And it coincides with revelation in a way that rules out the notion of "only" revelational, as if revelation does not disclose the reality. If we honor the intention, we can find a point of contact between the doctrine of the trinity and the life of the average congregation. For the congregation is responsive to the fact that it lives under the grace of the Lord Jesus Christ, the love of God, and the fellowship of the Holy Spirit. Realizing this, it knows that it is in touch with the reality of God in each case, and the reality of his salvation that is "with you all" (2 Corinthians 13:13).

True enough, there is a danger that the connection between the doctrine and the revelation may be clouded over. This happens in dogmatics when we begin talking about God in general, about his essence and attributes, and only later begin speaking of the trinity. In this way, the confession of the trinity looks like an afterthought, an appendage, be it a necessary one, to the more crucial "general" doctrine of God. Rahner is one theologian who points to the problem created by a two-track dogmatics: the dogma of the "one God" and the dogma of the "triune God." Isolating the dogma of the trinity in this way, says Rahner, is not right. And we might ask whether abstract notions of God do not begin with the general doctrine of God rather than with the trinity. The question is pressed on us when we read statements like this one, from Bavinck: with the trinity, he writes, "far

from its being a metaphysical concept or a philosophical speculation, we are at the heart and essence of the Christian religion"
(*Gereformeerde Dogmatiek*, II, pp. 343f.). Rahner is sure that
separating the doctrine of God in general from the doctrine of the
trinity has brought serious consequences with it. As it is, if anyone
concluded that the doctrine of the trinity is false, he would still
leave the largest part of religious literature unaffected. This would
certainly be true of much medieval discussion about the essence
of God. But it should be noted that the Belgic Confession also
begins with the one God and his attributes and only thereafter
speaks of the trinity. Is there here, too, an abstract idea of God's
unity and uniqueness, at the beginning, and only then an acknowl-
edgment of the riches of the trinitarian revelation?

We have only given a hint of the complications that the history of dogma has experienced, in its defenses and polemics, in
its formulas and its search for ways to avoid abstractions and
speculations, always without losing sight of the fact that revelation
discloses *reality*. We have seen enough to conclude that we
should be cautious before we brand reinterpretations of the trinity
as modalism. We should be cautious precisely because in the
stress on the revelational trinity there are perspectives for understanding the real intent of the traditional terminology. And there
are clues for avoiding classic modalism at the same time that
tritheism is shunned. And, with this, there is a greater possibility
of keeping the confession of the trinity in touch with the congregation, with preaching, with the sacraments and the benediction.

We began this last chapter by talking about the church's
concern for the faith. We did not use words like "disturbed" or
"alarmed." In many churches there *is* alarm and people *are* disturbed. And theology ought not keep itself above the dis-
turbances people experience, as though it has all wisdom and
can work with the truth above the heads of people in the congregation, as though it can afford to be unconcerned about the
anxieties of the plebeians of faith. Theologians do not like churchly
authorities who think of themselves as "guardians of the holy
place," who model themselves after "cherubim and sphinxes keeping motionless guard at some pagan temple." But theology likewise should not pretend to be an unmoved guardian of the truth.
As a matter of fact, theology shows little sign of serene immobility.
There is restless searching going on, a groping for ways to understand the gospel more clearly. We should not expect too much

from theology; it will at best only give us incomplete knowledge and inadequate understanding. If we forget that theology is always going to be partial, travelling along the way without ever arriving finally, we will be upset by theology's continued movement, and others will be alarmed and disturbed by it, seeing it as a threat to established truth. But those who long ago stopped expecting finality from theology, and are not intimidated by the fact that theology is on the move, have their own temptation; they can, after a while, lose their courage and lapse into skepticism. We are reminded of Lessing's famous remark about searching for the truth: "If God held all truth in his right hand and in his left the everlasting striving after truth, so that I should always and everlastingly be mistaken, and said to me, 'Choose,' with humility I would pick the left hand and say, 'Father, grant me that. Absolute truth is for thee alone.'" It is no wonder that this little parable has fascinated so many people through the years. Even if they do not make Lessing's choice, they find the prospect of search encouraging in a time in which there is so much confusion, uncertainty, and division in the theological arena.

But, conscious as we are of the unrest and the hesitations, the zigzag lines and the self-corrections, we not only are experiencing the limitations of all theological thought, but are receiving signals that theological unrest is part of the quest that has been given to the church of all times. It is the quest for a deeper and richer understanding of the unsearchable riches of the gospel. On this route, which has many travellers, each with his own cares, defeats, and discoveries, we also stand before another possibility: the correlation between seeking and finding. The light comes in the form of a promise: "Seek and ye shall find." This promise can be the stimulus to new courage and to new service.

Index of Names